SIR SYED AHMAD KHAN: VISION AND MISSION

Sir Syed Ahmad Khan: Vision and Mission

Edited by

SHAHABUDDIN IRAQI

CENTRE OF ADVANCED STUDY
Department of History
Aligarh Muslim Univesity

MANOHAR
2008

First published 2008

ISBN 81-7304-784-7

Published by
Ajay Kumar Jain for
Manohar Publishers & Distributors
4753/23 Ansari Road, Daryaganj
New Delhi 110 002

Typeset by
Kohli Print
Delhi 110 051

Printed at
Lordson Publishers Pvt. Ltd.
New Delhi 110 007

Contents

Preface

This volume contains papers selected for publication out of those presented at the International Seminar on 'Sir Syed Ahmad Khan: Vision and Mission', organized for the first time by the Centre of Advanced Study, Department of History, Aligarh Muslim University, Aligarh, on 5–7 November 2006. Earlier, the Old Boys of the University had celebrated the death centenary of Sir Syed in 1998 by organizing functions in different countries to commemorate the founder of this apex institution. Similarly, in Aligarh the Old Boys made efforts to organize seminars and other academic activities on a large scale but unfortunately the programme could not be carried out. This earnest desire was translated into action when our proposal for holding an International Seminar on Sir Syed Ahmad Khan under the auspices of the Centre of Advanced Study was approved by the Vice-Chancellor, Mr Naseem Ahmad, with the assurance of all support and cooperation.

The seminar was primarily a humble tribute to Sir Syed Ahmad Khan. The main objective in organizing it was to bring together scholars from India and abroad to assess and evaluate the great contributions of Sir Syed and the Aligarh movement, and to focus on their relevance in the present day situation of the Muslim community. In order to cover all relevant aspects, papers were invited on the following themes:

1. Sir Syed's Approach and Contribution to History: Edition and original works—*Tarikh-i Firoz Shahi, Ain-i Akbari, Tuzuk-i Jahangiri, Jäm-i Jam, Asbab-i Baghawat-i Hind, Sarkashi-i Zila Bijnor*; work on archaeology—*Asar-us Sanadid*; collection of artifacts.
2. Sir Syed's Religious Thoughts: *Tafsir-ul Qur'an*, *Tabin-ul Kalam, Khutbat-i Ahmadiyah*; rationalism and modern *Ilm-ul Kalam*.
3. Sir Syed's Mission of Muslim Education: MAO College, the first modern institution of Islam; Mohammedan Educational Conference; views about female education.

4. Sir Syed's Attitude Towards Western Thoughts: Role of the Scientific Society.
5. Sir Syed as a Social Reformer: Attitude Towards Secular Traditions: Role of the *Tahzib-ul Akhlaq*.
6. Sir Syed and Indian Nationalism: Attitude Towards the Indian National Congress and National Integration.
7. Sir Syed's Contribution to Literature.
8. Sir Syed as a Journalist.
9. Sir Syed's Contribution in the Field of Law.
10. Sir Syed's Relevance to Present Day Life.

SHAHABUDDIN IRAQI

Acknowledgements

I wish to express my grateful thanks to Mr M. Hamid Ansari, the Chairman of the National Commission for Minorities, who was kind enough to accept our invitation to participate as the chief guest in the inaugural function. I would also like to express my gratefulness to Mr Naseem Ahmad, Vice-Chancellor of Aligarh Muslim University, for sparing time to preside over the Seminar and for providing necessary facilities for holding it. I am extremely thankful to Prof. Mushirul Hasan, the Vice-Chancellor of the Jamia Millia Islamia, who considered our request to deliver the keynote address in spite of his multifarious responsibilities. Thanks are also due to Prof. (Mrs.) Hamida Ahmad for her remarks at the vote of thanks to the delegates and the guests. Our Centre is obliged to the University Grants Commission for extending financial assistance in organizing the Seminar. We also express our gratitude to Mr M.A.A. Fatmi, Union Minister of State, Human Resource Development, who was very helpful in this regard.

Our special thanks and gratitude are due to all the delegates who participated in the Seminar, presented papers and took part in the discussions. We are grateful to the authors for permitting us to include their papers in this volume. The Seminar was a great success only because of the whole-hearted support, cooperation and efforts of our colleagues, non-teaching staff and the students of the Department of History. Prof. B.L. Bhadani, Prof. Tariq Ahmad, Mrs Azra Alvi, Dr S. Liyaqat Moini, Dr M. Afzal Khan, Dr Ali Athar, Dr Iqbal Sabir, Dr Hasan Imam, Dr S. Chandni Bi, Dr M.K. Pundhir and Dr S. Bashir Hasan deserve special mention. Finally, thanks are due to Prof. Iqtidar Husain Siddiqui for rendering great help in preparing the text as a volume for publication.

SHAHABUDDIN IRAQI

Introduction

Sir Syed was a man of many talents, a writer both in Persian and Urdu, a religious thinker who laid down the foundation of modern *Ilm ul-Kalam* (Scholasticism in Islam), a social reformer, a historian who tried to bring the Muslims out of their century-old cultural stagnation through the reinterpretation of Islamic teachings, a fearless fighter for social justice and above all a scholar of comparative religion.

Long before Sir Syed, Muslim scholars had begun to take interest in acquiring knowledge of different religions of the world and wrote scholarly treatises relating to them. A specific genre of scholarly nature was thus created first in Arabic and then in Persian. The writings are marked by the objectivity of the writers. They are indicative of the fact that the main motive behind them was the writers' curiosity to know how the majesty of God found expression in other traditions. In South Asia, Al-Beruni was inspired to study the Hindu religion and science. But this tradition was abandoned in the eighteenth century, the period of decadence. Muslims became obscurantists the world over. It was because of this that Sir Syed Ahmad Khan (d.1898 AD) felt the need to revive this tradition in order to remove the cobweb from the mind of his co-religionists. He wrote a commentary on the Bible in Urdu and impressed upon Muslims that religio-cultural interaction between them and European Christians would be beneficial for them. For him, the acquisition of knowledge of different religions was a source of enlightenment. In his commentary on the Bible, entitled *Tabin al-Kalam,* the similarity in the two religions has been emphasized. Sir Syed had respect for all religions of the world and had all praise for the non-Muslim religious leaders who endeavoured to restore their religious tradition to its pristine purity.

Sir Syed's scholarship of Islam and his exegesis of the Koran was profound and *Hadith* and his approach was steeped in rational perspective. The motive behind his effort was to show that the teachings of the Koran do not conflict with modern sciences; that nothing has been mentioned in the Koran in contravention to the laws of nature laid down by God himself. While discussing the verses on polygamy (4:3), he justifies it on certain grounds, although he is in favour of monogamy. According to him, if there be no urge for a man, nature demands that he should have only one wife. He quotes the last part of the same verse 'if you fear you cannot do justice (to everyone of your wives) then marry one'.

Sir Syed was a pioneer in Urdu historiography. He edited medieval Persian texts, explored ruins and described the monuments in and around Delhi in his work *Asar-us Sanadid,* which is one of the classics of Urdu literature. He wrote on different themes and helped Urdu prose to develop into a vehicle of expression of philosophy and the sciences. In Urdu journalism too his contribution is substantial. Though, his religious writings suited the modern mind, he was vehemently opposed by the Muslim orthodoxy. Compelled by the need for cooperation and support from the Muslims for popularizing the teaching of modern sciences, he could not antagonize the Islamic orthodoxy any more.

The scientific society founded by Sir Syed in 1864 was joined both by Hindus and Muslims. The aim of the society was to provide Indians with Urdu translations of European works on modern sciences. His scheme resulted in the Aligarh movement and the establishment of the Mohammedan Anglo-Oriental College (at Aligarh) in 1877 to impart the knowledge of Islam with secular education, so that the faith of the students in their religion might not be weakened. It must be noted that the doors of the MAO College were kept open for non-Muslim students who were exempted from attending classes in Islamic theology, meant exclusively for the Muslims.

The graduates of the MAO College went out into the modern world as rationalists and young men of tolerant and progressive views. All this was possible because of the liberal atmosphere created by Sir Syed Ahmad Khan in the campus of the college. The college was the first modern institution of its kind in the entire Islamic world.

Sir Syed's contribution in the fields of education, religion, history, literature, journalism and politics was substantial and of far-reaching importance. The critical perspectives that have been brought recently to bear on his life's work reflect their width of his interests. The papers presented in this seminar not only contain the assessment of different aspects of Sir Syed's personality, and the achievements of the Aligarh movement but also highlights their relevance to the present day situation of Muslims in the world, not just South Asia. The papers contained in this volume will open new vistas for further investigation into different aspects of Sir Syed's life and mission and the Aligarh movement in the history of Islam in general and that of the Indian Muslim community in particular.

SHAHABUDDIN IRAQI

Report of the Seminar

The Centre of Advanced Study, Department of History organized for the first time an International Seminar on Sir Syed Ahmad on 5–7 November 2006. At its inaugural function in the Kennedy Hall Auditorium, the chief guest, Mr M. Hamid Ansari, Chairman, National Commission for Minorities (former Vice-Chancellor, AMU) accentuated six major challenges that the Muslim community was confronted with today. He called upon the Muslims to learn from Sir Syed's firm determination and to work in the light of his experiences. He stressed that in the competitive world of today Muslims have to keep in mind that education alone is the key to success in all spheres of life. They need to assess the success and failure of the Aligarh movement launched by Sir Syed with the founding of the MAO College at Aligarh. Mr Hamid emphasized that this self introspection of the Muslim community would enable them to chalk out their own agenda in order to compete and gain their due status in the present world.

Noted historian and Vice-Chancellor of Jamia Millia Islamia, Prof. Mushirul Hasan, in his keynote address said that Sir Syed was surrounded by people of inventiveness, which gave strength to his mission. Although there were differences in emphasis, his associates, Zakaullah, Nazir Ahmad and others, planted the seeds of a pluralist vision that could eventually become a touchstone of liberal and secular polity.

The Vice-Chancellor, Mr Naseem Ahmad in his presidential remarks said that Sir Syed's vision was very relevant in modern India and that we must try to live up to his ideals. He emphasized upon the need of carrying forward the legacy of Sir Syed's mission to greater heights of excellence.

Earlier in his welcome address, Prof. Shahabuddin Iraqi, Chairman and Coordinator, CAS, Department of History and Convener of the Seminar, said that the Seminar was a humble tribute to the founder of our Alma Mater. While enumerating Sir Syed's achievements, Prof. Iraqi pointed out that founding of an institution alone made him pre-eminent among all Muslim leaders and reformers of modern India. He said that his purpose of organizing the Seminar was to attract the attention of scholars of different fields towards Sir Syed's varied contributions. The Seminar was to provide an opportunity to them to exchange their views on the achievements of the Aligarh movement and to outline their relevance to the present circumstances of the Muslim community in the whole world.

Prof. Hamida Ahmad, Dean, Faculty of Social Sciences, delivered the vote of thanks to the distinguished scholars and guests. She emphasized the need for translating into action Sir Syed's mission that we generally keep in our hearts.

The three-day seminar was divided into seven academic sessions, each followed by fruitful discussions. The sessions were accordingly Chaired by Prof. Z.U. Malik, AMU, Prof. S.M. Azizuddin Husain, Jamia Millia Islamia, New Delhi, Prof. B. Sheikh Ali (former Vice-Chancellor, Goa and Mangalore Universities), Prof. Iftikhar H. Malik, Bath University, U.K., Prof. Alay Ahmad, Preston University, Peshawar, Pakistan, Ichhamuddin Sarkar, North Bengal University and by Prof. R.K. Trivedi, AMU. In all, fifty-eight papers were presented, some of which opened new vistas of knowledge regarding Sir Syed and his achievements in different fields.

The valedictory session, held at the Faculty Lounge on the evening of 7 November 2006, was presided by Prof. B. Sheikh Ali. Prof. B.L. Bhadani presented the report on the academic activities of the seminar. The delegates passed nine resolutions including the establishment of Sir Syed Study Centre, Sir Syed Award and Sir Syed Chair in the university. It also resolved that the proceedings of the Seminar be published by the Chairman, Department of History.

In his presidential remarks Prof. B. Sheikh Ali urged the Muslim community to take recourse to Sir Syed's mission to counter the challenges of the modern world.

Keynote Address

Hon'ble Vice-Chancellor, Mr S. Hamid Ansari, Chairman, National Commission for Minorities, Prof. Shahabuddin Iraqi, Prof. Hamida Ahmad and my friends and colleagues and co-author, Rakshanda Jalil, ladies and gentlemen.

Mr Vice-Chancellor, I am extremely grateful to you and your colleagues for inviting me to this conference and asking me to deliver the keynote address. This is an honour which I will cherish for long. I have chosen to speak not so much on Syed Ahmad Khan, the grand old man of Aligarh, but on his two illustrious friends, who were also connected with this great institution. They are Maulvi Nazir Ahmad and Maulvi Zakaullah. Central to my concern in this presentation is how the idea of *Ilm*, plurality and tolerance is reflected in the writings of these men of the second half of the nineteenth century.

Ilm was the pre-condition of worldly and otherworldly salvation—knowledge not only in the customary sense, but the combination of religious texts and the sciences in their time. '*Ilm* is your family's prized trophy (*tamgha-i-sharif*)', Nazir Ahmad reminded his son. Zakaullah's persuasive voice reflected this view as well, while the most intimate of his friends, Syed Ahmad Khan, expressed its rationale and the theoretical gist in more lucid terms. Like the Khorasan-born scholar-philosopher, Ghazali, he believed that right action follows where there is knowledge. The *Tahzib-ul Akhlaq*, as its name implies, was designed to cultivate among its readers enlightenment and social refinement, or correction of manners. Arguing that the kernel of meaning and values in society are embedded in education and nowhere else, Syed Ahmad, its editor, wanted to leaven his co-religionists by training and sending out men to preach the gospel of free enquiry, of large-hearted tolerance, and of pure morality. The modern college system he wanted to build was the tool for producing and reshaping knowledge rather than for simply transmitting centuries-old religious knowledge to future generations. 'Independence of mind and political liberation', he clarified after returning from England in 1869, 'were not symptoms of heterodoxy'.

Aware that education creates people's intellectual and cultural perspectives, their value system and their *Weltanschauung,* education for all, the 'haves' and the 'have nots', turned out to be the Aligarh reformer's main hobby. His concerns were often elitist, but he also believed that, in the ideal world, knowledge of science, history and literature ought to be attainable by all who desire it.

Syed Ahmad spent more than a few years outside Delhi, his birthplace, and yet he represented a distinctive example of an intellectual working within the context of his broader cultural heritages to respond to the challenges and experiences of the modern world. He was anxious not to stand on the sidelines or waste time in vain regrets. Without leaving any room for the vagaries of supernatural powers, he embarked on a momentous enterprise in order to navigate an era that was very different to what his forebears had experienced. His work is singularly important in the South Asian context, combining as it does a desire to see all things through science, reason, and rationality with a deep sensitivity to the religious underpinnings of human experience and the ache of the heart for guidance and happiness. Whilst according the high place of reason in the scale of values, he showed the compatibility of 'true Islam' with the findings of a mind free from the scourge of ignorance, prejudice, and superstition. He desired the door of *ijtehad* (interpretation) to be thrown open, and the people to rethink and reinterpret the problems of life and religion in accordance with the circumstances of their age.

He wanted the Sultan of Turkey and the Khedive of Egypt, to whom he had sent some of his published papers, to know that the onward march of science and enlightenment was in every respect compatible with Islam. To them most, but to all in some degree, he stated unequivocally that Islam would face extinction if people did not shun blind adherence, if they did not seek that light which can be found in the Koran and the Hadis, and if they did not adjust religion with the sciences.

Among the broad-minded and more far-seeing sections, the lamp lit by Syed Ahmad burned brightly. Zakaullah wrote an essay listing eight points to illustrate how and why *Tahzib-ul Akhlaq* ushered in a virtual social and intellectual revolution from Peshawar to Kanyakumari. Wahiduddin Salim, editor of *Maarif,* launched his magazine on 1 July 1898 paying his tribute to Syed Ahmad's contribution to Urdu language and literature through the *Tahzib-ul Akhlaq.* Azad devoured its every page. As an illustration of his consuming passion, he describes waiting for the copy of Hali's biography of Syed Ahmad in Urdu—*Hayat-i Javed*. Only thirteen years of age, he read it straight through, 1,000 pages in two nights. Mumtaz Ali (1860–1935), who began education at an Arabic *maktab* in Deoband and continued in Lahore, had his doubts about Syed Ahmad's commentary on the Koran answered after their meeting in December 1879. His faith reconfirmed, he published a pamphlet refuting the Ahl-i-Hadis attacks on Syed Ahmad. In *Lucknow: The Last of an Oriental Culture,* originally written as a series of articles over a period of years through the second decade of the twentieth century, Sharar, its author, observed that in *Tahzib-ul Akhlaq,* 'sorrow in regard to national tribulation was portrayed with seriousness and scholarly dignity. The phrasing was clear and analytical, incorporating ideas taken from the latest Western philosophy and literature with impressive discourses.'

This was not all. While Nazir Ahmad wrote approvingly of the formidably sober-minded Syed and his efforts, some others described him as his time's Ibn Sina (980–1037), the philosopher and scientist known to the medieval West as Avicenna. 'Which ever way I look, there is you and only you' (*Jidhar dekhta hun, udhar tu hi tu hai*), commented Shibli Numani, born in the year of the Great Rebellion, Professor of Persian at the MAO College from 1 February 1883 to May 1898, and one of the founders of Lucknow's Nadwat al-Ulama.

Syed Ahmad shaped the world of even those who differed with him, and by carrying the war to the enemy, he set the terms of most debates among Muslims in South Asia. In 1874, the Muslims of Lahore described him as their leader and spiritual preceptor, *pir-o-murshid*. Hali remembered when Muslim families in such places would refuse to send their children to the MAO College. A few years after Syed Ahmad's death, however, 700 boarders were drawn to Aligarh from Punjab, Bengal, Madras, Burma, Gujarat, Baluchistan, Afghanistan and Iran. In the country as a whole, intellectuals regarded themselves as the legitimate trustees of an intellectual development, which absorbed not only Islamic/Muslim thought, but also the field of Western rationalism. Later day historiography of the Aligarh movement has generally been conceived in a spirit of praise rather than blame, of appropriation rather than rejection. 'The world has seen,' Hali had stated, 'how one man has aroused a whole land, one man saved a caravan from destruction, and small boats sinking ships to the shore.'

NAZIR AHMAD AND SYED AHMAD'S WALK WITH DESTINY

Nazir Ahmad reflects the spirit of social, intellectual, and religious inquiry that had affected many educational institutions in north India. He and Syed Ahmad stand side by side as defenders of the same ideal, the harmony of faith and reason. Both wrote spiritedly, demonstrating their social awareness of those far-reaching forces that impinged on the lives of the people around them. Both wanted new windows to be opened to the light, and the new air of heaven admitted. That is how the community could travel from the shores of ignorance to the shores of knowledge and englightenment. No wonder, then, that the barrage of conflict and condemnation which both faced sprang from the familiar source, the party hostile to applying reason to revelation and theological dogma.

Nazir Ahmad and Syed Ahmad were both imbued with a profound contempt for the Congress, and an equal certainty that they and their chosen friends alone possessed the knowledge that could bring happiness to their community. Yet they diverged radically from each other on some other issues. Like Shibli Numani who took issue with some of Syed Ahmad's religious beliefs, Nazir Ahmad felt that 'too much of anything is bad'. He thought poorly of Syed Ahmad's commentary on the Koran, felt uncomfortable with his proximity to the government, and disagreed with his uncritical admiration of the West. It is true that he himself lavished praise on Western civilization and celebrated British rule as 'a blessing of God in every way', but he also disgraced and humiliated Ibnul Vaqt for aping the English lifestyle. Ibnul Vaqt is bluntly told: 'one door was closed on you and the other you could not reach. These are some of the worldly changes which are the results of your erratic plans.' Ultimately, though, Ibnul Vaqt mends his way, wears Indian dress, and questions certain British policies. To his son, Nazir Ahmad wrote:

> In short, those people who shout about 'English civilization, English civilization' don't get to the bottom of things, which is that different tastes are natural, and can't be changed. What I say is that everyone likes his own ways. It is these that give him pleasure and he is likely to continue in them to the end. We know that the English are making striking progress in every field, and not unmindful of the need to reform their way of life either. All the same, to imagine that their civilization has reached the highest stage of refinement would be a mistake. Matters of food and dress are minor ones.

There are things, very important things in their society that offend us. I have already spoken in passing of the position of women there. Now look at their drinking. [. . .].

Sir Syed preferred Western attire; Nazir Ahmad disapproved of 'tightly-fitting' clothes. In his opinion, it was the Englishman's dress which compelled him to slump about on chairs and couches morning, noon and night. This was not one-tenth as comfortable as siting on the floor. 'We have good reasons for the worthiness of our old things', he said to Farhatullah Beg. Commenting on the dress of English women, he commented: if that is a superior kind of dress then one can say without exaggeration that it is so only in the couplet:

Tan-i-uryani se behtar nahin dunya mein libas
Yeh voh jama hai keh jis-ka nahin sidha ulta.

There is no dress in the world superior to the body's nakedness
That is a dress which has no inside-out.

In his essays *Tariqa-i Tanawul-i Ta'am* (The Way to Eat a Meal) and *Tariqa-i Zindagi* (The Way of Life), Sir Syed reviled Indians for eating with their fingers and not using knives and forks. 'Deeds are known by intentions', said the Prophet. The Prophet also said, 'Whoever adopts the fashion of a people other than his own, becomes one of them'. Syed Ahmad quoted these words approvingly. Without casting doubt on the words of prophetic wisdom, Nazir Ahmad maintained that standards of personal cleanliness differed from nation to nation, and even from individual to individual. 'Matters of food and dress', he remarked, 'are minor ones. There are things, very important things in their [British] society that offend us.' 'I ask you', he put it to his son in plain words, though the message was intended to reach the appropriate quarters in Aligarh: 'Why would any foreigner want to live in a society where people keep themselves so much aloof from the others that two of them, members of the same nation, can live for long periods in the same hotel or travel on the same ship or eat every meal at the same table without being acquainted with each other.'

As if this was not enough, he pointed out that even though India's fortunes had diminished owing to prejudice, ignorance, short-sightedness and disunity of its people, 'the English-speaking brothers' share the blame. He observed:

If there is a speck in our eye there is a cataract in theirs. If we are one-eyed, they are blind. If wc stutter, they are dumb. If our English speakers had the capacity for high thinking, things would have been better than they are. They see only one fault in us—that we don't wear clothes like theirs, don't eat and drink, don't allow our women the freedom to rove around freely. As though these wise men of ours [this is a direct allusion to Syed Ahmad and other English speakers] thought that the worldly ascendancy of the English is the result of their civilized way of life.

Syed Mahmood grudged that Nazir Ahmad had caricatured his father for his Eurocentrism. His charge should not be taken seriously. Nazir Ahmad had announced quite early in life that, if he had to seek out a *pir* (spiritual leader), he would become Syed Ahmad's *murid* (disciple). Hence, his sharp reaction to Mahmood's reproach:

I am not Sir Syed's bard. If he were a spiritual guide, I am not his follower; if he were a teacher, I am not his pupil; if he were an elegist, I am not his weeper. If he is a rich man—and I know he is not—then I am not, nor shall ever be his dependent. But what is it? It is this, that I am a man and have wisdom enough to distinguish between a friend and a foe, and to understand the condition of the nation and its requirements.

Despite disagreements, Syed Ahmad remained not only Nazir Ahmad's determined idolizer but also rubbished his detractors. 'His stature is such that it would be impertinent on our part (*ma-o-shuma*) to dare comment', he confessed to his son. This is exemplified by his retort to the students' strike in 1907: 'You are slaves', the striking students were told. 'What can slaves do? Get back to your books and work.' He felt himself duty-bound to intervene, taking his cue, as always, from Syed Ahmad.

After Syed Ahmad's death in 1898, Nazir Ahmad withdrew from public gaze دولھا کے دم کے ساتھ یہ ساری برات تھی. He would say that, in the chain welded by Syed Ahmad, Syed Ahmad himself had been the strongest link, and his demise was bound to lead to disruption. In a moving speech at Lahore in June 1898, this is how he paid his tribute to Syed Ahmad:

If you are his friend, don't hurt or injure his spirit. . . . He did not want you to build a magnificent dome on his grave or to organize an annual *urs*. He did not want you to provide livelihood to his family. . . . What he desired and what his ultimate goal was that you live in this world honourably and with dignity. He had reached the pinnacle of his career. He was a Syed (by caste). He received knighthood, and a doctor (of philosophy). A truly honourable man, he founded the College. A reformer, he was an acknowledged Muslim leader.

In this succinct obituary, Nazir Ahmad invoked cultural symbols of reconciliation between a dead reformer and his detractors. He replied to his critics who came at him like a swarm of bees by urging them to chart a new course of spiritual and cultural life not in opposition to but in harmony with the winds of change. 'The good use of religion,' he had said in 1893, 'is that we should reform ourselves.'

If Ghalib had lived long enough to be acquainted with Nazir Ahmad's works, he may well have dedicated the following verse to him:

سب کہاں کچھ لالہ و گل میں نمایاں ہو گئیں　　خاک میں کیا صورتیں ہوں گی کہ پنہاں ہو گئیں

Only the survivors come forth in the rose, the tulip.
What faces have gone under the dust!

[Ghalib]

It will be instructive to end by pointing out that Ghalib may have paid similar tributes to Nazir Ahmad's intellectual partner on 'life's difficult journey'—Khan Bahadur Shamsul Ulama Maulvi Muhammad Zakaullah. Both grew up in the 'twilight of Delhi', and were exposed to the pressure of forces, old and new. Both experienced unprecedented movements of change, one welling up from below and embodied in the popular upsurge in 1857 and another that stemmed from above and was led by the colonial state. In consequence, they often worked out their thoughts amid the noise and heat of contemporary strife. Set within the problematic of the transition ushered in by the 1857 Rebellion, their writings, for all their variety, searched for ways to adapt a society to the new conditions. Yet both were essentially thinkers rather than men of action. While appearing on the national and provincial stage from time to time, they preferred living in the world of ideas rather than in the world of practical affairs.

A life-long friend of Syed Ahmad, Zakaullah endorsed not only the idea of founding the college at Aligarh and not elsewhere, but played a large part in its affairs as a trustee from 1892 onwards and as a member of the Board of Management. Nicknamed as *chihgham* or 'free from care' for the jokes he produced during the fund-raising tour of Punjab in 1885, he marched hand in hand with Syed Ahmad.

There was much bonhomie at a formal meeting in early July 1887. That is because Syed Ahmad announced that Zakaullah, appointed 'Life Honorary Professor of Mathematics', had decided to settle in Aligarh to devote his life to the college.

But Zakaullah was too sage, too tolerant, to force his way to worldly distinction. A very private person, he was too shy and nervous to speak in public. Like 'a nightingale of a thousand songs', he was 'tongue-tied', like a mute, in the presence of an audience. A man born to follow and not to lead, to serve and not to command, he needed a hero and found one in Syed Ahmad. His eyes lit up with eager enthusiasm at the mention of his name. He had his portrait in his living room, and stocked books relating to, or else written by Syed Ahmad. His idol dominated the stage, radiant, peerless, irresistible, and the saviour of Muslim society. When the students' strike in 1907 rocked the MAO College campus, he acted in concert with Nazir Ahmad and Andrews to resolve the deadlock. The hopes of Zakaullah's lifetime were centred in the college, 'the darling of our hearts, and the light of our eyes', and, if 'evil comes to it, the work of my life is ruined', he wrote.

Zakaullah's living hero was no other than Syed Ahmad, the man of destiny. Both recognized the importance of organized religion for maintaining sound morality, and were ill at ease with overzealous reformer's scepticism and materialism. Yet both laboured unceasingly to establish that 'without a full acceptance of the results of modern science and a full knowledge of them also, the East must inevitably fall behind the West'. For that reason, they recognized the necessity for progressive Islam to assimilate modern science and modern technical knowledge. Both held out the ideal of Muslim regeneration in unison with the British and, for this reason, saw the Congress endangering peace. Convinced that its methods and demands would lead to a violent upheaval, they, having experienced the 1857 stir, were unwilling to face the thought. Their fidelity was not to a political party, but to a set of values, which the government might best protect.

At the same time while Syed Ahmad felt politically energized after the founding of the Congress, Zakaullah despaired of public affairs and preferred instead the peaceful pastures of knowledge. This is not to suggest that he did not take public positions, though more often than not he remained studiously reserved in judging people and events. He wrote at least four articles in *Zamana,* an influential journal published from Kanpur, on the *swadeshi* movement and supported *swadeshi* but not the political motives behind the agitation. They allude to multiple themes, economy and education being the most important of them, and provide many insights. It can be said of their author that more often than not he regarded the political scene with a sublime and distant objectivity.

Opposition to the Congress did not mean that Syed Ahmad and Zakaullah were detached from the nation, variously referred to as *mulk, millat* and *qaum* and interchangeably used in public discourses. On the contrary, they exalted the nation as an indivisible entity that embraced castes, communities, and linguistic groups. This belief guided Syed Ahmad, who interacted closely with Rai Shankar Das (Ramchander's brother) when posted in Moradabad, to seek Raja Hardeo Narain Singh's help in founding a *madrasa* in Ghazipur, and enlisted the backing of Hindu patrons, such as Raja Jaikishen Das, for the Aligarh project. Deeply rooted in his country's traditions, he, like his contemporary Egyptian reformer, Muhammad Abduh, believed that the common history and interests of those who lived in the same country created a deep bond between them: for, 'since centuries we have been living on the same soil, eating the same fruit of the same land . . . breathing the same air of the same country'. He did not regard religion as the badge of nationhood, and advocated separation between matters religious and political. Spiritual and religious matters had no connection with worldly affairs; in fact, a true religion only set out cardinal principles comprising ethical values and only incidentally dealt with worldly dealings. Syed Ahmad disapproved of cow-slaughter on campus, and opposed tooth and nail the demand for appointing a teacher for the religious instruction of Muslim pupils. He believed that in a country of diverse faiths, a religiously neutral government should not extend preferential treatment to a particular community. The government heeded his advice and turned a blind eye to the earnest pleas that emanated from certain Muslim quarters.

In Zakaullah's writings, too, the ideas of nation, nationality, national belonging, and nationalism are paramount. 'Nothing gives [me] greater pleasure than one's city, fort (*qila*), and home, he wrote. 'For the sake of the country (*watan*) people give away their life.' His love for the country grew into a passionate desire for service. He discussed this devotion, or *hubul watani,* in another text. The reference point is *Khaslat-i Azeem,* or the great virtues and deeds guiding individual and collective life. Consider, for example, his impassioned plea:

India is our mother country, the country that gives us birth. We have made our homes here, married here, begotten children here, and here on this soil of India, which is mingled with the dust of our ancestors. For a thousand years, our own religion of Islam has been intimately bound up with India; and in India, Islam has won some of the greatest triumphs for its own peculiar form of civilization. We should love, therefore, the history and government of India, which have been shaped by such great monarch as Akbar the Great and his successors. I cannot bear to hear Indian Musalmans speaking without reverence and affection for India.

Even this kind of a rhetorical flourish has to be taken seriously. The words are carefully chosen in order to sum up the elements that, in both thought and action, went into the making of Zakaullah's world-view. Andrews, on his part, rounded off his assessment:

There were few subjects on which Munshi Zakaullah in his old age became more eloquent than this, and he never diverted for a moment from this position throughout the whole of his long life. . . . His nature was rooted like a tree in Indian soil and no storm or tempest from outside could ever shake it. Nobody knew this reality better than the writer of these lines.

Zakaullah had a purpose at the back of his historical studies—to reveal to his readers that tolerance of religious opinion was the first and last principle of good government. His ideal rulers were those who practised tolerance and bound together the divided people into one, instead of separating them by religious pride and bigotry.

Zakaullah and Syed Ahmad startled many of their Muslim friends by agreeing on another major issue that threatened to atomize the Muslim communities. Both rejected outright pan-Islamism. That is because they desired a new rapprochement with the government and allay its fear of a potential combination between religious and national sentiments that had created havoc in 1857. For them, as for so many other intellectuals, the Rebellion was a formative experience, crystallizing their notion of social responsibility. Yet commitment assumed amazing complexities when applied to real political choices. Syed Ahmad and Zakaullah emerged convinced that liberal education supplied the only tools to progress, and an *entente cordiale* with the rulers, the only concrete approach to reality.

Consequently, when they found some form of pan-Islamic sentiments threatening to wreck their effort to prop up the Anglo-Muslim alliance, they decided to cut the silver cord that tied Muslims to the Khilafat in Constantinople (now Istanbul). Critical of the weight of old, pan-Islamic traditions that still held the Muslims back, they recommended to them to forget their transnational links, and to build up, instead, their education and modernize social life. Both spoke against Turkophilia, arguing that they were legally bound to obey the writ, not of an external Khalifa, but of the British Indian government. In case of war between the government and a Muslim power, Zakaullah wanted Muslims to be loyal to the government. 'By all means', he would say,

> let us love our Musalman brethren in other countries, and feel their joys and sorrows; but let us love with all our hearts our own country and have nothing to do with the encouragement of those who tell us, that we, Musalmans, must always be looking outside India for our religious hopes and fulfilment.

While finding acceptance in some Muslim circles, quite a few prominent figures changed their opinion in the light of the outcry in the Balkan states. Shibli Numani pointed out how Muslims living under non-Muslim rule had remained loyal and obedient to their rulers in accordance with the Koran, the Prophetic traditions, and Islamic jurisprudence. However, when the European powers stirred up trouble in the Balkans, Shibli became a passionate pan-Islamist. Azad, the young editor of *Al-Hilal,* stressed that the bonding with the Turks was unique in so far as they were a part of the Islamic community (*Akhuwat*) as well as its last political centre (*Siyasi markaz*).

With Shibli's world-view transformed, he would have felt comfortable with Jamaluddin Afghani, the roving pan-Islamist who travelled through the Muslim lands in search of a major role against the hegemony of the European powers. During his stay in India, he published several articles in Hyderabad's *Muallim-i Shafiq*. In one of them, he attacked Syed Ahmad, Samiullah Khan, and other 'Materialists' for splitting the unity of the believers and strengthening the British government in India. 'This swindler (Samiullah) sets himself up as a preacher at Muslim gatherings, and his tears precede his words. He brings forth the utmost of his eloquence in order to destroy the pillars of the Islamic religion and nullify its fundamental beliefs.' The government rewarded 'this evident enemy of Islam' with the post of judge in Agra, and the Viceroy, Northbrook, used his services to alienate the Egyptians from the Ottoman government.

Whether or not Syed Ahmad knew of this indictment is unclear, but it was perhaps a coincidence that he, too, moved away from his old partner, Samiullah Khan. Part of the reason was that Samiullah had become, for a variety of reasons, the *bete noire* of the European staff at the MAO College, whereas part of Syed Ahmad's success in running the college lay in the excellent chemistry he shared with the English principals. The critical rupture took place over the Trustee Bill which provided that Syed Mahmood, the youngest son (Syed Hamid, the elder son was employed in the police service) would be Joint-Secretary during his father's lifetime and Secretary after his death. First of all, Mohsinul Mulk, Syed Ahmad's otherwise close associate, wildly contested the suggestion and sent off a strongly worded letter to him on 27 October 1889. Samiullah Khan, who did not want a successor to be appointed in Syed Ahmad's lifetime, followed. Syed Ahmad, who at times did not respond to counsels of prudence, put the matter to vote at the Fund Committee in December 1889. Aligharh's old guards, already at loggerheads with their guru on several issues, split irrevocably.

Syed Ahmad, an astute administrator, held out an olive branch to his friend Samiullah—a trusteeship—but that did not work. He then complained to Inayatullah, Zakaullah's son, of Samiullah's malice and rancour. In retrospect, though, Mohsinul Mulk and Samiullah had rightfully judged that Syed Mahmood, prone to heavy drinking and reckless in his public conduct, was unfit to undertake any serious responsibility. Shibli found Syed Mahmood, in February 1898, in a bad way. Hali not only agreed, but also sought his removal from the college. To cap it all, the father himself had a taste of his son's ill temper when he was turned out of his own house. This bizarre incident, which Hali suppresses in *Hayat-i Javed* but Shaikh Abdullah records, occurred just a few months before Syed Ahmad's death, 'Those who have lived through historical events, as I have', wrote Theodore Mommsen, the historian who brought Athens and Rome into the consciousness and culture of the modern world, 'begin to see that history is neither written nor made without love or hate'.

Abdullah describes what constituted friendship between Syed Ahmad and his colleagues. He and others like Syed Raza Ali considered loyalty and constancy in friendship as the hallmark of Sharif culture none of which Syed Mahmood possessed. Whenever they extolled the virtues of friendship, they held up the example of Zakaullah and Nazir Ahmad and scarcely mentioned those who violated Sharif codes. No wonder, Hali makes no mention of the Mahmood episode.

The account sketched above suggests that the dialogical element signalled an important step towards avoiding paradigms of encounter and undermining religious violence. The point is not to exaggerate its limitations or to debate whether or not such men were authentically modern, but to highlight their inventiveness. As people who had no conception of pacts and unity conferences that became the métier of peace in the 1920s for the sake of immediate political goals, they talked of building on the overarching shared ethical values and practices, and acknowledging each other's common visions.

MUSHIRUL HASAN

CHAPTER 1

Sir Syed's Asarus Sanadid: *A Historical Review, 1846 to 2006*

S.M. AZIZUDDIN HUSAIN

Siraj-ud-Daula's defeat in 1757 and Tipu Sultan's defeat in 1799 paved the way for the establishment of British Rule in India.

Iqbal highlighting the role of some Indian traitors had said:

جعفر از بنگال و صادق از دکن　　ننگ دنیا، ننگ دیں، ننگ وطن

Jafar from Bengal and Sadiq from Deccan both are shame for the world, faith and for the motherland.

Sir Syed had great reverence for eastern culture. By 1818 the entire subcontinent had been brought under British authority. Sir Syed knew that India's cultural heritage would be neglected and harmed, specially the monuments constructed since the twelfth century AD, beginning with Quwwatul Islam mosque in Mehrauli and ending with Safdar Jung's tomb, all telling stories of bygone days.

از نقش و نگار درو دیوار شکستہ　　آثار پدید است صنادید عجم را

From the broken walls and the *mehrab*, reflect the beauty of their makers from Iran.

Sir Syed again writes about the memories of the monuments of Delhi:

بیا د نقش عمارات شہر یاراں بیں　　کہ این سپہر جفا پیشہ چوں بہ لبست وشکست

Sir Syed wrote, 'I could not even bear to contemplate the miserable state of people. I wrestled with my grief, and believe me it made an old man of me.'

Lieutenant William Franklin in 1795 shared Sir Syed's feelings about the city of Delhi and its monuments, 'The environs of this once magnificent and celebrated city appear now nothing more than shapeless heaps of ruins.'[1]

Sir Syed knew that even Indian rulers like the Jats and the Marathas while holding power damaged these monuments of Agra and Delhi. Surajmal Jat damaged and looted Agra Fort in 1760. Now it was the turn of British to loot and damage these monuments.

> W.H. Russell wrote in 1860 I am hardly alone in being struck by this: the ruins of Delhi are something visitors have always been amazed by, perhaps especially in the eighteenth century, when the city was at the height of its decay and its mood most melancholic. For miles in every direction, half collapsed and overgrown, robbed and reoccupied, neglected by all, lay the remains of six hundred years of trans-Indian Imperialism—the wretched vestiges of a period when Delhi had been the greatest city between Constantinople and Canton. Hammams and garden palaces, thousand-pillared halls and mighty tombs, towers, empty mosques and deserted Sufi shrines—there seemed to be no end to the litter of ages. The prospect towards Delhi as far as the eye can reach is covered with the crumbling remains of gardens, pavilions, mosque and burying places.[2]

While Sir Syed was serving as munsif of Delhi he started working on the monuments of Delhi. At the same time his brother launched a newspaper, *Saiyad-ul Akhbar*, and Sir Syed began writing articles on the monuments of Delhi.

Sir Syed completed the draft of *Asarus Sanadid* and published the first edition in 1263/1846. For this he received support from Edward Thomas and Colonel Sixon asked Sir Syed to get it translated into English. Sir Syed writes in his Preface.[3]

> کرنیل سکسن صاحب بہادر نے فرمایا کہ اگر اس کتاب کا انگریزی میں بھی ترجمہ ہو تو بہت بہتر ہے۔ انہوں نے اس خاکسار کی شرکت سے اوس کتاب کا ترجمہ کرنا شروع کیا اوس وقت یہ بات خیال میں آئی کہ اگر از سر نو یہ کتاب بہت اچھی طرح سے مرتب کی جائے اور جو خرابیاں کہ پہلی کتاب میں ہوگئی ہیں وہ سب درست کی جائیں تو بہت اچھی بات ہے الحمدللہ کہ خدائے تعالی نے اوس آرزو کو پورا کیا اور جس طرح کہ دل چاہتا تھا اوسی طرح پر یہ کتاب پوری ہوئی۔ پہلی کتاب سے یہ کتاب بہت باتوں میں اچھی ہے۔

So in 1854 he prepared a revised version of *Asarus Sanadid*. He added new information to chapters I and II. In chapter III some monuments were also added. Incomplete history of some monuments in the earlier edition were completed in the revised edition. In this edition, the description of monuments is also more systematic. This edition also has references from historical sources. In the revised edition, the text of the inscriptions is also similar to the handwriting of the original text of the inscription.

Even today, historians of medieval Indian history serving in the three central universities in Delhi, University of Delhi (DU), Jamia Millia Islamia (JMI) and Jawaharlal Nehru University (JNU) are not aware of these monuments recorded by Sir Syed in 1846. The departments of History of DU and JNU do not have a paper on medieval architecture, and their students remain ignorant of monuments of Delhi. No work has been done on Sir Syed's *Asarus Sanadid* by any of the medievalists of DU, JNU, AMU or JMI. Several scholars of Urdu worked on the *Asarus Sanadid* and brought out editions of the *Asarus Sanadid*. Munshi Rehmatullah had published it in 1876, Khaliq Anjum in 1990 and Tanvir Ahmed Alavi in 2000. I appreciate the contribution of these scholars of Urdu but *Asarus Sanadid* though written in Urdu deals with history and architecture, which requires the attention of historians and architects.

Sir Syed revised his book in a short span of seven years but the historians of medieval Indian history did not bother to review this work after a passage of 160 years. Even Aligarh's Department of History and Department of Architecture which are the result of Sir Syed's contribution did not pay any attention to this significant work of Sir Syed. Credit goes to Prof. Shahabuddin Iraqi, the present Chairman, who is organizing for the first time a seminar on Sir Syed, the founder of this university. Prof. Iraqi has written a history of the History Department. Marxist and communal historians only condemned Sir Syed and said that he only promoted the interests of Muslims belonging to the upper sections of the society and never highlighted his contributions.

Several historical monuments were damaged by the Jats, Marathas and the British. Curzon is an exception among the Britishers. He paid attention to the preservation and publication of Arabic and Persian sources and to the conservation of some important monuments in Delhi and Agra. Even after the Partition of India, these monuments faced the frenzy of migrants from Pakistan. In Delhi, Agra and other towns, some monuments were converted into residences by them. In Delhi migrants occupied the dargah of Qutubuddin Bakhtiyar Kaki, Dargah-i-Shah-i-Mardan and other monuments in Mehrauli, Zamrudpur, Muneer ka Gaon, Hauz-i-Khas, Firoz Shah Kotla, Tughlaqabad Fort, etc. Injustice to these monuments was also done by the first planners of Delhi in 1952 who gave importance to only Lutyen's Delhi. No importance was given to these medieval monuments of Delhi. Parliament had passed a law that no construction of any sort will be allowed within 200 m of a monument. But we see that the Municipal Corporation of Delhi constructed a road at a distance of 10 m from Quwwat-ul Islam Mosque and the tomb of Iltutmish. Government agencies have broken government laws. In Hauz-i-Khas, the New Delhi Municipal Corporation has allowed the construction of houses in such a manner that they touch the walls of the Madrasa of Firoz Shah Tughlaq. Khirki Mosque which is the only covered mosque in India, is connected with a lane of 5 ft only. So we see that government agencies in free India have their equal share in harming and damaging these monuments of Delhi. But in Basti Nizamuddin Muslims themselves have damaged and converted some of these monuments into their residences or offices.

William Dalrymple rightly observes,

> Even after independence, the arts that were cultivated by the Mughals—the miniature painting tradition, the *ghazal*, the delicate forms of Mughal architecture—never really regained their full vitality or artistic prestige, and remained at least in some quarters—as discredited as the emperors who patronized them.

Hali, a contemporary of Sir Syed highlighting immense contribution of Sir Syed writes in his work *Hayat-i-Javed*.[4]

> باہر کی عمارتوں کی تحقیقات کرنی ایک نہایت مشکل کام تھا۔ بیسویں عمارتیں ٹوٹ پھوٹ کر کھنڈر ہو گئی تھیں۔ بعض عمارتوں کی حالت ایسی متغیر ہو گئی تھی کہ ان کی ماہیت معلوم ہونی مشکل تھی۔

Some of the buildings standing outside Shahjahnabad have already collapsed. And it has become very difficult even to identify those monuments. Again Hali writes about the importance of *Asarus Sanadid*.[5]

> سرزمین دہلی کے تین باب دیکھ کر سرزمین دہلی کی قدیم شان و شوکت اور عظمت کی تصویر آنکھوں کے آگے پھر جاتی ہے اور تھوڑی دیر کو دنیا سے دل سرد ہو جاتا ہے اور پہلے باب سے دلی کا آخر جھگڑا آنکھوں کے روبرو آ جاتا ہے۔

Through *Asarus Sanadid* one can peep into the grandeur and authority that Dilli had enjoyed during medieval period. And in this sense Sir Syed's *Asarus Sanadid* enjoys an important position as a source of our cultural history.

After the establishment of British rule in India, the Delhi Gate of Red Fort built by the Mughal Emperor Shahjahan was renamed Victoria Gate and the main gate of Agra Fort built by Akbar was renamed by the British as Amar Singh Gate.

Mushafi a Urdu poet laments about Delhi in these verses

ہے صاف تو یہ گلشن دہلی میں خزاں ہے

It is clear that the garden of Delhi is facing autumn.

And Ghalib writes to Nawab Alauddin Khan

میری جان یہ وہ دلی نہیں جہاں تم پیدا ہوئے تھے

My dear it is not that Dilli where you were born.

Though most of these monuments have already been erased from the map of Delhi, *Asarus Sanadid* will always enlighten us on the subject. To me the major contribution of Sir Syed is not the establishment of the MAO College at Aligarh but his work, *Asarus Sanadid.* Universities and colleges could have been established by anyone but no contemporary of Sir Syed had a vision of the monuments of Delhi as Sir Syed had.

QUTUB AREA

LAL-KOT

The Tomar Rajputs are believed to have first settled in the Surajkund area and later to have shifted some 10 km west, where Anangpal raised the citadel of Lal-Kot, now survived by its thick stone-built ramparts, a panoramic view of which may be obtained from the balconies of the Qutub Minar. Recent excavations have shown that the original citadel of Lal-Kot was oblong in plan, and the high stone walls to its west, which enlarge the original enclosure and are usually regarded as its part, are a later construction. Outside the ramparts ran a moat, now traceable only in some places. The later wall mentioned above is provided with massive towers and pierced by several gates, some with outworks, known as Ghazni, Sohan and Ranjit gates.

The rubble-built walls of the ramparts are 2.5 to 3 m thick, a stone footing on the exterior, over which was raised a thick brick revetment. Later, an elegant and impressive veneer of dressed local quartzite blocks, now extant only over some stretches, was raised in front of the brick-face, and provided with neat looking semi-circular bastions at irregular intervals. Ruins of several structures can be traced within the Lal-Kot, but no places have been located.

In AH 1262 / AD1846 the area was full of water as is shown in the sketch in *Asarus Sanadid*.

The walls of Lal-Kot have been pierced by the Delhi–Qutub, Badarpur–Qutub and Mehrauli–Qutub roads, and the visitor can have a glimpse of these while approaching this area from any of three directions, although they are not so apparent, while coming from Mehrauli. With the establishment of the Sultanate in Delhi a campus was developed in Mehrauli. One part of Mehrauli was occupied by palaces of sultans and mosque, etc., and the other part was occupied by the Chishti sufis but the road has totally shattered the plan of Mehrauli. Heavy traffic passes at a distance of only 20 m from the Quwwat-ul Islam Mosque and this poses a great hazard to the mosque and the Qutub Minar.

QUWWAT-UL ISLAM MASJID

Barring the pre-Sultanate monuments of Kutch district, this is the earliest extant mosque in northern India and consists of a rectangular court, 43.2 m by 33 m, enclosed by cloisters, erected with the carved columns of 27 Hindu and Jain temples demolished by Qutbu'd-Din Aibak.

Qutbu'd-Din calls the mosque Jami Masjid and states that on the original erection of each of the demolished temples a sum of 20 lakh of coins had been spent. Later it came to be called the Quwwat-ul Islam (might of Islam) Mosque. The western portion of the courtyard occupies the original site of one of the demolished temples. At the two ends of its eastern cloisters, an intermediate storey was raised to provide a compartment for women. An iron pillar from a Vishnu Temple of the fourth century, which had been earlier set up here by Anangpal, stands in front of the prayer hall.

The mosque was begun in 1192, immediately after the capture of Delhi by Qutbu'd-Din, and completed in 1198. Later, a massive stone screen was erected in front of the prayer hall, consisting of the central arch, 6.7 m wide and 16 m high, with two similar but smaller arches on either side, all ogee shaped. Except for the apex, where a few stones are laid in the manner of voussoirs, the arches are corbelled. The screen is beautifully carved with borders of inscriptions and geometrical and arabesque designs, but the hands of craftsmen used to Hindu motifs is clearly perceptible in the naturalistic representation of the serpentine tendrils and undulating leaves of its scroll work and even in the fine characters of Koranic inscriptions.

The extension of the mosque was done by two later Sultans. Shamsu'ddin Iltutmish (1211–36) successor of Qutbu'd-Din, doubled the size of the mosque in 1230 by extending its colonnades and prayer hall outside the original enclosure, with the result that the Qutub Minar now fell within the mosque's enclosure.

Alau'd-Din Khalji (1296–1316) again extended the mosque substantially by enlarging the enclosure—two gateways on the longer eastern side and one each on the north and south, the last one known as Alai-Darwaza and still extant in its entirety. In fact, he doubled the area of the mosque, and also commenced the construction of another minar, intended to be twice the size of Qutbu'd-Din's Minar, although it remained incomplete.

The main gate of Quwwat-ul Islam Mosque is badly damaged and its upper part is missing. Even the walls have collapsed. The central arch of the liwan of the mosque and the northern side arch have collapsed. The western wall also does not exist in the Syed's sketch. It seems that it was later repaired and now is well preserved.

QUTUB MINAR

Qutbu'd-Din Aibak laid the foundation of the now world-famous Qutub Minar, intended as a commemorative tower of victory but also as a minar attached to the Quwwat-ul Islam Mosque for the use of the mu'dhdhin to call the people to prayer. Qutbu'd-Din's construction was eventually completed by his successor Iltutmish. From the Nagari and Persian inscriptions on the minar, it appears that lightning twice, in 1326 and 1368, damaged the minar. The first damage occurred during Muhammad Tughlaq's reign (1325–51), and was repaired by him apparently in 1332. The second damage was attended by Firuz Tughlaq (1351–88). Later in 1503, Sikander Lodi (1498–1517) also carried out some restoration in the upper storeys, faced with red and buff stone. The uppermost storey which was damaged in 1368 during Firuz Tughlaq's reign, was replaced with two storeys by him, making free use of marble but leaving the lower portion of the fourth storey built with sand stone in its original condition.

The original three storeys are each laid out on a different plan, the lowest with alternate angular and circular flutings, the second with round ones and the third with angular ones only, with the same alignment of flutings, however, being carried through them all. Its projecting balconies have stalactite pendentive type brackets and decorative inscriptions. The minar has a diameter of 14.32 m at the base and about 2.75 m at the top. At a height of 72.5 m and 379 steps, it is the highest stone tower in India and the perfect example of a minar known to exist anywhere.

Originally it was surmounted by a cupola, which fell down during an earthquake and was replaced early in the nineteenth century by a new cupola in the late Mughal style by one Major Smith. It looked, however, so incongruous that it was brought down in 1848, and may now be seen on the lawns to the south-east of the minar.

LAL MAHAL

Outside Chaunsath-Khamba a red sandstone building in private occupation, attracts attention. Known as Lal Mahal or 'red palace', it has a central domed room with verandahs on all the sides. The verandahs have a flat roof supported on pillars and lintels. It is identified sometimes with Koshak-i-Lal (red palace), built by Ghiyasu'd-Din Balban (1266–86). Only one part of Lal Mahal is preserved which is now called Urs Mahal but other parts which are shown in *Asarus Sanadid* do not exist.

BALBAN'S TOMB

On the western side of the Mehrauli bypass to Gurgaon there are extensive ruins of old Mehrauli, now deserted. Among these, as the visitor proceeds from the Qutub Minar, he first encounters a domeless and extremely dilapidated rubble-built square chamber with arched openings on all its four sides. This occupies an important place in the development of Indo-Central Asian architecture, as we find here for the first time the use of a true arch and dome.

A ruined rectangular chamber on its east is believed to have contained the grave of Balban's son, Muhammad, who was popularly known as Khan-i-Shahid (i.e. the Khan who became a martyr), after he died fighting in a battle against the Mongols near Multan in 1285. There exists also another tomb not very far away to the south, which is also popularly known as that of Khan Shahid. Its dome was demolished on Mahabat Khan's (a noble of Aurangzeb's reign) initiative. The sketch done by Sir Syed shows it standing in a very poor condition. Recently the Archaeological Survey of India (ASI) has repaired it but the cenotaph of the grave of Balban was not rebuilt by the ASI. The Khan-i-Shahid's grave is there in its original form but it requires repairs.

HAUZ-I-SHAMSI

We get references about Hauz-i-Shamsi in contemporary Persian chronicles like Barani's *Tarikh-e Firozshahi.*

The famous Moorish traveller Ibn-Battuta was struck by the vastness of this tank which was supplied by rain water and in whose centre stood a double-storied stone pavilion, reached only by boats when the tank was full. A red sandstone domed pavilion resting on twelve pillars located near the south-western corner of the tank, but originally believed to have been situated in its centre, is identified with the pavilion built by Iltutmish. The water in the tank was regarded sacred, and several graves of Muslim saints lie around it. The procession for the fair called Phulwalon-ki-Sair or Sair-i-Gulfaroshan, when flower-vendors present flower-bedecked large fans at the *dargah* of Qutub Sahib and at the Jogamaya Temple, starts from the overflow outlet of this tank, called Jharna.

But now it is very dilapidated. The pavilion and other buildings of Hauz-i-Shamsi have already collapsed and a monument standing in the centre of Hauz needs repair otherwise we shall lose this monument also.

Probably the original stone with the footprint of Hazrat Ali is believed to have been removed and brought to the present Dargah Shah-e-Marda in a newly developed locality called Aliganj. And it might be possible that because of the footprint this place was called Aliganj. Mirza Sangeen Baig, Sir Syed and Bashiruddin do not give any opinion on it.

DARGAH OF QUTUBUDDIN BAKHTIYAR KAKI

Khwaja Qutubuddin Bakhtiyar Kaki was popularly known as Qutub Sahib. He came to India with the earliest Muslim conquerors after journeying through Khurasan and Baghdad and became a disciple, and later a spiritual successor, of Khawaja Muinuddin Chishti of Ajmer. He lived during the reign of Iltutmish (1211–36) and died in 1236.

His grave, originally plain and earthen, but now enclosed within the marble balustrades and surmounted by a dome resting on pillars, completed as late as 1944, is the máin tomb. It lies in the middle of a rectangular enclosure, which has been embellished by different rulers of Delhi, the most pleasing part being the western wall containing floral multi-coloured tiles, said to have been fixed by Aurangzeb.

The sufi saint was held in high esteem by different rulers, and several of them lie buried in the various enclosures around his grave, the whole place being turned into a kind of necropolis. Among those buried here are Bahadur Shah I (1707–12), Shah Alam II (1759–1806), Akbar II (1806–37) and members of their families. Bahadur Shah II (1837–57) prepared a grave here for his burial, but it remained unutilized, as he was deported to Rangoon where he died and was buried.

The Dargah is provided with several gates, halls for different purposes, such as the Naubat-khana (drum-house), Majlis-khana (assembly-house) and Tosha-khana (robe-chamber), mosques, tanks and a baoli. According to an inscription on its main northern gate, it was erected in 1542, during Sher Shah's reign (1538–45) by Shaikh Khalil, a descendent of Shaikh Fariduddin Ganj-i-Shakar, who was himself a disciple and successor of Khwaja Qutubuddin Bakhtiyar Kaki. Among the important mosques is the small marble-built Moti Masjid (pearl mosque), with three arched openings and double-storeyed minars at the eastern corner of its courtyard. It is believed to have been built about 1709 by Bahadur Shah I. Farrukh Siyar (1713–19) added two gates to the enclosure of the *dargah*.

Outside the western entrance of the *dargah*, known as the Ajmeri Gate, are the ruins of Zafar Mahal, a palace built by Akbar II, the main gateway of which is said to have been reconstructed by Bahadur Shah II and named after his nom de plume Zafar. Built of red sandstone relieved by marbles, it is a lofty, three storeyed imposing structure, with arcades inside it flanked by rooms on the same pattern as in the Chhatta Chowk in the Red Fort.

In Sir Syed's sketch, there is a tent on the grave of Qutubuddin Bakhtiyar Kaki, but now it is encircled with arches and over that a beautiful dome has been constructed. It shows that up to 1847, there was no dome on the grave. It is added later on. It is also damaged by the people controlling the *dargah*. New constructions are coming up when it is against the ASI's laws. The floor of the *dargah* is also damaged by steel poles piercing it to make space frames and covering the courtyards. The *dargah* also passed into the illegal occupation of migrants from Pakistan in 1947. They started living inside the *dargah* and damaged the marble screens at several places which is an irreparable loss.

TUGHLAQABAD FORT

The fortress of Tughlaqabad stands on a rocky hill about 8 km from the Qutub Minar. Built by Ghiyasu'd-Din Tughlaq (1321–51), it constitutes the third city of Delhi, with a perimeter of 6.5 km. Its high rubble-built walls are provided with bastions and gates at intervals. On its south was a vast reservoir created through bunds between the hills to its east. A causeway connected it with Ghiyasu'din's Tomb, standing amidst waters, while a wide embankment near its south-eastern corner gave access to the fortress of Adilabad, built a little later, on the opposite hill.

Tughlaqabad was divided mainly into three portions. To the east of the present entrance from the Qutub–Badarpur Road, the rectangular area with high walls and bastions served as the citadel. A wider area immediately to its west, bounded by double walls and bastions, housed the palaces. Beyond this to the north lay the city, now marked by ruins of houses. The streets in the city, some of which can be traced even now, run in grids between gates on two opposite sides. Inside the citadel enclosure is a tower known as Bijai-Mandal and remains of several halls, including a long underground passage. Inside the fort only one small mosque and a royal stable are standing while the rest of the buildings have already collapsed. Sir Syed does not give any description or sketch of these monuments. So it shows that the buildings of Tughlaqabad Fort had already collapsed during his time.

Near the embankment connecting it with Adilabad are sluice gates through which water was controlled for irrigating the fields below.

Sir Syed's sketch shows that the area was surrounded with water and the fort was connected with the tomb via a bridge. Later the bridge was broken in the middle to construct the Mehrauli–Badarpur Road. As a result the whole campus of Tughlaqabad was shattered by the government of the NCR. Unauthorized colonies also came up within the fore walls of the Tughlaqabad Fort after the Partition of India. Only now has the ASI woken up to reclaim its lost property and is fighting for its recovery in the courts of Delhi, but it is too late.

ADILABAD FORT

The fort of Adilabad, south of Tughlaqabad, was built by Muhammad bin Tughluq (1325–51). Architecturally it is not much different from Tughlaqabad. The walls of the embankment connecting it with Tughlaqabad are carried over the hills as the outer walls of the city, and provided with two gates, one with barbicans between two bastions on the south-east and another on the south-west. Inside it, separated by a bailey, is a citadel consisting of walls, bastions and gates within which lay the palaces. The fortress is also known as Muhammadabad. Sir Syed's sketch of Adilabad shows it in a better condition than now. It is badly ruined because of the negligence of those agencies which are supposed to carry out its protection and preservation.

HAZRAT NIZAMUDDIN AULIA'S DARGAH

Shaikh Nizamuddin was born at Budaun in 1236. He became the disciple of the famous saint Shaikh Fariduddin Ganj-i-Shakar, who appointed him as his successor. Both Alau'd-Din Khalji (1296–1316) and Muhammad Tughluq were devoted to him.

Hazrat Nizamuddin died in 1325. His original tomb does not exist any longer. It was repaired and decorated by Firuz Shah Tughluq (1351–88), but even the repaired building has disappeared. The present structure was built in AH 970 by Faridu'n Khan, a noble of Shahjahan's reign, and has been added to or repaired later by several persons. It consist of a square chamber surrounded by verandahs, which are pierced by arched openings. The dome is ornamented by vertical stripes of black marble and is crowned by a lotus cresting. The area around the tomb was regarded as sacred, with the result that a large number of persons, including those from the royalty, lie buried there.

HAUZ-I-KHAS

A road branching off the Delhi–Mehrauli Road (now named Sri Aurobindo Marg) south of Green Park terminates at Hauz-i-Khas. Alau'd-Din Khalji excavated a large tank here for the use of the inhabitants of Siri, the second city of Delhi founded by him. It was then known as Hauz-i-Ala'i. Firuz Shah Tughluq desilted it and repaired it, and built several buildings on its southern and eastern banks, which are now known as Hauz-i-Khas, and are enclosed partly within modern walls.

Firuz Shah's tomb, a rubble built but plastered square chamber with high but slightly battered walls and a lofty dome, is the most prominent among these buildings. The monotonous austere look of its exterior is broken by a string-course of red carved sandstone battlements. The tomb is entered through a door on the south, with a courtyard enclosed within stone railings. The intrados and ceiling of the dome and squinch-pendentives are decorated with plaster-work, Sikander Lodi undertook some repairs to the tomb and AH 913 (1507) is incised on the wall. The doorway spanned by a lintel and the stone railings outside it are feature of Indian construction, which have been pleasantly mingled with characteristics of Central Asia architecture. Among the four graves inside the chamber, the central one is believed to be that of Firuz Shah and two of his sons and a grandson.

Contiguous with the tombs to its west and north and rising from the bank of the tank are a series of two-storeyed halls and chambers that were built by Firuz Shah around 1352 as a *madrasa* or college for imparting education. At their northern extremity is a mosque. These buildings are sited on an L-shaped plan. With their latticed windows, medallions in stucco, lotus motif, paintings on ceilings, balconied windows and deep niches, possibly for keeping books, these wings stand out as a unique complex in their class. The independent building on the south-western corner could have served possibly as the principal's residence.

One of the old entrances to the area is from the west, now closed. There are several staircases leading down to the tank from the upper stories of the *madrasa*. Scattered over the area, including the neighbour-hood of the tank, are several tombs of different designs, but the people buried in them are not known, although some of these could be the teachers of the college.

In 1398, after defeating Mahmud Tughluq, Timur encamped at the tank and his historian Sharifuddin Yazdi was highly impressed by its large size. He however, wrongly ascribed the construction of the tank to Firuz Shah Tughluq. During Sir Syed's time there was one small village but now it has become a market centre and one of Delhi's posh colonies has come up.

The Indian Parliament has passed a law that no construction of any sort will be done within 200 m of historic monuments but the NDMC has allowed the construction of houses whose walls are touching the walls of the *madrasa* at Hauz-i-Khas and there are hotels in the courtyard of the mosque of this *madrasa*! It shows that the Government of India and the Government of Delhi has no check on such unauthorized constructions. We ourselves are damaging these beautiful monuments.

DARGAH-I-CHIRAGH-I-DILLI

The village of Chiragh-i-Dilli, on Malviya Nagar–Kalkaji Road, grew up slowly around the tomb of Nasiru'd-Din Mahmud entitled Raushan Chiragh-i-Dilli (illuminated lamp of Delhi), Khalifa of Hazrat Nizamuddin whom he succeeded as head of Chishti Silsilah. He died in 1356. The village was enclosed earlier within a large rubble-built rectangular enclosure with a gateway on each side, by Firuz Shah Tughluq. The tomb consists of a twelve-pillared square chamber, enclosed within perforated screens and surmounted by a plastered dome rising from an octagonal drum, with small domed turrets at the four corners. It has been renovated, decorated and provided with several halls from time to time, such as a Majlis-khana (assembly hall) and mosques among which one was built by the Mughal Emperor Farrukh Siyar. There exist also numerous tombs and graves inside the enclosure of the *dargah*.

PURANA QILA AREA

The Purana Qila occupies the ancient mound which conceals perhaps the ruins of the city of Indraprastha mentioned in the *Mahabharata*. Sher Shah Suri demolished the city of Dinpanah built by Humayun and on the same site raised this citadel. It is irregularly oblong on plan, with bastions on the corners and in the western wall. Its ramparts cover a perimeter of nearly 2 km. It has three main gates on the north, south, and the west, the last one functioning as the entrance now. The gates are double-storeyed, built with red sandstone and surmounted by *chhatris*. On the inside, against the enclosure wall run cells two-bay in depth. Of the three main gates, the northern one is called the Talaqi-darwaza (forbidden gate). Why and when the entrance through it was forbidden is not known. Above the oriel windows on its front are carved marble pleogryphs engaged in combat with a man. The exterior of the gates was originally decorated with coloured tiles, and the rooms with incised plaster-work. It is believed that Sher Shah left the Purana Qila unfinished, and it was completed by Humayun, and it is possible, therefore, that if the gate was not constructed by Humayun it was at least repaired by him. On the southern gate, which is called the Humayun-darwaza, there existed a similar inscription in ink mentioning Sher Shah and the date AH 950 (1543–4).

Purana Qila originally lay on the bank of the Yamuna. The general depression on the northern and western sides of the fortress suggests that a wide moat connected with the river existed on these sides, which were approached through a causeway connecting the fortress with the mainland. Most of the buildings of the fort have now collapsed.

QILA-I-MUBARAK

After transferring his capital from Agra to Delhi in 1638 Shahjahan commenced the construction of Shahjahanabad, and a little later, on 16 April 1639, he also laid the foundation of his citadel, Qila-i-Mubarak, known also by other names in contemporary accounts. It was completed after nine years on 16 April 1648. The entire fort is said to have cost about Rs. 59 lakh, half of it on the palaces.

The Red Fort, so-called because of the red colour of the stone largely used in it, is octagonal in plan, with two longer sides on the east and west. On the north, the fort is connected by a bridge to Salimgarh. It measures about 900 m by 550 m, with its rampart walls covering a perimeter of 2.41 km and rising to a height of 33.5 m on the town side and 18 m along the river. Outside the ramparts runs a moat, originally connected with the river Yamuna.

The palaces lie along the eastern side of the fort, while two imposing three-storeyed buildings flanked by semi-octagonal towers and consisting of several apartments are located in the centre of the western and southern sides and are known as Lahori and Delhi gates. On the outside, the Delhi Gate is flanked by the statues of two elephants renewed in 1903 by Lord Curzon in place of the ones which had been demolished long ago by Aurangzeb. The main entrance to the fort lies through the Lahori Gate and palaces are reached through the roofed passage, flanked by arcaded apartments called Chhatta Chowk and now used as shops. The other portions were originally the residences of the courtiers and the retinue. Both the gates were built by Aurangzeb. There exist three other entrances on the other sides, now largely closed.

After the British occupied it in 1857, they constructed some new buildings inside the fort which totally damaged its campus. When Delhi was connected with rail, the railway tracks were built close to the Red Fort by demolishing one of its bastions.

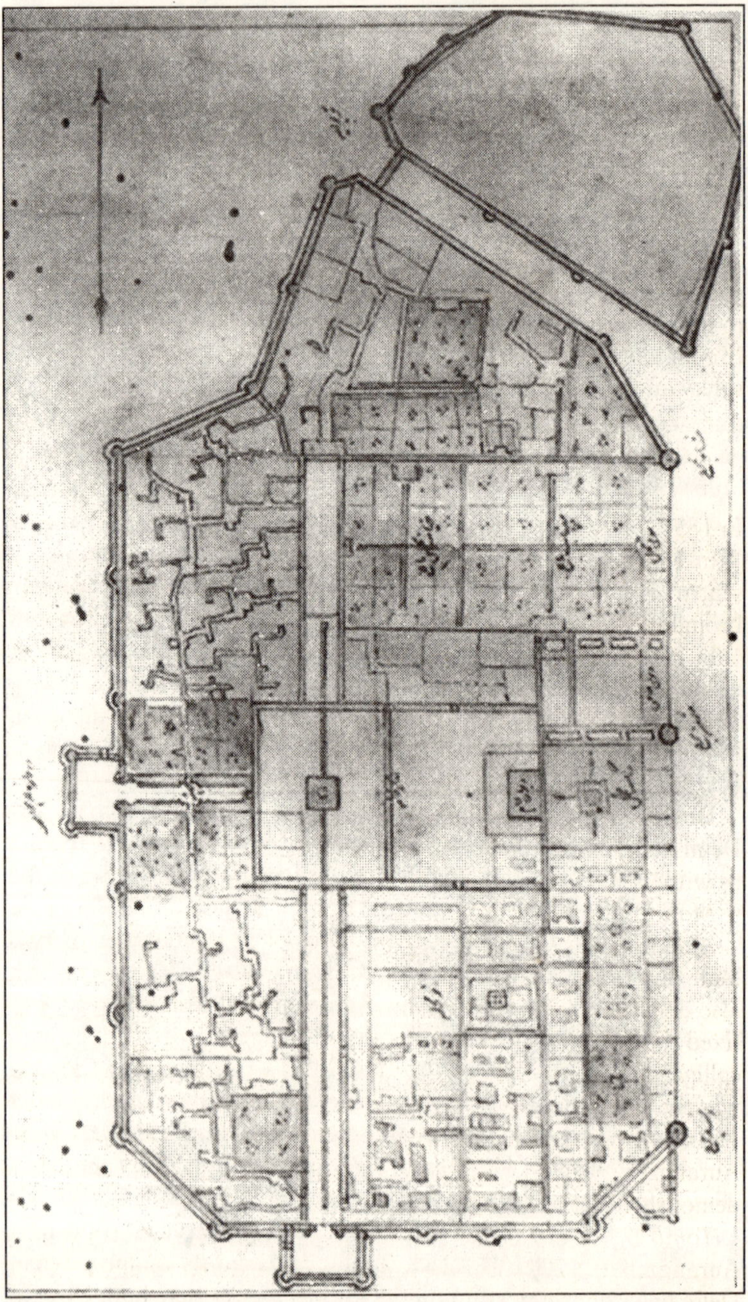

The British demolished Mehtab Bagh and half of Bagh-i-Hayat Baksh. In the courtyard of the Diwan-i-Am, kitchen, Tosha-khana were also demolished. Behind the Diwan-i-Am, there was Wali Ahad ka Mahal which too was demolished and the *hauz* was filled with mud.

There was a bridge over the Yamuna between the Red Fort and Salimgarh. Now it is part of the Ring Road.

The Red Fort was occupied by the British Army in 1857 and even after 15 August 1947, some of its portions remained under the occupation and use of the Indian Army and much damage was caused to the structure. In 2003 it was vacated by the Indian Army because Mr Jagmohan, former Minister of Culture, took an interest in the safety and conservation of the Red Fort.

STRUCTURES DAMAGED AND DEMOLISHED

In 1857, *Shah Burj's* dome was demolished.

In 1857, some paintings hanging there were taken out and were sent to English museums. But Curzon repaired them in 1906 and brought them back to India.

In 1904, some repair was done by Lord Curzon. Nasheman-i-Zill-i-Ilahi was reconstructed.

Tasbih Khana: Persian verses were inscribed here in gold water but now those verses are not there. But the same verses have been documented by Sir Syed Ahmed Khan in his *Asarus Sanadid*.

Diwan-i-Khas: Here Bahadur Shah II was declared Emperor of Delhi in 1857 and here itself the court called Bahadur Shah to appear as witness to answer his crimes relating to mutiny of 1857.

Moti Mahal was demolished after 1857.

Akbarabadi Mosque: Akbarabadi Begum, a wife of Shahjahan built this mosque which is now in Subhash Park. After 1857 it was also demolished and Sir Syed purchased the Koranic inscription and fixed those at the Jama Mosque at Aligarh Muslim University. The calligrapher of the inscriptions at the Taj Mahal and this mosque was the same person.

Aurangabadi Mosque: This mosque was built by a wife of Aurangzeb. When Delhi was connected with railways it was also demolished in 1857.

Tomb of Zebun Nisa: The tomb was built for a daughter of Aurangzeb (d. 1702) near the Kabuli Gate of Shahjahanabad. When Delhi was connected with railways it was also demolished.

In 2002–3 the Ministry of Culture, gave a grant for its preservation. Now we see a new life in the Red Fort which had remained neglected since 1857. Credit goes to Jagmohan, for he paid attention for the first time to the protection of the Red Fort in free India. Since the British conquest of Delhi in 1857, it remained under the occupation of the British Army who filled the inside of the fort with ugly barracks. I do not agree with William Dalrymple when he says, 'the barracks should of course have been torn down years ago,' no these barracks should be given full protection so that we and future generations can see how the British defaced Qila-i-Mubarak built by Shahjahan. There is a law of the ASI that no new constructions of any kind can be done inside or outside the monument. This is the case of a law abiding nation whom our intellectual class was considering in 1857 that Indians should not oppose as the Britishers would modernize India.

William Dalrymple writes

Meanwhile, what remained of the Mughals' Red Fort became a grey British Barrack. The Naqqar Khana became the quarters of British Staff Sergeant. The Diwan-i-Am became a lounge for officers, the emperor's private entrance a canteen, and the Rang Mahal was turned into a military officers' mess. The Mumtaz Mahal was turned into a military prison. The magnificent Lahore Darwaza was renamed the Victoria Gate. Pavillions of Hayat Bakhsh Bagh were turned into urinals.[6]

Hindu traders and bankers even bought up two of the city's most famous mosques: Chuna Mal bought Fatehpuri Masjid, while a Hindu banker bought the Zinatul Masjid. Madarsa-i-Rahimiya was auctioned off to Ramji Das.[7]

William Dalrymple quotes the great Victorian historian of architecture, James Fergusson, no whining liberal. Fergusson's horror is recorded at what had happened in his *History of Indian and Eastern Architecture*: 'Those who carried out this fearful piece of vandalism', he wrote, did not even think 'to make a plan of what they are destroying, or preserving any record of the most splendid palace of the world . . . the engineers perceived that by gutting the palace they could provide at no expense a well round their barrack yard . . . the palace was sacrificed.'[8] One Urdu poet rightly sums up the destruction of Shahjahanabad by the British.

مٹ گئے تیرے مٹانے کے نشاں بھی اب تو   اے فلک! اس سے زیادہ نہ مٹانا ہرگز

When the revolution came to Iran in 1979 and the Shah left Iran, not a single article in his palace was touched or disturbed by any Iranian. The West calls Iran a country of fundamentalists. British politicians and bureaucrats should go to Tehran and compare the vandalism caused by British officers at the Qila-i-Mubarak of Delhi in 1857. And see how the Iranians have protected the palace of the Shah.

OLD DELHI RAILWAY STATION

The station was built within the four walls of Shahjahanabad by demolishing the bastion of the Red Fort, the tomb of Zebun Nisa and Aurangabadi's Mosque. The entrances of Shiatus Safa Mosque and Punja Sharif's were blocked by the railway line and separated by the populated area of Shahjahanabad. This was intentionally done by British planners otherwise they could have built it just in front of Mori Gate as New Delhi Railway Station is in front of Ajmeri Gate. The British had two intentions by doing so:

1. They wanted an entry into Shahjahanabad through rail so that arms and ammunition could be transported easily inside Shahjahanabad. They had taken a railway line right into the Red Fort by demolishing some of its portions for the same reason.
2. They wanted to tease Muslims by demolishing the bastions of Red Fort, Zebun Nisa's Tomb and Aurangzeb's wife Aurangabadi's Mosque were demolished in 1852 so that Muslims would know that now the British were the masters of Hindustan.

PUNJA SHARIF

Punja Sharif lies near Old Delhi Railway Station. It is related to the relic of Imam Hussain. The whole building has been renovated.

GHAZI-UD-DIN KHAN'S MADRASA AND TOMB

These monuments lie outside the Ajmeri Gate of Shahjahanabad. They consist of a large enclosure of arcaded apartments with a gate on the east and a three-domed mosque on the west, with an enclosure of perforated stone screens, both on the latter's north and south. Ghazi-ud-din Khan's grave is one of the three in the southern enclosure. Red stone has been used as a facing veneer in most of the monuments.

Ghazi-ud-din Khan was an influential courtier during the reigns of Aurangzeb (1658–1707) and his son and ultimate successor Shah Alam I (1707–12). His son, Mir Qamaruddin was appointed the Governor of the Deccan by Muhammad Shah (1719–48) and became the founder of the Nizami of Hyderabad.

The arcaded apartments were used as a *madrasa*, which became first the Anglo-Arabic school and later the Anglo-Arabic college, and is now known as the Delhi College.

After Partition it was occupied by some unauthorized persons. They badly damaged the marble tomb of Ghazi-ud-din Khan.

In 2003, the Ministry of Culture had given a grant to bring this monument back to its old glory. A lot of restoration work has been taken up but a lot needs to be done.

KHAN-I-KHANAN'S TOMB

The tomb of Abdur Rahim Khan who had the title of Khan-i-Khanan, lies east of the Mathura Road opposite Nizamuddin. It is a massive square edifice rising from a high platform faced by a arched cells. Double-storeyed, with a high and deeply recessed central arch on each side and several shallow arches on the flanks in each storey, it follows the pattern of Humayun's Tomb. The interior of the tomb is decorated with incised and painted plaster with beautiful designs, especially on the ceiling. Around the double dome are disposed *chhatris* at the corners and *dalans* (open) halls in the middle of the sides. The red sandstone, marble and other stones which faced it originally were later removed and used in Safdar Jang's Tomb.

Abdur Rahim Khan-i-Khanan was the son of Bairam Khan, regent of Akbar, and served both Akbar and Jahangir. He knew several languages and composed couplets in Hindi under the familiar name of Rahim. He died in 1626–7.

The sketch in *Asarus Sanadid* shows the bad condition of this monument but now it is well preserved.

SAFDAR JANG'S TOMB

The tomb of Mirza Muqim Abu'l Mansur Khan, entitled Safdar Jang (1739–54), viceroy of Oudh under Muhammad Shah and later his Prime Minister is the last example of the garden tomb layout, which began with Humayun's Tomb. It was built in AH 1167 (1753–4), by Nawab Shuja'ud Daula, Safdar Jang's son. Its extensive garden enclosure, over 300 sq m, is divided into four squares by wide pathways and tanks, which are again divided into smaller squares by passages on the pattern of Mughal gardens (*chaharbagh*). The high rubble walls of the enclosure, with channels over them to carry water to different pavilions, contain a series of recessed arches on the interior and octagonal towers (*chhatris*) in the four corners. In the centre of the eastern side is the double-storeyed impressive gateway to the enclosure with several apartments, a courtyard and a mosque. The same position on the other side is occupied by multi-chambered spacious pavilions, known originally as Moti Mahal, Badshah Pasand (king's favourite), and Jangli Mahal (sylvan palace), on the north, south and west respectively. The mosque, built with red sandstone on the second storey, was obviously added later.

The double-storeyed mausoleum, 18.28 sq m built with red and buffstone relieved by marble, stands in the centre of the garden and rises from a high platform faced by a verandah, broken by arched openings, leading to a series of cells on the inside. The central chambers of the mausoleum are square with eight apartments around it, the corner apartments being octagonal and the others rectangular. There is one cenotaph in the central chamber, but two graves are located below ground under the centre of the platform, presumably, one of Safdar Jang and the other of his wife. The ceilings of different apartments are ornamented with incised and painted plaster-work. The large dome with its bulbous outline rises from a sixteen-sided drum. The corners of the mausoleum are occupied by polygonal towers picked with inlaid marble designs, and covered by *chhatris*. The arched entrances to the tomb chambers from all the four sides are located within high recessed engrailed arches.

NOTES

1. William Dalrymple, *The Fall of the Dynasty*, Noida, 2006, p. 8.
2. Ibid.
3. Sir Syed Ahmad Khan, *Asarus Sanadid*, New Delhi, 2000, p. 18.
4. Altaf Hussain Hali, *Hayat-i-Javed*, Delhi, 1971, p. 11.
5. Ibid., p. 12.
6. Dalrymple, p. 460.
7. Ibid., pp. 460–1.
8. Ibid., p. 7.

CHAPTER 2

Political Thought of Sir Syed

B. SHEIKH ALI

Sir Syed holds the rare distinction of changing the course of history. It was he who brought about a renaissance in the thought process of Indian Muslims, who lifted them up from the depths of despondency to hope and faith, who made them march in the direction of modernity, who reconciled intellectualism of the West with the traditionalism of the East, and who laid more emphasis on mind than on matter, more on realism than on idealism, and more on liberalism than on conservatism. As a social reformer, as a religious thinker, as a political leader, and as a builder of institutions, he has left deep impressions on the sands of time.

However, it must be said that politics was not his cup of tea. It was education, it was social reform, it was religious thought, it was history, philosophy, literature, law, theology, archaeology, science and journalism. Such a person was reluctantly drawn into politics, which involved policy-making. It is said, 'No wise man has a policy. A policy is the black-mail levelled on the fool by the unforeseen.' Therefore, Sir Syed's politics should be viewed in the context of a social reformer pushed into the vortex of politics where he took short-term measures of immediate benefits rather than adopt long-term strategy that could have averted the later tragedy. In Sir Syed's entire life there are only two areas where his critics could point a finger. One is his political thought and the other, his religious ideas. His religious ideas are only of academic interest, having no impact on history, but his political ideas changed the course of history. Politics is a difficult game where expediency rather than principles play a vital role, and where rules are often violated to score a point.

Sir Syed's political thoughts had worldwide impact. They affected the Islamic world, the Western world and the Indian subcontinent. On the Islamic world they had such a profound effect as to produce reformers of the order of Shaikh Muhammad Abdahu, Rashid Raza, Shakeeb Arsalan, Abdul Khadir Maghrabi, Jamaluddin Afghani and Mustafa Kamal Ataturk. On the European scene, he was able to put across his ideas in England on such great personalities as Marquis of Lorne, close relation of Queen Victoria; Duke of Argyll, Secretary of State for India; Lord Lawrence, former Governor-General of India, Lord Stanley, former Ambasador to Constantinople; Thomas Carlyle, the renowned thinker; John William Kaye, historian of the Mutiny; Sir John Strachey, the great administrator, and an intellectual, and others, with whom he did not simply sing a song of Western superiority, but laid bare the points where they went wrong. He published in England his famous pamphlet *Strictures Upon the Present Government System in India,* which was highly critical of British policy in India. In this pamphlet, for instance, he stated that the English had reduced the Indian members of the district Educational Committees to such a low level that they were no better than the 'wax figures taken from Madam Tussaud's exhibition'.[1] It required great moral courage for a guest to be so critical of the host in a foreign land. As for the Indian scenario, his impact was so great that the entire history of our freedom movement is nothing but a triangle: on one side, the colonials, on the second side, the nationalists and on the third side, the defenders of Sir Syed's political thoughts.

Sir Syed's politics is characterized as loyalism, whose basic parameters were five forces, namely fear, hope, appreciation, commitment, and pragmatism. It is the fear complex that haunted him most. He had witnessed the events of 1857, and would do anything to avoid their recurrence. He was like the French man who boasted that he played a vital role in the French Revolution, and on asking what role that was, he said, 'I survived the Revolution'. Sir Syed had done something more. Not only did he survive, but he really played a great humanitarian role, and had analysed threadbare the causes for the revolt. He would shudder to recall what a havoc it was.

Secondly, he lived on hope, and wrote a good deal on hope. His hope was to rebuild a destroyed society, to make it stand on its own, to revive its health, its morals and manners, and to integrate it with something modern. For this purpose he had started the Aligarh College, had instituted the *Aligarh Gazette*, had established the Scientific Society and had organized the All India Educational Conferences. He had launched a programme of social reforms and had inaugurated a literary renaissance. More than all, he had initiated a policy of rapprochement with the administration which would end a century-old confrontation with the British. All these hopes would be shattered if he joined the mainstream of national agitation.

Thirdly, he appreciated Western learning, their advance in science and technology, their economic and social progress, and their development in every field. He felt India was far behind them in several sectors. He was in the service of the East India Company and knew well their organizing abilities. His visit to England made him love their institutions. What impressed him most was their educational system, which gave them superiority of mind. He appreciated their universities so much that he desired to plant a Cambridge in India as well.

Fourthly, his deep commitment was to bring about a social change. He had newly entered into the race of social reforms. The Hindus were ahead of him by half a century. In order to catch up with them, he would not offend the administration, without whose help he could not run the college even for a day. His own community was most unhelpful. Far from supporting the college, they bitterly opposed him and called him a heretic.

Lastly, his pragmatism made him adopt the policy of loyalism in order to bring immediate relief to his community. He had bitter experience in 1867 when Hindi agitation was started to displace Urdu. He was very sensitive to cultural change. He told Shakespeare, then Collector of Benares, that he was not hopeful Hindus and Muslims would get on smoothly. When Shakespeare was greatly surprised at his new trend, as Sir Syed had always stood for Hindu–Muslim unity, he said that this was only the beginning of a divergence, and that more was to follow in future. He regretted it was a bad trend, but it was inevitable as it was in the nature of things. Events proved him prophetic. Even from his deathbed in 1898 he wrote a powerful article for the retention of Urdu as official language. Urdu–Hindi controversy loomed large in later years acting as a potent factor in the rift between Hindus and Muslims. Therefore, his pragmatism made him think that in a democracy where majority view would prevail, the interests of the Muslim minority might suffer. His loyalism was based on such apprehensions.

The areas where his political thoughts were reflected were his analysis of the causes of the events of 1857; his great efforts to avert the persecution of the Muslims in the wake of those events; his refutation of Hunter's allegations against the Wahhabi movement;

his role in the Viceroy's Legislative Council; his participation in the educational reforms; his relations with the Hindus; and his confrontation with the Indian National Congress. For over four decades from 1857 he was actively involved simultaneously in several sectors of life—society, religion, literacy, education and politics. Perhaps, no other leader of the nineteenth century had so much to do in so many areas of human development.

THE CAUSES OF THE INDIAN REVOLT

We many call the masterpiece of Sir Syed's political wisdom was his book, *The Causes of the Indian Revolt*. It was more an indictment of English rule than an apology for what had happened in 1857. He listed both important and unimportant causes. The distribution of chapattis, the role of Bahadur Shah Zafar in the movement, the involvement of the Iranian government in the annexation of Oudh, the formation of the National League, the planning of *jihad*, the *fatwa* of *jihad*, the question of cartridges, were all in his view, unimportant causes. The real causes according to him were the divorce of *de jure* from *de facto* power in India. The absence of a machinery to know the grievances of the people, the passing of the provocative laws which offended the people, the apprehensions of the people as to the intentions of the government, the ignorance of the administration about the problems of the people, the absence of the essential elements of good governance in the land, and the lapses of the army. The whole treatise was a long indictment of the Company's rule in India.

He said the distribution of chapattis was no sign of a deep conspiracy as it was merely 'a kind of talisman to keep off the cholera, the superstitious Hindustanees being in the habit of using such talismans'.[2] On the issue of Iranian involvement in the affair, Sir Syed said, 'As between Roman Catholics and Protestants, so between the Mussalmans of Persia and of Hindustan, cordial cooperation is impossible.'[3] About the proclamation which was found in the tent of a Persian prince, he said it was no proof of conspiracy as it might have been posted after the break-out of the mutiny.

Sir Syed denied Bahadur Shah Zafar could have been a cause of the rebellion. Sir Syed observed, 'Such an imbecile was the ex-king that had one assured him that the angels of heaven were his slaves, he would have welcomed the assurance, and would have caused half a dozen *farmans* to be prepared immediately.'[4] He said the annexation of Oudh at worst could have caused irritation, as the English had broken their treaties, but the irritation was confined to nobles, princes and talukdars, and not to the general public, much less to the mutineers who were sepoys, not the governing class.[5] About the National League he said the sepoys had fought many wars for the English in the past and at no time they had protested. He asked 'How then can it be supposed that the present revolt originated from hatred on the part of the Mussalman against those who had wrenched the kingdom from them?'[6] In 1827 Amherst openly declared that sovereignty of India belonged to the British government and nobody questioned that position.[7]

Sir Syed refuted the argument of *jihad*, as the English had not interfered in the religious practices of the Muslims. The events of 1857 were not a religious war, and no preparations were made for it before 10 May 1857.[8] He said, 'the fact seems to be that some scoundrels prompted by greed and hoping to gain their end by deceiving fools and increasing their own numbers gave the disturbances the like of a religious war'.[9] The printed *fatwa* of *jihad* was a counterfeit. Sir Syed asserted, 'I have gone into the question, and I found very strong proof to the effect that this *fatwa* was a forgery . . . a noted scoundrel stamped it, by the way, with the seal of a man who had died before the commencement of the mutinees.'[10] Sir Syed said that 'even the question of new cartridges was not a serious problem, as the sepoys believed that the government would not insist on their use and the order was withdrawn on 2 May 1857'.[11]

Sir Syed then took up the real causes and said the political structure the British had raised in India was faulty, and that the divorce of *de jure* from *de facto* power caused all the confusion. He said, 'The King of Delhi was a spark from a furnace which wasted by the wind, eventually set all Hindustan in a blaze.'[12] The people thought the Mughals were still ruling over India, whereas the reality was quite different when the British were in effective power.

The second lapse Sir Syed pointed out was the absence of a machinery to redress the grievances of the people. No member of the legislative council was an Indian, and the Europeans who were different from Indians in religion, customs, habits and manners could not understand the real problems. Sir Syed said that the people should have a voice in the council, and that alone could 'check the errors in the bud, and warn us of the danger before they are burst upon. . . . A needle may dam the gushing rivulet. An elephant must turn aside from the swollen torrent.'[13] Sir Syed added, 'There is no reason why the natives of his country should be excluded from the Legislative Council, and there it is that you come upon the one great root of all this evil. Here is the origin of all the troubles that have befallen Hindustan.'[14]

Sir Syed furnished five more causes:

1. Ignorance on the part of the people by which I mean apprehension of the intentions of the government.
2. The passing of such laws and regulations and forms of procedure as jarred the established custom and practice of Hindustan, and the introduction of such as were in themselves objectionable.
3. Ignorance on the part of the government of the condition of the people, of their mode of thought and life, and of the grievances through which their hearts were becoming estranged.
4. The neglect on the part of the rulers of such points as were essential for the good government of Hindustan.
5. The bad management, and disaffection of the army.

He elaborated these five points, and illustrated in each case how the government had gone wrong. The interference in matters of religion was undesirable. Both Hindus and Muslims thought that the government was forcing Christianity on them. It was taking advantage of the poverty and ignorance of the people and inducing them to change religion by offer of jobs to them. The missionaries had intensified their preaching of the gospel in schools and colleges. The destitutes of the famine of 1837 were given relief on accepting Christianity. The Bishop of Calcutta, Revd. E. Edmund, issued a circular letter to all offices stating that when the whole of India was unified through rails and telegraphs, 'it was right, therefore, that we should all become Christians'.[15] This circular made the people mad. 'They cried out that the long expected hour had indeed arrived. The servants of government were first to be made Christians, then the mass of the people.'[16] This circular was more repugnant to the Muslims as they were more sensitive in religious matters.

Sir Syed was highly critical of the military administration. He listed quite a few defects and suggested reforms. The paucity of Europeans in the army made the sepoys feel 'it was they who conquered India from Burma to Kabul'.[17] Thus the whole treatise was a long indictment of British policy in India. It was packed with irritants to any imperialist. But they drew right lessons. Its impact was such that they exonerated the Muslims from the charges of conspiracy, and placed the blame on the shoulders of the administration.

REVIEW OF HUNTER'S BOOK

Hunter's book, *Indian Mussalmans* was concentrated poison on Muslims of India. He had said, 'The Mussalmans of India are, and have been for many years, a source of chronic danger to the British power in India.'[18] He referred to the Wahhabi movement in Bengal which had affected the masses. Sir Syed refuted all arguments of Hunter and said Wahhabism was pure theism free from rituals of medieval time. He traced the entire history up to the days of Syed Ahmed Shaheed and effectively replied all contentious issues which Hunter had raised.

In 1878 Lord Lytton made Sir Syed a member of his Legislative Council and Lord Ripon renewed the term in 1880. Sir Syed took keen interest in welfare measures of the public. He vehemently supported the Agricultural Relief Bill, the Vaccination Bill, the Educational Reforms Bill, the appointment of Qazis, and the local self-government measures. He sketched the conditions of the peasants and said the 'Marwaris were particularly obnoxious to them'.[19] The main issue was rural indebtedness. It is surprising how well Sir Syed had understood the rural problems of India. He fought tooth and nail for the passage of compulsory vaccination, which was opposed by his own countrymen on superstitious ground, and saw to it that it was finally passed. He played a major role in the educational reforms and removed many of their shortcomings.

RELATIONS WITH HINDUS

Sir Syed did not desire anything at the expense of the Hindus. He regarded the Hindus and Muslims as 'Two eyes of a beautiful bride whose face would be disfigured if either one or the other were to be injured.' In recent years he is wrongly held responsible for the two-nation theory. Objective study will reveal that he advocated all national causes. As late as 1883, he said, 'Now both of us live on the air of India, drink the holy water of Ganga and Jamuna. We both feed upon the products of the Indian soil. We are together in life and death; living in India both of us have changed; ill-feelings are sure to destroy us.'[20] Addressing the Hindus in the Punjab he had said, 'You have used the term Hindu for yourselves. This is not correct. For in my opinion the word Hindu does not denote a particular religion, but on the contrary, everyone who lives in India has the right to call himself a Hindu. I am therefore sorry that although I live in India, you do not consider me a Hindu.'[21] He had said in Patna, 'Please remember that the Hindu, Muslim or Christian, are by virtue of the fact of their residence, one nation. The time is past when merely on the ground of religion the inhabitants of this country could be regarded as members of two nations.'[22] He repeated the same sentiments at Gurdaspur on 27 January 1884, 'We (Hindus and Muslims) should try to become one heart and soul and act in unison, if united we can support each other. If not, the effect of one against the other would tend to destruction and downfall of both.'[23] He forcefully advised the Muslims to give up the sacrifice of cows for religious rituals. He said the friendship of the Hindus was far more valuable than a little satisfaction of religious rights.[24]

These sentiments amply reflect his relations with the Hindus. Yet why was there divergence? It was because of two reasons, positive and negative. The positive side was his mission to modernize the Muslims and bring them up to the level of the Hindus. The negative was his advice to the Muslims to go slow on politics, as that would alienate the British whose support was crucial to remove their backwardness. He was not, unlike the Hindus, in a hurry to unfold the drama of human freedom which in the absence of an enlightened public would present a picture of chaos.

The more negative factors widened the gulf. One was Hindu revivalism in the wake of Western learning and the other was British policy of divide and rule. What hurt the thinking of Sir Syed was the view of some Hindu intellectuals, who spoke only of a Hindu nation. In one of the lectures in 1872 Rajnarain Bose said, 'I see in my mind the noble and puissant Hindu nation rousing herself after sleep and rushing headlong towards progress with divine powers. I see this rejuvenated nation illumining the world by her knowledge, spirituality and culture and the glory of the Hindu nation again spreading over the whole world.'[25] Bankim Chandra Chatterji's novel *Anand Math* was an open attack on Muslim culture. A new kind of history came to be written in which every Rajput warrior was depicted a hero and his rival, a devil. Sir Syed was greatly agitated by the attempts to substitute Hindi in the place of Urdu.

In such a situation Sir Syed was perplexed by an attack on Muslims from three different directions, one from the British who held Muslims responsible for the events of 1857, the second from his own co-religionists who wanted to stick to traditionalism and the third from Hindu revivalists who wanted Hindu nationalism to prevail. His sole purpose was to save the sinking ship of the Muslims and to bring it safely to shore. The strategy he adopted for this purpose was loyalism which would effectively answer the challenges from all the three directions. His policy towards the Indian National Congress should be viewed in this perspective.

INDIAN NATIONAL CONGRESS

Sir Syed's differences with the Congress were so serious that they ultimately changed the course of history. It should also be said that he was not responsible for what subsequently happened, and that what happened was not what he wanted. He was a nationalist to the core who had quarreled with his friends for not calling him a Hindu, and who had called Hindus and Muslims as two eyes of a beautiful bride. His differences with the Congress arose because of his loyalism to the British and also because of the great role the European staff of Aligarh College played in the politics of the country. His rift with the Congress was also because of his conviction that the West was so far ahead of the East that until the East caught up with the West any agitative politics of the Congress was not desirable. It would be more suicidal to the Muslims, who were not on par even with their own countrymen, much less with the Europeans. The fear element that worked on his conscience was how the Muslims had suffered more than the Hindus in the events of 1857. Just at a time when a recovery seemed possible, he would not break with the British.

Moreover, Sir Syed was aware of the fact that the Muslims lagged behind the Hindus by half a century, as Hindu renaissance started in 1830 under Raja Rammohun Roy, whereas the Muslims woke up only in the 1880s. Yet another reason was his apprehension that the Congress demand for dominion status on the pattern of Canada would mean majority rule which might adversely affect the interests of the minorities. As the Muslims were one-fourth of the Hindus, the balance of power would be tilted in favour of the Hindus.

When the Congress was established in 1885, Sir Syed remained aloof. Surendranath Banerji wrote to him, 'no assembly of national delegates would be complete without your presence'.[26] The Congress was disappointed by his silence. Earlier he had supported the claims which the Congress was now forcefully demanding, namely to hold competitive examinations in India. As a member of the Viceregal Council he had supported local self-government and the right of Indian judges to try Europeans, opposing the Ilbert Bill. He had himself started the British Indian Association, and when he revived it in 1877 at Aligarh, Banerji attended its session. As late as 1884 Banerji visited Aligarh again to start another political organization, the National Fund, and made Sir Syed its President. Six months later the picture was completely changed.

Three theories are advanced for this change. One was Sir Syed's own assessment that too much involvement in agatitive politics was not in the best interests of the Muslims. The second was the influence of two Muslim leaders of Calcutta, Syed Amir Ali and Abdul Latif, who thought democracy would adversely affect the Muslims. The third theory was the role of Theodore Beck, the Principal of Aligarh College, through whom the British arm-twisted Sir Syed. Beck was a symbol of British Paramountcy both in intellectual and political areas, and a staunch supporter of Muslim recovery. A few think that if Beck was not there, Muslims would have joined the Congress. He realized British interests would be served better if Muslims were kept away from the Hindus. When Banerji came to Aligarh, Beck expressed the opinion Bengalis would knock off all government jobs, if competitions were held in India.[27] He wrote in the college magazine, that the Congress leaders were 'no better than ungrateful school boys dealing with subjects far above their comprehension and like ill-bred creatures biting the hands that feed them'.[28] He bitterly criticized the Congress and excited communal passion, saying the 'object of anti-cow killing movement is to prevent Muhammadans and Englishmen alike from killing cows for food'.[29]

Beck went to the extent of saying that the students of Aligarh College should be ready 'to face bullets and bayonets in defence of the glorious empire'.[30] In an article appeared in the *Pioneer*, 26 November 1893, he said Lord Dufferin should not have yielded to the demand of the elective councils, and that the Parliament should not have agreed to holding competitive examinations simultaneously both in England and in India.[31] He founded a parallel organization in August 1888 known as 'The United Indian Patriotic Association' against the Indian National Congress in order to inform the Parliament that the zamindars and princes were not with the Congress. In December 1893 he set up the Mohammedan Anglo-Oriental Defence Association of Upper India for the alleged purpose of protecting Muslim interests in India.[32] Thus Beck had a hand in shaping the political policy of Aligarh. He was in the good books of Sir Syed, but there is no evidence to believe that Sir Syed had surrendered his judgement to Beck. Sir Syed had snubbed Beck on many occasions, if he did anything against his desires.

It was only in 1887 Sir Syed came out openly against the Congress when Badruddin Tyabji was installed as the President. Sir Syed set up a rival organization, Mohammedan Educational Conference which met in Lucknow at the same time that the Congress held its session in Madras. It was the first meeting of great political importance, well attended by intellectuals, aristocrats, civil servants, army officers, lawyers, journalists, Syeds, Sheikhs, Mughals, Pathans, Shias and Sunnis. The conference made out a case that the proper representatives of Indian opinion in the councils of the government should be on the basis of 'social position' as determined by ancestry, and not merely on the basis of a degree, BA or MA, to rule over them. Sir Syed said that even the Hindus of UP would not be able to compete with the Bengalis. Not only would the Muslims be denied jobs but also the brave Rajputs, and they would be ruled by a Bengali 'who at the sight of a table-knife would crawl under the chair'.[33] Sir Syed added, 'therefore, if any of you, men of good position, *raises, nawabs,* men of the middle classes, men of noble family to whom God has given sentiments of honour . . . if you accept that the country should groan under the yoke of the Bengali rule and its people lick the Bengali shoes, then, in the name of God, jump into the train, sit down, and be off to Madras, be off to Madras!'[34]

Addressing the Muslims, he said,

> Weep at your conditions! Have you such wealth that you can compete with the Hindus? In the normal case no single Mohammedan will secure a seat in the Viceroy's Council. The whole Council will consist of Babu so-and-so Mitter, Babu so-and-so Ghosh, and Babu so-and-so Chukerbuthy.[35]

Speaking of the unfair results of the election system, he said,

> In Calcutta an old bearded Mohamedan of noble family met me and said that a terrible calamity had befallen them. In his town there were eighteen elected members, not one was a Mohammedan, all were Hindus. . . . I can assure that the only thing which can raise you to a high rank is high educa-

tion. Until our nation can give birth to highly educated people it will remain degraded; it will be below others and will not attain such honours as I desire for it.[36]

This Lucknow speech set the tune for his subsequent policy, which hardened itself against the Congress. The same arguments were repeated that the new trends were not in the best interests of the Muslims. Perhaps the European staff of the college had a hand in strengthening this conviction. He was quite conscious of the power in the hands of the bureaucrats, and unless a part of it fell to the share of the Muslims, the Hindu–Muslim problem would not be solved. Here was the seed of the communal problem which the colonials would not fail to exploit. Badruddin Tyabji attempted to remove Sir Syed's apprehension, but he was not successful.

CONCLUSION

In conclusion we may say Sir Syed's policy was dictated by fear; hope, commitment and pragmatism. He was for national unity, but the rising trends of Hindu nationalism desirous of eliminating Islamic impact, the obvious tilting of power towards majority in the democratic system, the pathetic conditions of the Muslim society, his commitment to lift them up from a desperate situation, his own historical consciousness of the rich heritage of Islamic culture, together with the colonial shrewdness to perpetuate their own rule through divide and rule, brought about wide divergence between the Hindus and the Muslims. However, he had no idea at that time what it would ultimately lead to. It was all a struggle to meet the challenges of the time.

There is one more important point to note in Sir Syed's policy. He loved nature and resented nationalism. Nature is God's creativity which is so beautiful, perfect and harmonious, while nationalism is the product of man's mind which sows seeds of discord. In the name of nationalism Europe fought so many wars. Democracy and nationalism were two Western concepts, and Sir Syed disliked them both. He thought the pluralist society with illiterate masses was not yet fit for either of these concepts. India had not known any other form of government than monarchy. Democracy is not a heaven of liberty, but it is a powerful despotism in the hands of a gifted group of politicians who sweeten the ears to catch votes and come to power.

They would create a situation where the people would be compelled to count their heads rather than break the heads. In such circumstances Sir Syed would not opt for the Indian National Congress which stood for democracy.

Sir Syed's greatest contribution was to excite in Muslims not political but social, cultural, religious and rational consciousness. He launched a social reform movement which brought about a renaissance in the thought process of the Muslims. The instruments he used for this purpose were the Aligarh College, the Scientific Society, the media *Tahzib-ul-Akhlaq*, and the annual Mohammedan Education Conferences. He made Aligarh the hub of all his activities. Ironically, the Aligarh movement which he initiated switched over from social reforms to political activity to such an extent that it changed the course of history. Even Aligarh boys had a hand in shaping the destiny of Indian Muslims. Sir Syed wanted the Muslims to remain aloof from politics, but events made Aligarh the cockpit of politics.

NOTES

1. Quoted in G.F.R. Graham, *Syed Ahmed Khan,* rpt., Delhi: Idarah-i-Adabiyat-i Delhi, 1885, pp. 311–12.
2. Syed Ahmed Khan, *The Causes of the Indian Revolt* (Urdu); 1858, English tr., 1873, republished by Hafiz Malik, pp. 134–5.
3. Ibid., p. 135.
4. Ibid., p. 136.
5. Ibid.
6. Ibid., p. 137.
7. Ibid., p. 138.
8. Ibid.
9. Ibid., p. 139.
10. Ibid.
11. Ibid., p. 140.
12. Ibid., p. 141.
13. Ibid., p. 142.
14. Ibid.
15. Ibid., p. 149.
16. Ibid.
17. Ibid., p. 171.
18. Syed Ahmed Khan, *Review on Dr. Hunter's Indian Mussalmans,* p. 270.

19. Graham, *Syed Ahmed Khan*, pp. 290–1.
20. Khwaja Altaf Husain Hali, *Hayat-i Javed*, Lahore: Academy Punjab, 1957, p. 872.
21. Syed Ahmed Khan, *Akhri Mazamin*, Lahore, p. 1.
22. Ibid., p. 3.
23. Ibid.
24. Ibid., pp. 71–2.
25. Quoted in R.C. Majumdar, *History of the Freedom Movement*, vol. I, Calcutta: Firma K.L. Mukhopadhyay, 1962–3, p. 333.
26. Quoted in David Lelyveld, *Aligarh's First Generation*, New Delhi: Oxford University Press, 1978, p. 305.
27. Tufail Ahmed, *Mussalmanon-ka-Roshan Mustaqbil*, Lahore: Hammad Al-Katbi, 1937, p. 275.
28. Quoted in S.K. Bhatnagar, *The History of M.A.O. College*, Aligarh: S.S. Hall, 1969, pp. 86–7.
29. Ibid., p. 87.
30. Ibid.
31. Ibid., p. 88.
32. Ibid., p. 89.
33. Hafeez Malik, *Political Profile of Sir Syed Ahmed Khan*, Islamabad: Deptt. of Culture, Islamic University, 1982, pp. 347–8.
34. Ibid., p. 348.
35. Ibid., pp. 348–9.
36. Ibid., pp. 354–5.

CHAPTER 3

Sir Syed Ahmad Khan on the Response of Indian Muslims to the Turko–Russian Wars: An Appraisal

Z.U. MALIK

INTRODUCTION

Sir Syed Ahmad Khan (1817–98) was a versatile genius, endowed with penetrating intellect, marvellous memory, sharp and quick comprehension, brilliant skill in speculative and logical argumentation, and incisive insight into the dynamics of complex forces of national life released by the colonial system of governance in India. Combined with such rare mental abilities were his broad humanism, rationalism, unshakable confidence and sense of purpose, and an untiring effort to pursue the avowed mission of educational and socio-religious reforms in the colonial milieu of the nineteenth century. His vision was rooted in the Indian ethos. He was engaged exclusively to the concerns and needs, especially of the Muslims, during the post-mutiny era. Though educated through classical curriculum and an ardent admirer of the greatness of civilizational and cultural achievements attained in Medieval India, he was a modernist, forwardlooking, and committed to the introduction and diffusion of the English language, adoption and application of Western knowledge in sciences, technologies, and disciplined ways of life. He regarded modern education as *sine qua non* for the rise and progress of the country to new heights. Opposed to politicized religiosity, religious fanaticism as he was, he assiduously advocated intercommunal harmony, and totally rejected violent and agitational means used by religious and political groups to gain political objectives.

In spite of his preoccupations with the multifarious activities of public life,[1] Sir Syed Ahmad Khan found time to devote himself to study and writing. His literary output was undoubtedly formidable, in volume and variety, and proved seminal in its impact on contemporary thought and outlook and to posterity a source of inspiration and guidance. Besides many original research studies on miscellaneous subjects—religion, history, archaeology, politics, current affairs—well-known to scholars to merit enumerating here, he contributed innumerable essays, articles, editorials on encyclopedic topics of perennial academic importance, mainly in the two periodicals, *Aligarh Institute Gazette* (97 editorials) and *Tahzib-ul Akhlaq* (208 articles) both launched by him in 1866 and 1870 respectively.[2] He outdistanced other contemporary Urdu journalists and writers in the techniques of analysis and synthesis, emphasis on inquiry, logic, and historic objectivity, clarity, simplicity, and authenticity of narrative. He opened up new dimensions of essay writing, gave new orientation and a Western-style paradigm to Urdu journalism of his times. These voluminous writings have been put together and separately published in thirteen carefully arranged volumes,[3] constituting the foundation of original source-material, at once most informative and reliable. It is indispensable to explore and explain the socio-economic conditions, the relative backwardness in modern education of the Muslim community, the nature, form, and characteristics of its responses to problems and challenges threatening its cultural identity and economic prospects in the colonial context.

The last set of the collected works include nearly fifteen essays which deal with events of the Turko–Russian wars during nineteenth century (Crimean War, 1854–6; Turko–Russian War, 1877; Graeco–Turkish War, 1897), the changing policies and attitudes of the major European states, Britain and France, towards Turkey in these hostilities, repercussions of the momentous happenings on Indian Muslims, and the modes and manner of their reaction to all of them. Though Sir Syed Ahmad Khan espoused the cause of Turkey emphatically and expressed deep sympathy for the Turks, he, nevertheless, cautioned the Muslims to behave circumspectly in celebrating the victory of Turkey over Greece in the war of 1897. There are essays written in defence of Islam, Turkish civilization and culture, delineating the bright aspects of the character and style of life of Sultan Abdul Aziz (1861–76) and Sultan Abdul Hamid II (1876–1909). Most importantly, a few essays are centred on the discourse about such contentious issues of Khilafat, Imamat, *jihad* and allied themes, intensely debated at that time in some sections of Muslim society. Moreover, two other essays of special interests are related to peace and concord between Christians and Muslims, and Hindu–Muslim unity. These essays, while reflecting commanding reservoirs of knowledge, bring to light the ideals of humanism, secularism and nationalism which Sir Syed Ahmad Khan had persistently propounded and stated categorically in his previous writings, speeches, and addresses. The underlying message to Indian Muslims contained in the essays selected for analysis here is that they should concentrate their whole genius on self-development, progress in education, economy, cultivating noble and virtuous character, as other communities were engaged in, under the peaceful atmosphere created by the British government of India.

But no detailed study of the subjects covered in these essays has been published, excepting the elucidation of the great author's theoretical propositions on the phenomenon of the Khilafat, since it has been a theme of continuous disquisition until today, and that, too, in a perfunctory manner. In fact, the chronicles recorded in the *Aligarh Institute Gazette* are so widely spread that even their cataloguing[4] cannot possibly be made in the following brief descriptive narrative. This deserves a separate treatment in a full-fledged research undertaking, meant for the compilation of comprehensive historical account of war events, political occurrences in Turkey during the period under consideration, as viewed from the nationalist perspective by the greatest Indian Muslim leader of the age.

The present study seeks to present some glimpses gleaned from the vast and varied source-material referred to above. It is divided into four sections. The first section gives an outline of various political and economic developments in nineteenth-century Europe, and is intended to serve as a preliminary survey and background to understanding the significance of events and changes in Turkey described in the subsequent narrative. The second offers a summary of the four wars Turkey fought with Greece and Russia, and the general state of affairs in Turkey under the regime of Sultan Abdul Hamid II. The third section offers analysis, not translation, of a few selected essays, highlighting the strands of thought of Sir Syed Ahmad Khan in relation to these specific historical events. The fourth section provides a conclusion.

Nineteenth-century Europe had witnessed not only the most amazing economic revolutions, but also the emergence of the two closely connected movements of nationalism and democracy in several parts of the continent. The Industrial Revolution, brought about by unprecedented scientific and technological advancement, transformed the economic and social structure in many states of Europe. One of the tremendous technological contributions of the age was the construction and opening of the Suez Canal in 1869, that linked the Mediterranean and Red Sea and became a vital part of the British Empire's life-line, 'the Queen's highway to India'. The Industrial Revolution gave rise to the factory system which created two classes—the factory owners and wage-earners, and out of their conflicting interests there developed schools of economic thought, both liberal and radical with far-reaching effects on capitalistic order and society.[5]

At the end of nineteenth century the spirit of aggressive imperialism was rekindled in the newly industralized, united and militarily superior states of Western Europe—England, France, Germany, Holland, and Belgium. The British were the unrivalled industrialists of the world, their products went in large quantities to every corner of the globe unimpeded by tarrifs. The other European States being freed from their internal troubles began to feel intensely the need for overseas expansion, in search of markets for their surplus products, raw materials, and settlements for their growing populations. In the words of Marx and Engels, 'the need of constantly expanding markets for its products chases the bourgeoisie over the whole surface of the globe'. Besides this economic factor, nationalsm, military supremacy, combined with political and cultural ascendancy were other potent causes for imperialistic expansion during its recent phase that began about 1880. Imperialism, however, threw Europe into a state of turmoil, fomented mutual rivalries and strife, and divided the major imperial powers into blocks.[6]

Of all the achievements of the nineteenth century in science, industry, philosophy and politics, the most striking symbol of progress was the growing spirit of nationalism, political freedom and liberal representative government. Nationalism and liberalism were the motivating forces in the revolutions of 1820, 1830 and 1848 in which workers and peasants played a pivotal role. They demanded redress of their grievances about wages, jobs, food and shelter. The new political order and system of alliances by the Congress of Vienna in 1815 and in 1820, mainly through the efforts of Prince von Metternich (1773–1856), an astute diplomat and chancellor of Habsburg empire of Austria under Joseph Francis. It was based on the principles of legitimacy, stability and tranquility, and it resisted the rising tide of nationalism and individual liberty in Spain, France and Austria. But these revolutionary movements were so dynamic that at the end of the century they emerged triumphant, defeating the system of alliances established by the great powers of Europe. This international machinery of suppressing the widespread revolts broke down by 1848 when Metternich, its chief architect, fled from Vienna to seek refuge in England.[7]

II

THE GREEK REVOLT: 1821–1829

The waves of insurgency which had swept across West Europe in the first half of the nineteenth century swiftly spread to Greece and the Balkania in Eastern Europe, split into distinctive races and nationalities. Whereas political and economic issues dominated the ideologies and strategies of revolutionary movements in West Europe, the Greek revolt against non-Christian Muslim Turks was marked by a religious character that changed its complexion and trajectory. Its object was the explusion of the Turks from Europe and the re-establishment of the Greek Empire. Since the conquest of Constantinople by Sultan Muhammad II (1451–81) and the concordat established with George Gennadios Scholarios, the supreme Patriarch of the Christians,[8] the Greeks had enjoyed absolute religious freedom, retained their religious identity in the Greek tradition of the Orthodox Patriarch. The Turks had made no attempt to root out Christianity, obliterate language or culture in this ancient land, the citadel of Orthodox Church. The Ottoman Sultans continued their anti-Latin policy, and actively supported the Protestants, including the Huguenots in France. Encouraged by this sympathetic attitude the Calvinists built a stronghold in southern Hungry, then under the Ottoman rule.[9] The Greeks constituted a superior class of Christians, and as skilful mariners held high positions in the Turkish navy, and a large number of them had been employed in civil administration. They along with other religious minorities like Jews and Armenians had a major share in the economic development of the empire, trade, business and banking.[10] The Christians were the first agents of Western capitalism, the first harbingers of Western culture, and the collaborators of Western powers, and they received extensive rewards and political support from these external sources. They became the richest people in Turkey. Western culture spread among the Muslim intelligentsia only later.[11]

In the light of the above facts the allegations of persecution and ill-treatment are false. 'The rampant nationalist thought which swamped the Ottoman lands have blurred and distorted the writers' and scholars' intellectual vision.' One expert on the subject pertaining to the causes of Greek Revolt writes:

> The ideological manifestation of the new concept of political organization was nationalism based on language, ethnicity, race, history, and local or traditional attachments. Religion lost its Gnostic character, and became secularized ingredient of nationality and nationalism, a mere cultural dimension of national identity rather than universal fraternity. The notions of ethnic nationalism and secularism that inspired the revolution were still unacceptable to Patriarchate. Sultan Muhammad II (1803–48) did not understand the dynamics of the Greek revolutions or the basic anti-secularist and anti-nationalist position of the Patriarchate, and unjustly held him responsible for the revolt.[12]

However, the Greeks under foreign influence and inspired by their own scholar-patriots—Philgas and Adsmatios Coraes (1748–1833)—organized themselves to take up arms against the Turkish authorities for liberation and resuscitation of their country. Early in the nineteenth century they launched military aggression on Turkish garrisons and crushed it in Morea. A severe and prolonged fighting ensued, carried out with extreme brutality by both sides. In 1821 the Greek massacred Muslims who had shut themselves in Tripolitz. Mahmud II, the Sultan of Turkey (1802–39), retaliated by ordering the massacre of Christians in Chios. Even the Greek Patriarch of Constantinople, the titular head of entire Eastern Europe, was executed.[13]

The orgy of this retaliatory violence and terror caused revulsion against the Sultan, provoked the ire of the entire Christiandom, and the backlash showed up in all its alarming dimensions. The liberals, intellectuals, and political leaders in France, Britain, and Germany came under the spell of Greece, and they stood up to defend the cause of Greek freedom, to preserve the rich heritage of Hellas that had been once the cradle of European civilization. Hellenic societies were formed, large loans floated, gifts of canons and munitions were sent, and adventurers enlisted to reach the battlefield. Lord Byron, the foremost literary figure in Europe, went to Greece and died in her cause at Missolonghi in 1824. Czar Nicholas I (1825–55) was opposed in principle to rebellion against a legally constituted regime, but he hated Sultan Mahmud II, and the Muslim Turks, and looked for an opportunity to invade Turkey and annex the Dardanelles by military force. Armed intervention in the continuing standoff between Greece and Turkey obviously seemed the needed strategy for the realization of the long-cherished national objective. The Russian government, therefore, as champion of the Orthodox Church, allied itself with Western powers—Britain (led by Canning), and France (under Charles X), all being excited to win the glories of a crusade in driving the despised infidels out of Europe. The attitude of Metternich, not on friendly terms with Nicholas, was based on the policy of non-interference. He announced, 'True, *the Turk was a Muslim*, and he had not shared in the treaties of Vienna, nevertheless was a legitimate sovereign and Greeks were rebels.'[14]

In 1826 the three allied powers sent a fleet to the harbour of Navarina which destroyed the Egyptian navy, having drowned sixty Muslim ships with six thousand men. In 1828 Czar Nicholas I declared war against Turkey, and his mighty army crossing through the Balkans reached Danube and seized Adrianople within a striking distance of Constantinople. In terror, at last Sultan Mahmud II, by the Treaty of Adrianople (September 1829) conceded the establishment of independent kingdom of Greece; Serbia was also given formal recognition of an autonomous principality.[15]

THE CRIMEAN WAR: 1854–1856

The Ottoman Empire had ceded important territories to Austria and Russia in the eighteenth century (1718, 1774), yet it still held sway over the Balkan peninsula, mostly mountainous and rugged where Christians were predominantly concentrated. Here, Serbs, Bulgars and Rumanians, stimulated by the example of Greek independence, and incited by the Russian diplomacy started a fierce struggle for liberation from the Islamic rule of the Turks in mid-nineteenth century. The Bulgars had become through the process of infusion over centuries wholly Slavic in character and culture, their ethnic and linguistic structure transformed, and they borrowed their religious practices from the Greeks of Constantinople. The Russian government took keen interest in the formation of a united, independent state of Bulgaria with a view to making it a future satrapy. In the pursuit of his political agenda Czar Nicholas used the religious plank, and exerted pressure on the Sultan of Turkey, Sultan Abdul Majid (1839–61) to set up an 'exarch' (a Bishop appointed by the Church of Constantinople) in Bulgaria to rule the local Christians. Faced with the threat of invasion the Sultan conceded the demand. Czar Nicholas had developed deep conviction of the imminent liquidation and ultimate partition of the declining Ottoman Empire in Europe, and he accordingly shaped his conception of carving out a large space in order to secure control of Constantinople and through it gain an entrance from the Black Sea to the Mediterranean Sea. An ordinary dispute over the Holy places—Jerusalem and Bethlehem—in Palestine between Greek and Latin Christian monks afforded the Russian despot an opportunity to fish in the troubled waters. He demanded a Protectorate over all Greek Christians. The Sultan did not yield to this threatening demand as it clearly infringed the sovereign rights of Turkey.[16]

On 17 May 1853 the Turkish government rejected the Russian demands, and on 21 May Menshikov, the Ambassador left Constantinople. With his departure the diplomatic relations broke off, and war clouds began to gather. The Russian armies invaded Turkey in 1853, and occupied the line of Danube. At Sinope, in November 1853, the Russian Black Sea Squadron made of Paixhans, small ships with its guns, annihilated a Turkish wooden fleet.[17]

For nearly two centuries there was a war between Russia and Turkey. In October 1853 the ninth of this series (the Crimean war) began. But from the outset it was radically different from its predecessors. Europe was ranged with the Muslim Sultan against the orthodox Czar.[18]

Both France and Britain vigorously supported Turkey and sent their fleets to the Aegean, and their combined armies attacked Russian Crimea and besieged the great fortress of Sebastople. In fact, 'no power in Europe entertained the intention of overthrowing the Turkish empire'.

'There can be no doubt that Russia with Petersburg and Constantinople in the same hands would be an object of alarm to Europe, but especially to England, and France, and Austria.[19]

Sebastople held out gallantly for a year on the strength of a vast system of Russian entrenchments. Nicholas, overwhelmed with mortification, died on 2 March 1855, and in the same year Russian General Menchikov evacuated the city. This brought the Crimean war to an end. The French had lost 97,000 men, of whom 20,000 had fallen in action. France succeeded in striking a severe blow to the prestige of Russia and smashing its formidable war machine. Russia, under the new Czar Alexandar II (1855–81) was forced to undertake the guarantee for the integrity of the Ottoman Empire, that earlier seemed threatened with disintegration. All these exertions and sacrifices made by the victorious powers, though for their security concerns and maintaining balance of power in Europe, resulted in saving the Ottoman Empire from dismemberment.[20]

By the terms of the Peace of Paris, March 1856, Russia was compelled to cede Bessarabia to Moldavia (Northern Rumania) in order to prevent the Czars from controlling the mouths of the Danube. Russia was also forbidden to maintain warships upon the Black Sea, and asked to abandon any claims to the exclusive protectorate of the Turkish Christians. The principalities of Rumania and Serbia were confirmed in their rights of self-government, and were placed under the protection of all the great Western powers. The principalities of Moldavia and Wallachia were to remain under the suzerainty of the Porte. Kars was to be restored to the Turks and Crimea to Russia.[21]

TURKO–RUSSIAN WAR: 1877

Peace in the Balkan peninsula was again menaced by the recrudence of disorders in its principalities of Serbia, Bosnia and Rumania. The Pan-Slavic movement, commenced and organized by the Christian striving for the union of all Slavdom in one confederation gained strength with the rise in their material resources and fervent outside support of their cause. The Russian people were zealous adherents to the Orthdox Church, considered themselves the best Slavic race, and expected that under the impact of pervading idealistic chauvinism the new state of Bulgaria would function under the protection and guidance of their government. The suzerainty of the Ottoman Sultan over this medley of diverse nationalities, was little more than a name, the people maintained their local institutions, retained the old class of nobility, and kept a Christian *hospadar* to rule over each principality.

The central government of the Ottoman Empire failed to hold these petty nations under its sovereign authority, or try to turn over a new leaf in its relationship with them.

In 1859 Rumania, better organized politically and economically than Serbia and Bulgaria succeeded in uniting the two principalities of Wallachia and Moldavia under one single government. Lord Alfred Tennyson (1809–92) admired these revolutionaries in these words, 'Of freedom, warriors beating back the swarms of *Turkish Islam* for five hundred years.' In 1875 the peasants of Herzegovina, a district in Bosnia, infuriated by taxes levied by Turkish officials rose in arms, and defeated a small Turkish corps with the help of Slavic brethren in Serbia and Montenegro. In Bulgaria about 100 Turks were killed, and Sultan Abdul Hamid (1876–1909) sent a Turkish army of regulars to repress the revolt. The army slaughtered 5,000 Bulgarians, without anticipating the severity of reaction that would come from the Christian population.[22]

The massacre of Bulgarians, sanguinary and frightful as it was, raised a storm of intense indignation, bitterness and animosity in the Christian world against the perpetrators. It was interpreted as 'perhaps the most heinous crime that has stained the history of the present century'. It caused alienation of those states of the continent which had previously professed cordial sympathy and friendship towards Turkey. William E. Gladstone, Prime Minister of England (1868–74) demanded that action be taken against the Turks, and they get out of the Balkans immediately. He wrote a pamphlet entitled , *Bulgarian Horrors and the Question of the East* (London, 1876). In this he stated, 'No government ever has so sinned, none has so proved itself incorrigible, or which is the same, so impotent for reformation. Let the Turks now carry away their abuses in the only possible manner, by carrying off themselves (pp. 61, 63).'

Though Czar Alexander II (1855–81) was a peace-loving despot, he could not ignore the summons from the Orthodox Church, nor the resounding and clear clarion call of the Russian people to launch a crusade against the infidel Turks and rescue their Christian brethren from their yoke. He, therefore, declared war against the Ottoman Turks in 1877. The Russians forces rapidly pushed into the Turkish territory across Rumania and surrounded the Turkish General Osman Pasha at Plevna. The siege lasted till the beginning of December, when Osman Pasha was forced to surrender along with 40,000 soldiers after severe fighting in which Russians lost 21,000 men. In

Asia, in the Caucasus, the Turks suffered disastrous defeats; they lost Kars and Sofia. The military power of Turkey completely collapsed, and the triumphant Russians stood at the gates of Constantinople. The Cossacks raged and raided the Muslims in the region around Yanina in Empirus and around Adrianople and massacred them with brutality that was unabashedly connived by the Russian government and treated with appalling insensitivity by the outside public. At this critical juncture Sultan Abdul Hamid had no alternative to an armistice which he accepted, but the terms of the treaty of San Stefano dictated by Czar Alexander caused profound perturbation in England, and the English opinion took an ever-increasing alarm at the Russian occupation of Constantinople, the gateway to India. England had proclaimed neutrality in the present war, but now refused to participate in any scheme leading to the disintegration of the Ottoman Empire.[23]

Edward Henry Stanley Derby, Foreign Secretary of England (1874–8) wrote to Count Shuvaloff, Russian Ambassador in London: 'The vast importance of Constantinople, whether in a military, a political, or a commercial point of view, is too well understood to require explanation, England is not prepared to witness with indifference into other hands than those of its present possessors, of a capital so peculiar and commanding a position.'[24]

Benjamin Disraeli, first Earl of Beaconsfield (1804–81), then Prime Minister of England expressed his viewpoint on the current situation as developed by the harsh and unfair terms of peace between Turkey and Russia stipulated in the Treaty of Stefano, in these words: 'Moreover, it (the Treaty) is asking us to sanction them in putting a knife to the throat of Turkey, whether we like it or not.'[25]

Since the Treaty of Stefano jeopardized the security concerns of England the British government decided to bring military pressure to bear upon Russia to get the strict and severe conditions contained in it modified. The British fleet was accordingly ordered to move into the sea of Marmara inside the Dardanelles and challenge the Russian troops standing at the gates of Constantinople. These signs of resolute action in the defence of Turkey by England discouraged the Russians. In consequence, they agreed to revise the malignant clauses of the Treaty of Stefano. But Disraeli exacted price for the armed aid from the helpless Sultan without which Turkey would have succumbed. The Ottoman Sultan, ignorant of the secret deal, allowed the British government to occupy and administer the rich island of Cyprus, and he promised to introduce necessary reforms for the Armenian Christians (4 June 1878).[26]

At the suggestion of Otto von Bismark (1815–98) the iron chancellor of Germany under William I, the Congress of European great powers—England, France, Italy, Germany, Austria, and Russia—was held at Berlin (June–July 1878) to reconsider and re-write the Treaty of Stefano. England was represented by her Prime Minister Disraeli and Foreign Secretary Lord Salisbury (1830–1903), Austria by Count Andrassy, and Russia by Prince Gorchakov, the Chancellor, the following re-adjustments were made at the Congress of Berlin:

1. In Asia Minor, Russia was compelled to disgorge part of her conquests, although she retained the strong fortress of Kars.
2. Great Bulgaria was partitioned into three.
3. Bosnia and Herzegovina were assigned to Austria, to be occupied and administered until peace and prosperity returned to the region.
4. The great island of Crete was taken away from Greece, and left under the rule of Turkish government for 34 years.
5. Bessarabia was detached from Rumania, and given to Russia.

By the Treaty of Berlin, Turkey lost two-thirds of its territory in Europe. The Sultan now a mere shadow, saw some 65,000 sq miles of his former dominions, 'divided between Thracy, Macedonia and Albania'. About six million people lived in Turkey in Europe, the majority of them were Christians.[27]

GRAECO–TURKISH WAR: 1897

As mentioned above, the Berlin Congress had not awarded greater portions of Thessaly and Epirus to Greece, and Crete, a large island with strong Christian majority was given back to Turkey. This island had been subjugated by the Turks in 1669. Since the Greek Revolt in the early-nineteenth century the island had been perpetually in revolt (sixteen in number) and seen constant civil strife between Christians and Muslims. Its administration had been placed under the charge of Muhammad Ali by the Sultan of Turkey in 1830, but by the treaty of London it was restored to the Porte in 1840. The fundamental object of insurrections was the union of Crete with mainland Greece. In the spring of 1896 the islanders of Crete started warring to conquer these areas and drive out the Muslims from cities and towns. The King of Greece sent a torpedo flotilla supported by the army to Crete. The warships of the great powers prevented the explusion of the Turkish garrison, and general fighting followed on the frontiers. On 17 April 1897 Turkey declared war and the Turkish army under the command of Edhem Pasha occupied Larissa and won two decisive battles at Phars and Eomoks. In this 30-days war no great power of Europe, neither Russia nor Bulgaria, backed the Greeks in their reckless enterprise. However, under their pressure Sultan Abdul Hamid agreed to the terms of armistice, December 1897, according to which the Greeks were to pay a heavy war indemnity amounting to $20,000,000, and cede to Turkey certain strategically located villages. But in 1898, the Great Powers set up an autonomous government on the island of Crete, 'with the preponderance granted to the Christians'.[28]

SULTAN ABDUL HAMID II: 1876–1909

Sultan Abdul Aziz had been deposed in May 1876 in favour of his nephew Murad, who three months later was deposed for mental derangement, and was succeeded by his younger brother Abdul Hamid aged 34. In 1867 Napoleon III of France had invited Sultan Abdul Aziz to visit an International Exhibition at Paris, and during the course of his journey to Western Europe he was received at the Courts of Paris, London, Vienna and also met the King of Prussia. Murad had accompanied his uncle in this European tour, and was highly impressed by the great achievements of Western nations in science, industry, and military organization. He took keen interest in French literature and culture. Sultan Abdul Aziz was a despot and soon fell out of favour of the Reform Party. The ministers who had propelled Sultan Abdul Hamid on the throne had obtained from him the prior promise of introducing a constitution and other liberal reforms they had prepared.

Soon after the accession of Abdul Hamid II the Turko–Russian war began, and the Russian armies advanced almost to the gates of Istanbul on 14 February 1878. In these dangerous conditions of war the Sultan prorogued the parliament, and at the same time the constitution was also suspended. 'From this time on, Sultan Abdul Hamid II ruled as an absolute monarch for 30 years.' Nineteenth-century European historians and statesmen have projected him in their writings as a reactionary tyrant, underpinning their reasoning with illustration of the bloody repression of the Armenians and other acts of cruelty, but modern historians of Turkey have underlined the culmination of the process of reforms (*tanzimat*) during his regime that was further marked by the spectacular development of the means of communication, construction of telegraph lines, and network of railway lines through-out the empire by the British and French companies.[29]

Sultan Abdul Hamid was a frugal and hardworking ruler who administered imperial finances in such an efficient manner that the government borrowed very little from abroad and it paid off its old foreign debts. British and French companies were the main important companies in the country, over 90 per cent of the industrial establishments were owned by non-Muslims, and 10 per cent traditional handicrafts were in the hands of local Muslims. In schools, the percentage of Muslim students was lower as compared with Christians. In this period economic activities increased in consequence of trade with the West. Tobacco cultivation, a major export item spread, so did the silk industry, coal mines were opened, and the gradual liberalization of the land code drastically changed the traditional structure in rural areas.[30] Tanzimat played a definite role in the transformation of the Ottoman Empire, it accomplished a great deal in reforming legal and administrative systems, educational institutions, and laid the foundation for modernizing Turkey which became the corner stone of policies pursued by the Young Turks in the nineteenth and early-twentieth centuries.[31]

However, the disasters of the 1877–8 war both in terms of loss of territory and human tragedy had set a mood of reaction against European civilization and the doctrine of pan-Turanism based on common origin, common language, and common national interests. Besides the loss of nearly a third of the empire's territory comprising 20 per cent of its population, the immigration of over a million Muslims following the wholesale killings of Muslim villagers and townsmen by Russians to which Western Europe turned a blind eye added more woes, and gave impetus to the rising wave of reaction. The prestige of France had reduced in the wake of its defeat in the Franco–Prussian war, 1871, the process of reforms weakened, and Ali Pasa became isolated. The British occupation of Egypt and Cyprus in Levant seriously strained its relations with the Porte. In these changed conditions in the Ottoman Empire Sultan Abdul Hamid II, a ruler of pious nature and ascetic nature, sought to define and categorize identity and solidarity on the basis of religious affiliation, and stressed the need for Islamic unity, Islamic character of the empire, in opposition to secular policies, common citizenship and forces of Westernization. The doctrine of Islamic unity was more actively advanced when the Sultan claimed to be the Caliph of all Muslims of the world, the rallying centre for the liberation of Muslim lands from the bondage of European powers. The survival of the empire lay in the consolidation and unity of its Muslim subjects, preserving Arab loyalty, and stemming the tide of European aggression and expansion. Jamaluddin Afghani (1839–97), the ideologue of pan-Islamism who was forced to leave the country in 1871, was invited back and honoured in 1894–7. The new ideology, an alternative as well as response to challenges confronting the Ottoman Empire won considerable support in society and struck a responsive cord among religious-minded and traditionalist Muslims outside Turkey. The Sultan sent his agents to India, also to other lands to gain moral support to his regime by arousing religious feelings of Muslims against Russian and other imperialist powers of Western Europe like England and France.[32]

III

RESPONSE OF THE INDIAN MUSLIMS

It is against this background of Russian persistent military aggression to conquer Turkey and drive out Muslim Turks (Turk and Muslim being synonymous terms) out of Europe,[33] the religious fervour in the Christiandom against Muslims in general, and the seizure of Muslim lands in north Africa and the Levant by Britain and France, that aspects of response of the Indian Muslims may be understood in clear historical perspective. Moreover, the hostile approach of European Orientalists, historians, and writers interpreting Islam and Islamic civilization evoked profound reaction among the educated classes of Muslim India, and generated an atmosphere of disappointment and distrust especially against Britain. Sir William Muir, in his *Life of Mahomet* (1857–61), Aloys Sprenger (1813–93), Wellhausen (1844–1918), Leopold Von Ranke (1795–1886), Ignaz Goldhizer (1850–1921) and a group of others, treated Islam as a world religion in confrontation with Christian Europe and repudiated Islamic civilization for its total failure in making any substantial contribution to the progress of mankind since the thirteenth century.[34] During times of war in the nineteenth century, strong religious leaders, statesmen, poets and intellectuals of Western Europe, Russia and Greece, portrayed Turks as fanatics, barbarians, the Sultan an incompetent, luxurious, oriental despot, and their civilization primitive. The unfriendly, unjust statements of Gladstone and his party comrades, outrageous tirade by writers published in the newspapers in England which found expression in a section of the Indian Press, English and vernacular, hurt the consciousness of Muslim readership, elite and ordinary alike. The Muslims perceived their writings blatantly partisan, based on superficial, unauthentic facts, reflecting deep-rooted enmity and injustice of the detractors of Muslims and Islam.

In response to the denigration of Islam the distinguished Muslim leaders and intellectuals in India compiled erudite and comprehensive works to prove the falsity of suppositions and formulations underlying the religious and historical literature on Islam brought out by the above-mentioned Western orientalists. In this regard the scholarly contributions of Sir Syed Ahmad Khan, Amir Ali (1849–1928), Maulana Shibli Numani (1872–1914), Maulana Ubaidullah Sindhi (1872–1944), Abdul Halim Sharar (1860–1926), and Saiyid Ali Bilgrami, and others were most outstanding and in effect paved the way for the new interpretation of Islamic history and civilization by the new generation of Muslim intellectuals and writers in India. The second response of Muslims to the contemporary situation in India and their religious brethren outside it was the active support to the movement of pan-Islamism, initiated by Sultan Abdul Hamid II in Turkey, and vigorously propagated in India by Jamaluddin Al-Afghani, its most celebrated theorist, and those who came under his spell. It envisaged political unification of Muslim countries under one government, symbolized by the ecclesiastical designation of Khilafat, while retaining their distinct national identities. The beliefs underpinning Khilafat converged with the aspirations and interests of a class of theologians who now surrounded Abdul Hamid, and they in collaboration with other like-minded persons worked to mobilize public opinion in support of the doctrine. The construction of Hijaz Railway from Damascus to Medina largely from voluntary contributions between 1901–8 was a great success of Islamist policies and agenda pursued by Sultan Abdul Hamid, demonstrating the measure of influence and esteem he commanded in different strata of Muslim population.[35]

Al-Afghani spent considerable time in India, from 1857 to 1865, and again in 1879, during which period he visited Bombay, Hyderabad, Bhopal and Calcutta where he addressed the local elite leaders of Muslims, explained the meaning and objectives of pan-Islamism, or universal Islamic unity, and urged his Indian Muslim audience to get free of the shackles imposed by the European political and cultural hegemony.[36] His lectures and writings stimulated feelings of sympathy and solidarity with Turkey, supposedly the only surviving rallying centre for the Muslim world, among Muslims of India, and some zealous adherents declared Sultan Abdul Hamid as their *Amir al Mu'muminin* and *Padshah-i-Musalmanan*, and even gave call to *jihad*. The British government was well aware of the lurking dangers of such agitational activities by the supporters of Khilafat to the peace and order in the country, but it sought to control rather than suppress it.[37] The categorization, institutionalization, and mass mobilization of the movement were still underway when it turned into a massive popular upsurge in the first decades of the twentieth century. Sir Syed Ahmad Khan, ever restless, and ceaselessly active, with a subtle and reflective mind raised questions in respect of the historical and constitutional premises, intents and efficacy of attempting to recreate the institution of Khilafat which had lost its significance to the Indian Muslims 300 years back. In a series of articles he expressed his apprehensions about the involvement of the Muslims in the politics and ideology of extra-territorial movements that could not offer any answers to their educational and socio-economic problems.

MUSLIM RESPONSE TO TURKISH VICTORY

The Muslims of India celebrated the victory of the Turks over Greeks in the war of 1896–7 with excessive enthusiasm and display of emotions. However, Sir Syed Ahmad Khan cautioned them to behave with restraint and exercise circumspection in expressing their happiness on this occasion. He stated that all Muslims, including himself, felt delighted at this memorable event. But, they should refrain from bringing in the sacred name of Islam. It was the victory of a Muslim state, a Muslim king. A defeat would have foreboded the catastrophe of both. The triumph of Islam, based on Islamic Monotheism (*Tauhid ar Rubuiyyah*), Oneness of the Lordship of Allah had been, in fact, announced by the grace of Almighty God on the peaceful, glorious entry of His Messenger Prophet Muhammad (peace be upon him) into Makkah long ago, towards the end of January 630 (AH 8). He had exclaimed, 'Truth has come and falsehood hath vanished.' Therefore, to call the victory of Turkey as the victory of Islam was wrong, and to associate Islam in such matters, and say 'Islam, Islam', was in his opinion extremely unwise. Success and defeat come from God. God bestows success or inflicts defeat on whomsoever He wills. He alone changes the position from one side to the other. Sometimes non-believers prevail on believers in warfare. When the Turks defeated Russians with the help of England and France (in the Crimean war, 1854–6) by what name would this success be proclaimed, and when the Turks suffered defeat at the hands of Russians (in the Turko–Russian war, 1876–7), was it, God forbidding, the defeat of Islam? The dignified and exalted name of Islam should not be linked with worldly affairs and causation which constantly undergo alternations.[38] We must be glad and contented that a Muslim kingdom won success. But it was not an extraordinary victory which should have produced so much clamour, because compared with military strength and material resources of Turkey Greece was inferior, and it also failed to receive succour from any European power (1897). Britain's foreign policy was not affected by the speeches of Mr Gladstone who pleaded for coercion of Turkey, nor did the British government of India pay any serious attention to the emotional outbursts of the Indian Muslims.[39]

Turkey did not fight these defensive wars against Russia in the name of religion; had its government given religious complexion to her ceaseless struggles for security, the Christian powers of Western Europe would not have supported it. Whatever policies these states pursued in the future these would be founded on political expendicies and not on antagonism towards Islam. Sir Syed Ahmad writes that exceptional enthusiasm and fervour demonstrated by Muslims in rejoicing the victory may be accounted for by the hypercritical speeches of Mr Gladstone,[40] and the sinister and biased approach of the English newspapers towards the Turks and their King. By their onslaughts they sought to humiliate and ridicule the Turks which pained and agitated the Muslims in India. In contrast, the Turks after victory treated the wounded soldiers of the vanquished army and other victims of war. They gave them food and provided medical aid and general facilities. 'We are Indian Muslims, and we can not afford to entangle ourselves in the internal affairs of a foreign Muslim kingdom. We must behave prudently, sagaciously, and avoid doing acts that may arouse suspicion of the British government about our loyalty to it.'[41]

CRIMEAN AND TURKO–RUSSIAN WARS: RESPONSE OF INDIAN MUSLIMS

'If any person who saves the life of our friend and helps him in times of trouble it is obligatory on us to express our gratitude to him', wrote Sir Syed Ahmad Khan. The most critical time of pressure and distress for Turks was when Russia launched aggression on Turkey in 1855, the war that ensued is famous as the Crimean war known to every one. At that time England and France showed sympathy with Turkey, and helped her militarily and materially. Had these states not aided her, Turkey would have certainly been extinguished. Now, the pertinent question is, why did the Muslims of India not express their thanks to the governments of England and France after winning the war of Crimea, if they were sincerely sympathic towards Turkey? Why were prayers not held for the success of the Turks in mosques and places of worship, and why were telegrams and addresses of gratefulness not dispatched to these supporting governments? Sir Syed Ahmad asked. On this strange behaviour of Muslims in India one Englishman observed that they were ungrateful, because during the period they had sacrificed their lives and wealth to save Turkey the Muslims here revolted to overthrow the British government. Syed Ahmad did not agree with this point of view. He reiterated his thesis that in 1857 no one had any intentions of revolting against the Englishmen, and according to one historian J.W. Kaye it was not a rebellion but a political war. The disturbances that arose in its wake were owing to the break-down of law and order enforcement agencies, for these subsided soon after the suppression of the mutiny. Even then, there seems no plausible answer to the question why the Muslims of India failed to pay the debt of gratitude they owed to the governments of England and France.[42]

Again, in 1876 hostilities broke out between Russia and Turkey in which the latter suffered disastrous and unmitigated defeat, despite the feats of valour exhibited by the excellent infantry men and their commander Usman Pasha, unique in tenacity and skill amongst the Turkish generals. The legions of Russia streamed across Wallachia, speedily forced their way over the Danube and pushed on towards

Constantinople. In their onward march the invaders had neglected to spread terror over the small town of Plevana, which Usman Pasha seized without delay. Nearly 50,000 soldiers were under his command. Having received reinforcements from Rumania the Russian forces turned to besiege the Turkish commander at Plevana, but he held on for five months, and cost the Russians 21,000 men. When no help came from Constantinople and the soldiers began to starve, Usman Pasha tried to cut his way through the besiegers, and in this desperate attempt he was hemmed in by the superior numbers, which forced him to surrender in December 1877. In comparison with the heroic deeds and sacrifices of Usman Pasha the performance of Odhem Pasha in the recent war with Greeks (1897) was not so conspicuous as to have claimed praise and gratefulness articulated in messages of congratulations from the Indian Muslims who had denied this privilege 20 years earlier to the former. This kind of response was inexplicable and worrisome to Sir Syed Ahmad Khan. Even after the armistice of San Stefano the armies of Russia and Turkey stood in a grim position of standoff before the walls of Constantinople. It was at this moment of extreme anxiety and uncertainty that the British fleet sailed into the sea of Marmara inside the Dardanelles, and British canons thundered on the sea. The Russian monarch Alexandar II was forced to withdraw his forces from the theatre of war and submit his entire scheme of the partition of the Ottoman Empire contained in the treaty of San Stefano for revision and modification to a congress of the powers that later met at Berlin in 1878.[43]

About the position of the Sultan of Turkey Sir Syed stated that acknowledging Caliph (*Khalifa*) signifies nothing more except that the Bani 'Ummayyah and Bani Abbasid were known by this title. None amongst the Muslims considers the orders of the Sultan binding in manner that the commands of the Pope are obeyed by the Christians, or like the ordinances and rules of the first four rightly-guided Caliphs were religiously followed. He further said that Sultan Abdul Hamid declined to surrender Thessaly demanded by the European Powers. How this problem would be solved in the period ahead is not known.

We also want that Thessaly should be kept under the possession of the Sultan. Which powers would support his avowed objective, and which would oppose or remain neutral is at the moment unpredictable. But it is purely a political matter, religious question is not at issue. Every state in Europe pursues foreign policy based on principles of national enlightened interest, least guided by religious considerations. In this period all wars have been fought for territorial expansion, political ascendancy and promotion of national economy.[44]

COLLECTION OF RELIEF FUNDS IN INDIA

Sir Syed praised the humanitarian endeavours of the Indian Muslims for mitigating the sufferings and deprivation of the people of Turkey, caused by unending wars, raids and rapine. The Muslims collected funds for medical aid and other relief for the wounded, the widows and the orphans. In this connection committees were set up in big cities—Bombay, Calcutta, Hyderabad, Lahore and Madras—to which are associated some very respectable, dignified and highly educated personalities. For example, one Calcutta Maulawi Abdul Latif Khan, and Saiyid Amir Ali Khan Bahadur took active interest in the programme and the working of the local committee, and the Muslim gentry and wealthy groups of the city collected thousands of rupees. The money so gathered was remitted through the District Magistrate to the Central Committee. The British government did not object to this kind of relief work since that was done to provide comfort and solace to the needy and helpless people, and not to strengthen the sinews of warfare. In London social activists raised funds and sent the amount directly for treatment of the wounded in Serbia, and some Englishmen reached there to help their Christian brethren. Sir Syed felt angry at the rejection of an application for collecting funds by the district court of Saharanpur. This action of the judge was unjust and wrong he said.[45]

SULTAN OF CONSTANTINOPLE AND INDIAN MUSLIMS

Under this heading the *Pioneer* published a telegram received from Constantinople, dated 17 June 1897.

It was in response to the letters of congratulations sent by Muslims of India to the Sultan of Turkey on the Turkish victory over the Greeks. In this lengthy letter the obligations of a true Muslim towards the Caliph are explained in great detail. At the end it emphasized that the real strength of Islam lay in the unity and cooperation amongst Muslims. It was reported that the copies of this letter would be sent through special messengers to the 'Ulama and Shaikhs of India, Egypt and Arbia'. In the context of Indian Muslims the sermon of the Turkish Sultan was neither relevant nor valid, simply because they did not constitute his subject population like the people of Egypt and Arabia. This fact the Sultan understood, for he sent replies to messages of congratulations not directly to the Muslim citizens of Bombay, Simla and other cities but through the embassy of his government in India. In case of Simla, the Turkish government transmitted the message of thanks through its ambassador posted in London as it had no embassy there. The Sultan thus acted in accordance with the prevalent international law and conventions. The subject matter of the Sultan's letter mainly related to the duties of a Muslim which he has to perform in promoting the cause of his Khilafat, and that in consequence of non-performance of these he would suffer material, moral and physical losses. But why Muslims of India, who are not his subjects, should submit to the authority of the *Khalifa* of a foreign kingdom, obey his orders, and in what way they would suffer losses indicated by him in the letter as a result of non-compliance is beyond comprehension, wrote Sir Syed.[46]

POSITION OF SHAIKH-UL ISLAM OF TURKEY

Shaikh-ul Islam holds a very superior position among ministers and officials in the central government of Turkey. On account of his expertise in the Hanafi jurisprudence he wields wide authority and influence not only in the judiciary but also in the civil, executive and military bureaucratic set up. All civil, military appointments, decisions on war and peace, deposition and accession of kings bear the seal of his assent. In rank and status Shaikh-ul Islam is considered equal to the Catholic Pope of Rome. Of late, however, the scope and impact of his powers have been reduced in the regime of Sultan Muhammad II who had appointed a second Shaikh-ul Islam in the process of reforms in the system governance. The Muslims of India are not duty-bound to obey his decrees and judgements in political or religious issues for they are not nationals of Turkey or subject people of the Ottoman Empire. The concept that the Sultan of Turkey is a religious leader of the Muslims is ill-conceived, devoid of factual reality. It is reported that both Sultan Abdul Hamid and Shaikh-ul Islam wear European dress, coat, pants, shoes, eat food sitting on chairs, and using knife and fork at the table. In external appearance they resemble infidels.[47]

Sir Syed has disapproved the deposition of Sultan Abdul Aziz and his replacement by Sultan Abdul Hamid as sovereign of Turkey. He has criticized the council of ministers for obtaining a decree (*fatwa*) from Shaikh-ul Islam to legitmize a measure of such an import. In Sir Syed's estimate Sultan Abdul Aziz was a more capable and farsighted ruler than the present one, in whose regime Turkey has fallen into the grip of chaos, how she will come out of it is difficult to say.[48] He concludes: 'If his (referring to Sultan Abdul Hamid) indefatigable but divided energy could have been devoted entirely to Islam as a system of human belief and conduct, the world of Islam, intellectually speaking, would have been on a much more solid ground today.'[49]

It is being informed that the brave Turks are sacrificing their lives in fighting with the rebellious Christian nationalities of Serbia, known for their barbarism and inhuman atrocities. Serbia is not an independent, consolidated separate kingdom; it is a tributary state under the suzerainty of the Ottoman Empire. Turkey is under pressure to put hostilities to an end, but the terms of a peaceful settlement with the defeated insurgents set forth by the Turkish government are not in accord with the foreign policy concerns of England. The Sultan has demanded a war indemnity since the secessionists of Serbia had started armed revolt, constructed railways, and surrender all the big forts and dismantle the small ones. It is expected that the counsels of Edward Stanley Derby, the Foreign Secretary of England (1874–8), a sagacious, sympathetic, wise diplomat, would prevail over the religious, and ethnocentric predilections of Gladstone.[50]

ISLAM AND TURKISH CIVILIZATION

Sir Syed Ahmad Khan wrote constantly and voluminously, in defence of Islam against outrageous theories, and vilest expressions framed by Western writers and intellectuals in that period. In one essay of this genre he argued that Islam invests human beings with the truth of spiritual, moral and cultural values, creates trust in God, and to surrender unconditionally to the will of Supreme Being, and to endure all troubles and difficulties with pure heart and genuine intentions, without feeling sad. Islam teaches all people to treat every human being with friendliness, implicit sincerity and generosity, speak the truth in every matter, shun pride, ego, and refrain from treachery, deceit and hypocrisy. These qualities are the distinctive hallmarks of a Muslim, and the living symbols of Islam. Alas, we have stained Islam by our failure in practising these cardinal precepts in daily life.[51]

In Constantinople, the ladies of upper classes like all other women live in the house, *rabat* with the difference that in their families there is greater unity. The husbands are faithful and obedient to their wives, the evil custom of polygamy does not prevail in the wealthy and aristocratic classes. The Turks, men and women, bear all troubles and difficulties with patience and thankfulness to God. The women of respectable families are pious, truthful, honest, and relying on the mercy of God they endure grief and distress with courage and firmness. 'The Turks live in love and cooperation with each other. They take care of their parents, and are obedient to them; their families are very refined and civilized. The Turkish seraglio (*harem sara*), a palace or house, is not filled with beautiful women for the satisfaction of the Sultan, but it is a place of security and comfort.' The Turk is as much attached to his house as any European may be fond of his own residence. Here only one woman lives and within its walls her control is absolute. She is master of her husband's purse. In domestic affairs she is an efficient manager, and is highly respected by the family members. She is well-educated, cultured, upholds high moral standards, capable of overcoming all kinds of strains and stresses patiently, is flourishing and resplendent. The education and training of children is her exclusive responsibility. The Turks are mild and soft-spoken, civil and large-hearted in providing hospitality to guests and strangers. But they do not allow their children to come into contact and mix with European boys and girls whom they consider lazy, disobedient and obstinate, with notions of individual liberty. For this reason the Turks live at distant places, far away from the European settlements.[52]

The view that Sultan Abdul Hamid II has gathered a large number of women around him and spends his time in their company is completely blurred, and far from the truth. He is, on the contrary, a religious-minded, pious, ascetic, economical, hard-working king, and keeps only one wife. He is extremely respectful towards his mother, obeys her implicitly, does not sit before her without permission. In civilizational standards, the Turks are not inferior to people of any other civilized regions in the world. The assumption that the religious beliefs of Muslims are obstructions to the development of civilization and efflorescence of culture, good manners and etiquette is based on antagonism to Islam. The Turks are orthodox Muslims, and their religion is wholly civilized. This is a different issue that we may call any people civilized while the other uncivilized.[53]

CHRISTIAN–MUSLIM HARMONY

Islam is wide, universal and all-embracing; it has its own dynamics and resilience, offers broad guidelines to cope with challenges any time and under all circumstances. It demands patience and refined manners. It recognizes all the prophets revered either by the Jews or Christians, and commands to accommodate their followers with tolerance and forbearance. Excepting the religion of Islam no other religion in the world has manifested deference to Jesus Christ, and given due regard to his teachings as the Muslims have done. Undoubtedly, Christians and Muslims disagreed and disputed, and they also confronted each other in battle, but such differentiations and collisions stemmed actually from political and economic issues rather than religion. There exists no religious animosity between Islam and Christianity. Driven by political ambition, the rival Christian nations waged wars against each other, the same has been true of Muslims who fought amongst themselves for territory and wordly riches. It may be admitted that hostilities between people of opposite ideologies were generally fuelled and accelerated by religious passions and communal hatred which belligerents on both sides stirred to accomplish their political purposes and plans. This may be illustrated by the example of religious crusades the Christian nations of Europe had launched against Muslim states from 1096 to 1270, likewise the Muslims accorded the title *jihad* (holy war) to fighting with non-Muslims, though the essential cause of all such wars had been the promotion of political and economic interests.[54]

The historical events of the period under consideration confirm the fact that the priorities set by European powers in assisting the Muslim kingdom of Turkey, exhausted and forlorn, were primarily determined by the fundamental principle of balance of power and common stakes in free passage of trade, commerce, and security of their old and new colonies in Africa and Asia. The independent existence of a Muslim country was strategically vital for the realization of these political and economic ends. The Christian states have stood aside from the continuing stand off between Turkey and Greek (1896–7). Now the Armenians, aided and abetted by the Greeks, have unfurled the flag of insurrection, and committed bloody excesses to attain their political objective of carving out a separate principality. They contrived a pretext of persecution of Christians in order to instigate public opinion in the Christian world and gain their sympathy and support for the success of their incredible cause. The allegation of misgovernment should not be a rational justification of revolt and violence. Their religious freedom and rights are so unassailably entrenched under Turkish rule which could hardly be witnessed in any other regime. It is regrettable that both Christians and Muslims are covering these national conflicts with a religious garb, and in the name of religion inciting people. The real sufferers would surely be those who are influenced by the slogan of 'religion, religion', proving beyond doubt their ignorance and shortsightedness. Turkey is a Muslim country,[55] if it is afflicted with some catastrophe, either because of internal convulsions or external invasions; it is natural that Muslims would feel concerned and express sympathy in a positive way, as in the case of Afghanistan, Iran and Morocco. The other religious communities also react in similar manner when their co-religionists are found in dire straits. Beyond this extent, giving religious or communal colour to such occurrences in the context of altering pattern of international relationship is misplaced, erodes intercommunal harmony, and misrepresents the religion itself.[56]

THREE SHINING EXAMPLES OF HINDU–MUSLIM AFFINITY

Sir Syed was deeply impressed and pleased with the public demonstration of sincere friendship between Hindus and Muslims at three places in the country during this period. In the Deccan the Hindus along with Muslims celebrated the victory over the Greeks, lighted lamps, illuminated markets and streets, held meetings, and sent telegrams of congratulation to the Sultan. This is a sufficient proof of fraternity between the two communities. Secondly, the Muslims of Bareilly did not sacrifice cows on 'Idu'z Zuha, and the Hindus promised to arrange free supply of drinking water (*sabeel*) and share in their sorrow and help them in trouble. Thirdly, Hindus and Muslims together organized a committee to raise funds for the construction of a mosque in the civil division of Manakpurganj in the district of Dacca, and both are collecting money for this purpose. As religious differences cannot be an impediment to social behaviour, mutual friendship and sympathy for each other, so the dissensions in political matters should not be an obstacle to cordial, humane relationship.[57]

CONCLUSION

In his factual narrative of wars between Turkey and Russia Sir Syed supported the cause of the former and explained that the sympathy of Muslims of India for a Muslim country and their co-religionists was inherent. He glorified the Turkish civilization, portrayed in lurid colours by the European critics, denounced their anti-Muslim tirade, and brought forth bright aspects of Sultan Abdul Hamid II's character, though he differed from his political policies. He earnestly hoped that Turkey might recover its former prowess, and ranked amongst the strong and prosperous nations. In the given circumstances the Muslims showed great sympathy with the Turks, marked by public demonstration of jubilation on the Turkish victory over Greece in 1897. They raised subscriptions for the relief of widows, orphans, war victims and needy people in that country. Sir Syed also felt happy on this occasion, enthusiastically participated in the relief programme, held a meeting at his house in Aligarh, and due to his influence and exertions, an amount of Rs. 6,807 was collected. He appreciated the cooperation and sympathetic attitude of the non-Muslims in the south, Bengal and other provinces in these well-meaning humanitarian efforts which underlined the valued traditions of tolerance and generosity of the Indian society.

However, Sir Syed suggested that the Muslims should maintain self-discipline in their ebullition of sympathy and happiness, and desist from associating with the agenda and activities of a complex political movement that originated and was organized in a foreign land. This kind of foreign connection would bring to them more problems and create a lot of confusion in their thought processes, and may even corrode the better understanding they now enjoyed with the British government that seemed keen to ensure their loyalty, he apprehended. The letter written by Lytton, the Viceroy (1876–80) to Salisbury the Secretary of State of India, unravels the current situation:

So far I can judge the feelings of our Mahomedan subjects at present is eminently satisfactory, but if Indian Muslims suspected British hand in the dissolution of Turkey their loyalty would dissipate. . . . It is my strong impression that, at the present moment, the lives of all your officers and European subjects in India mainly depend on the course of your Eastern policy and its freedom from all appearance of subserviency to Russia.[58]

Salisbury answered, 'It is somewhat startling to have our foreign policy in Europe prescribed to us by the people whom we conquered in the East.'[59] The British government of India became alert and closely watched the nature and extent of contacts between Indian Muslims and the Muslim world at large and Turkey in particular. The pan-Islamic Council at Constantinople had established its branches in India, while Sultan Abdul Hamid sent emissaries and agents to induce Muslims to rally round his flag. At the same time Jamaluddin al-Afghani preached the gospel of pan-Islamism through his speeches, writings and interaction with Muslim elites in the cities of India. He held that 'the decline of Islam as a religious system was due to its loss of political power, and a strong pan-Islamic society could alone reverse the process of decadence'.

On the basis of historical evidence Sir Syed repudiated the theory of a single universal Caliphate and unilateral leadership of the Muslim world, split up into diverse national entities and socio-economic interests. He argued that at one time there were three independent Caliphs in the Muslim world: the Abbasid Caliphs in Baghdad, the Fatimid Caliphs in Egypt, and Abdul Rahman Nasir and his successors in Spain. After the sack of Baghdad by Hulagu in 1258 and murder of al-Mustasm, the Abbasid Caliph (1242–58), the Caliphate vanished. In fact, it had been reduced to the lowest ebb of humiliation and degradation in the regime of Caliph Muqtadir (908–32) who was twice deposed and then killed. The institution of the Caliphate as the unified centre of dominance over the Muslim lands had ceased to exist, and the word Caliph that once inspired awe and reverence had lost its significance. Sultan Selim (1512–20), the conqueror of Egypt was the first Ottoman king who assumed the title of the Caliph in 1517. The Mughal Emperors of India did not recognize the successors of Sultan Selim as Caliphs, for according to their political concept every Muslim emperor was also the Caliph in his dominion. They called themselves Caliphs, and the capital city of their government was named *dar-ul-Khilafah,* though they kept up diplomatic and cordial relationship with Turkey.[60] At the end of eighteenth century Tipu Sultan of Mysore (1782–99) secured Caliphate patent from the Ottoman Khalifa, Sultan Selim III (1798–1805), who advised him to come to terms with the East India Company and sever all ties of friendship with the French. During the Mutiny of 1857, the British government of India obtained a proclamation of the Ottoman Sultan, Abdul Majid (1839–61) asking the Indian Muslims to remain loyal to the British government.[61]

It was against this historical background that Sir Syed challenged the claim of Sultan Abdul Hamid II's to being the Caliph of the whole Muslim world, including the Muslims of India. Without joining issue with those who questioned his ethnic identity or credentials of religious leadership, Sir Syed admitted that Abdul Hamid was the Caliph of his dominions. But, he insisted, that kingship or Khilafat of the Ottoman Sultan will remain confined within the frontiers of territories under his control, and will not be extended to those Muslims who lived beyond the pale of its jurisdiction. He was not the ruler of India, was not legally authorized to exercise his sovereign authority over the Indian Muslims, he could not defend them, and had no power to enforce laws of *Shariat* to strengthen the religion, the essential functions, forming the *raison d'être* of Khilafat. This fact admits of no disputation. It, therefore, follows that whatever revolutions take place in Turkey, and whatever ordinances are issued in that foreign land shall have no effect on the lives of Muslims in India. Sultan Abdul Hamid was not the *Khalifah* of the Indian Muslims and none here owed obedience to him. Drawing comparison between the true model of early Khilafat (632–61) and those which succeeded it Sir Syed wrote:

> The title of Caliph properly belongs to the first four rightly guided Caliphs. Only they deserved to be called Caliphs. The religious position which they hold in the eyes of the Muslims is not shared by any other ruler. Other rulers can be called Sultans or Amirs but not Caliphs. Therefore, the rulers of other Muslim countries are not successors of Prophet Muhammad (peace and blessings be upon him) even though they may call themselves Caliphs.[62]

On the controversial issue of Khilafat the views of Ali Abdul Raziq (b. 1888) are incongruous with those articulated by Sir Syed. Abdul Raziq in his book disproved the thesis that the Caliphate was an obligatory institution of Islam. 'The ulema had been unable to produce a single verse of the Quran in order to prove the thesis that the appointment of an Imam (leader) is a religious duty of the Muslims . . . what is true of the Quran is also true of the Hadis.' He further stated, the study of Islamic history show that the 'preservation of religion and the maintenance of religious rites do not depend on that particular form of government which the legists (*fuqaha*) called Caliphate or on the rulers whom they call Caliphs. Far from being a source of strength, the historical Caliphate was actually a source of weakness and it gave rise to many evils.' After its abolition in 1924, attempts to revive the dead institution were made, [63] but none amongst the Muslim rulers was prepared to assume the responsibilities of such an exalted office. King Faud I of Egypt could not succeed in his ambition of becoming the Caliph, Sharif Hussain of Hejaz gave up the idea, and Ibn-i Saud of Saudi Arabia declined to accept the position offered to him.[64] This situation confirmed the hypothesis of Sir Syed. He had postulated: 'If we look deeply into the present conditions, we shall come to the conclusion that there is not a single person in these days who can occupy the status of Imam, nor is any one entitled to be called the Caliph (successor).'[65]

The movement of pan-Islamism had passed its crucial stage, the arguments 'for' and 'against' still continue, their fuller comprehension is not part of the present endeavour. These essays served the needs of the contemporary Muslim audience in enriching their understanding of the changing realities in Turkey and Europe and developing an alternative pragmatic paradigm to deal with their impact on their lives and thought in the Indian environment. The central thesis emerging from the oeuvre was the overriding concern of Sir Syed for the alleviation of the educationally and economically backward Muslim community of India. The horizon of his political thought, educational and social reforms trajectory was that of modern India in which the Muslims could become an important part of the mainstream through their own strivings in the direction of building educational, cultural institutions and industries. Altaf Husain Hali (1837–1914) had indicated in his famous long poem how non-Muslim communities in Gujarat, Bombay and Bengal had modulated with the colonial order, and made rapid strides in education and industrial development. The other specific theme permeating the writings is related to his unflinching commitment to the ideology of goodwill and peaceful coexistence in society. Sir Syed censured the politicians who insidiously used religion as an instrument for accomplishing their political aims. In one essay he explained that in the past and modern times terrible wars between people of divergent religious ideologies as well as of common faith were waged for territorial expansion, political ascendancy and material gains, and religion had not been the fulcrum of such hostilities. The Christian powers of Western Europe would not have helped Turkey in the Crimean war, 1856–7, or at the Berlin Conference of 1878, or remained neutral in the Greek war, 1897, had Turkey fought against its foes in the name of religion. By his analysis and critique of the wars in historical perspective he proved that religion was not at the core.[66]

NOTES

1. Some of these activities may be mentioned in connection with the management of the Scientific Society (1863–4), MAO College (1877), Muslim Educational Conference (1886), participation in the debates on legislation of laws in the Viceroy's Council as its member (1878).
2. For details see, Asghar Abbas, *Sir Syed ki Sahafat,* Lahore, 2002, pp. 57–98. Shafey Kidwai, 'Sir Syed as a Journalist', in Asloob Ahmad Ansari, ed., *Sir Syed Ahmad Khan: A Centenary Tribute,* New Delhi, 2001, pp. 389, 390, 394.
3. Maulana Muhammad Ismail Panipati, ed., *Maqalat Sir Syed,* vol. 13, Lahore, 1963; Maulawi Imamuddin and Maulawi Ahmad Baba, eds., *Sir Syed Ke Akhri Mazamin*, Lahore: Mansur Press.
4. A list of articles prepared chronologically will follows this model (1897)– 15 May, 'Mutual Cordiality and Unity between Christians and Muslims'; 22 May, 'We Must Pay Regard to the Religious Leaders of Other Creeds'; 17 July, 'The Sympathy of Muslims of India for the Turks'; 5 June, 'Khilafat wa Khalifa'; 13 June, 'Greeks and Turks'; 31 July, 'Turkey and Greece'; 11 September, 'Khilafat'; 18 September, 'Imam and Imamat'; (1892); 28 June, 'Asiatic and Islamic System of Government'. (1877); 4 May, 'Funds Collection for Turks in Hyderabad'; 11 May, 'Places of Fighting'; 25 May, 'Turks and Indian Muslims'; 22 June, 'Russia and Turkey'; 3 July, 'Pro-Russian and Pro-Turkey'; 7 July, 'Funds for Turkey'; 28 July, 'Suleman Pasha'; 25 September, 'Victory of Sultan and Defeat of Russia'; 13 November, 'Ambassador of Turkey, and '*Madrasat-ul-Uloom*'; 15 December, 'Turkey and Russia';

18 December, 'Expediency of England and Turkey'; 9 March, 'Islam from Constantinople to Calcutta', for details see Asghar Abbas, *Sir Syed ki Sahafat*, Delhi: Anjuman Taraqqi Urdu, 1975, pp. 212–23.

5. The liberal school of thought was represented by Jeremy Benthem (1748–1832) who advocated that liberty, democracy and rationalism should form the basis for politics, economics, law and religion. His theory of utilitarianism, emphasizing the greatest good of the greatest number was explained and popularized by his disciples, James Mill and John Stuart Mill (1806–13). Karl Marx (1818–83) put forward his formulation of scientific socialism. In 1848 he in collaboration with Friedrich Engels issued the *Communist Manifesto* that called on the workers to unite and overthrow their exploiters. Marx's *Das Kapital* proved an epoch-making economic treatise. His significant contribution to social philosophy and historiography was the thesis that economic conditions have been the principal means of changing the course of human history, and issues of discussion relating to patriotism, religion and culture are only 'ideological veils' to obscure the fundamental economic forces, class conflicts, poverty of workers and peasants.
6. Tunisia became a protectorate of France in 1881, and Morocco in 1911, while Algeria became an integral domain of it in 1847. By 1883 Britain occupied and administered Egypt, and in 1898 it conquered the area of the headwaters of the Nile in Sudan. These were generally Muslim majority areas which now passed under the control of European powers. Between 1864 and 1869 the Russians conquered several Muslim lands in Central Asia, Tchemkend (1864), Tashkent (1865), Khojend, Khan of Khokand, Khanate of Bukhara (1867), Syr Daria, Samarkand, capital of Bukhara (1868), Khan of Khiva (1874). The occupation of Cape Colony in South Africa, Ceylon, Malta, and the Gulf of Aden by the British were primarily aimed at founding naval bases to protect its trade and commerce. In 1911 the British annexed the island of Madagascar. Belgium acquired extensive rubber areas in the Congo, ten times as large as Belgium. The Dutch had a great Island Empire in the Dutch East Indies.
7. In 1815 a revolt broke out in Spain against the repression and tyranny of Ferdinand VII, the Bourbon King and the rebels forced him to restore the liberal constitution of 1812. The news of the successful Spanish revolt stimulated insurgents in Naples and Sicily in Italy, and Sardinia, to carry on their revolutionary struggle against monarchical rule. In consequence, Greece gained its independence in 1829; two years later the Belgians succeeded in separating themselves from the Dutch. The process of unification in Italy and Germany culminated in 1871, owing to the superb qualities of Cavour (1810–61), Giuseppe Garibaldi (1807–82) and Otto von Bismark (1815–98). In France, under the pressure of

popular uprisings Charles X was deposed in 1830, and Louis Philippe I met similar fate in 1848.

8. 'Ottoman Views and Politics Towards the Orthodox Christian Church', in *Studies on Ottoman Social and Political History,* ed. Kemal H. Karpat, Leiden, 2002. He is also the author of *Politicization of Islam*, pp. 590–2.
9. Ibid., p. 593.
10. J.A.R. Marriott, *The Eastern Question,* Oxford, 1917, pp. 193–203.
11. Bernard Lewis, *The Emergence of Modern Turkey,* Oxford, 1968 pp. 38–50.
12. Karpat, pp. 601–4.
13. Marriott, p. 205.
14. For detail see, 'Protocol of St Petersburg', 4 April 1826 (a result of the diplomatic efforts of Duke of Wellington), *Eastern Question,* pp. 210–15. *The New Cambridge Modern History*, vol. IX, pp. 547–9.
15. For details see, *The New Cambridge Modern History*, vol. IX, p. 549. The Treaty of London, 14 September 1829. 'The War of independence could not have been won by the Greeks without foreign intervention; but equally the movement could hardly have been suppressed if the powers had held aloof', p. 548.
16. 'The War was not brought about by the deliberate cunning of Napolean II of France, nor by the machinations of Palmerston and Stratford de Redcliffe, still less was it brought by British economic interests. War began because a nationalist Turkey would not yield to Russian demands which she held to be humiliating and threatening to the maintenance of her empire.' For details see, *The New Cambridge Modern History*, vol. X (*1830–70*), ed. J.P.I. Bury.
17. *The New Cambridge Modern History,* vol. X, p. 281.
18. Ibid., p. 468.
19. Kenneth Bourne, *The Foreign Policy of Victorian England, 1830–1902*, Russel's memorandum on 'Russia and Turkey', 19 June 1853; Palmerston, Prime Minister, 1855–8; Lord John Russel, Colonial Secretary, February 1855–July 1855, Prime Minister, 1865–6; Lord Aberdeen, Prime Minister, 1852–5.
20. *The New Cambridge Modern History,* vol. X, pp. 280–1, 480–92.
21. *Eastern Question,* pp. 249, 266–75. In May 1853 Mustapha Pasha was appointed Grand Wazir of Turkey, Rashid Pasha, the Foreign Minister, Muhammad Ali, Minister of War, and Omar Pasha, Commander of a large army in Bulgaria. It was during this war that Florence Nightingale had set an extraordinary example of dedication and self-sacrifice by providing medical assistance to the wounded and sick soldiers at the base level. The establishment of the International Red Cross in 1866 was another major landmark in the humanitarian movement.

22. *The New Cambridge Modern History,* ed. F.S. Hinsley, vol. XI, pp. 567–70.
23. For details see, ibid., pp. 571–2.
24. Bourne, p. 408.
25. Ibid., p. 405.
26. Ibid., p. 573.
27. Ibid.
28. *The Eastern Question,* pp. 375–82.
29. Erik J. Zurcher, *Turkey: A Modern History*, paperback edn., New York, 1994, pp. 80–1.
30. Karpat, pp. 50–65.
31. Lewis, pp. 122–5.
32. Zurcher, pp. 83, 85, 341–2.
33. The Greek War of Independence was avowedly a war of extermination. 'The Turk shall live no longer, neither in the Morea, nor in the whole earth', was the popular song in Greece. *The Eastern Question*, p. 205.
34. P. Hardy, *The Muslims of British India*, Cambridge, 1972, pp. 175–6.
35. Zurcher, pp. 81–3.
36. Mushirul Hasan, ed., *Communal and Pan-Islamic Trends in Colonial India,* New Delhi: Manohar, 1985, pp. 2–42.
37. Hardy, p. 177.
38. Maulawi Imam al Din and Maulawi Ahmad Baba, eds., *Akhri Mazamin, 1896–7*, Lahore: Mansura Press, p. 49.
39. *Akhri Mazamin,* p. 49.
40. Bourne, extracts from the speeches and addresses of Mr Gladstone, pp. 420–3.
41. *Akhri Mazamin,* p. 50.
42. Maulana Muhammad Ismail Panipati, ed., *Maqalat Sir Syed,* vol. 13, Lahore, 1963, p. 430.
43. Ibid. It may be noted here that in this essay Sir Syed omitted to mention the occupation of Cyprus in return for military help to Turkey. The helpless Turks did not know that Britain and Russia had reached a working adjustment five days before the Cyprus convention was signed (4 June 1878). Alexander II was aware that his formidable war machine was no match for the combined military strength of England and France which would not allow him to decide the fate of the afflicted country. Sir Syed also left out the territorial losses sustained by Turkey in Europe on the morrow of the signature of the Treaty of Berlin. Turkey was consolidated, as announced by Benjamin Disraeli (1st Earl of Beaconsfield), Prime Minister of England 1874–80, only by expelling her from two-thirds of its territory in Europe, and migration of lakhs of Muslim Turks from there.
44. Ibid.

45. *Akhbar Scientific Society Aligarh*, 22 December 1876, *Maqalat Sir Syed*, vol. 13, pp. 458–60.
46. *Maqalat Sir Syed*, pp. 425–37.
47. *Tahzib-ul Akhlaq*, 1877; *Maqalat Sir Syed*, pp. 436–40; *Shamsul Akhbar*, 9 Shaban 1293. *Maqalat*, pp. 464–6 (*Tahzib-ul Akhlaq*, vol. VI, 1 Ramzan 1292, pp. 142–4).
48. *Akhbar Scientific Society Aligarh*, 22 December 1876; *Maqalat*, pp. 441–3.
49. Ibid.
50. Ibid., pp. 441–6.
51. Ibid., pp. 407–8.
52. *Tahzib-ul Akhlaq*, 1871, *Jamadi* II, 1288 M; *Maqalat*, pp. 405–10.
53. *Akhbar Scientific Society Aligarh*, 17 March 1876; *Maqalat*, pp. 419–24.
54. *Akhri Mazamin*, pp. 53–5.
55. Ibid., p. 56.
56. Ibid., pp. 57–8.
57. Ibid., pp. 70–1.
58. Rajkumar Trivedi, *The Critical Triangle, India, Britain and Turkey*, Jaipur, 1993, p. 4.
59. Ibid., p. 4.
60. Naimur Rehman Farooqui, *Mughal Ottoman Relations (1556–1748)*, Delhi, 1989, pp. 190–8.
61. Yusuf Husain Khan, 'Indian Muslims and the Caliphate', in S.T. Lokhandwalla, ed., *India and Contemporary Islam*, Simla, 1971, pp. 170–3.
62. *Maqalat*, pp. 425–9, 432, 437–8; *Akhri Mazamin*, pp. 33, 34, 40–4.
63. *Akhri Mazamin*, p. 35. Mazheruddin Siddiqui, *Modern Reformist Thought in the Muslim World*, Islamabad, 1982, pp. 155–6. Similar views about the true Caliphate had been expressed long back by Ziyauddin Barni. He stated, the true Caliphate had really ceased after four Caliphs, who alone were able, either due to their nearness to the Prophet's time or one of his miracles that just for one generation the pious Caliphs were able to exercise the powers of government and keep the world in order in spite of their spiritual life and austerity (*darweshi*). 'Islam and such Mussalmans are not left that can govern them after the manners of Abu Bakr and Umar (632–64).' For a detailed discussion of the aspects of transformation of the early pious Caliphate into *Mumlakat* (temporal sovereignty) by the Umayyads (661–750) and under the despotic rule of the Abbasids (750–1258), Abul Ala Maududi, *Khalafat wa Mamlukiyat*, Delhi, 1974, pp. 77–81, 92, 145, 192. According to Maulana Shibli Numani (1857–1914) the *Khalifah* should belong to the Guriesh family as this rule had been in vogue throughout

in the history of Khilafat. *Maqalat-i-Shibli*, vol. IV, Azamgadh, 1930, pp. 182–7. Muhammad Habib, *The Political Theory of the Delhi Sultanate,* p. 34.

64. Siddiqui, pp. 157–9.
65. *Akhri Mazamin (Imam aur Imamat)*, p. 43.
66. *Musaddas Hali,* Khuda Bakhsh Library edition, Patna, 1995, pp. 47, 146.

BIBLIOGRAPHY

Arnold, Sir Thomas W., *The Caliphate*, London: 1965.

Azad, Abul Kalam, *Masla-i-Khilafat*, Lahore, 1985.

Emin, Ahmed, *Turkey in the World War*, Yale University Press, 1930.

Farooqi, Naimur Rehman, *Mughal Ottoman Relations (1556–1748)*, Delhi, 1989.

Forbes, N. et al., *The Balkans*, 1919.

Gooch, G.P., *Nationalism*, 1920.

Habib, Mohammed and Afsar Umar Salim Khan, *The Political Theory of the Delhi Sultanate*, Allahabad: Kitab Mahal, 1961.

Hull, W.P. and W.S. Davis, *The Course of Europe Since Waterloo*, 1941.

Hamdani, Raza, *Jamaluddin Afghani*, Lahore, 1951.

Hardy, P., *The Muslims of British India*, Cambridge, 1972.

Holt, P.M., ed., *Cambridge History of Islam*, 2 vols, 1971.

Kasaba, Resat, *The Ottoman Empire and the World Economy: The Nineteenth Century,* New York, 1988.

Kohn, H., *Prophets and People: Studies in Nineteenth Century Nationalism*, 1946.

Lewis, Bernard, *The Emergence of Modern Turkey*, Oxford, 1968.

Lewis, Geoffrey, *Modern Turkey*, Cambridge, 1977.

Lipson, E., *Europe in the 19th and 20th Century*, Bombay, 1984.

Malik, Hafeez, *Muslim Nationalism in India and Pakistan*, Washington, D.C., 1963.

Maqalat-i-Shibli, vol. IV, Azamgarh, 1938.

Marriott, J.A.R., *The Eastern Question*, Oxford, 1917.

Miller, W., *The Ottoman Empire and its Successors, 1801–1927*, 1936.

Miller, W., *A Short History of Greek People 1821–1921*, 1922.

Minault, Gail, *The Khilafat Movement: Religions Symbolism and Political Mobilization in India, Britain and Turkey*, Delhi, 1973.

Mowdude, Abul Ala, *Khilafat Wa Malukiyat*, Delhi, 1974.

Muhammad, Shan, *Sir Syed Ahmad Khan: A Political Biography*, Meerut, 1969.

Mushirul Hasan, ed., *Communal and Pan-Islamic Trends in Colonial India*, Delhi, 1985.

Nizami, Khalif Ahmad, 'Syed Ahmad Khan and Syed Jamaluddin Afghani', in *Sir Syed Aur Aligarh Tehrik*, Aligarh, 1982, pp. 27–59.

Shaw, Stanford and Ezel, *History of the Ottoman Empire and Modern Turkey*, Cambridge, 1977.

Shukla, R.L., *Britain, India and the Turkish Empire*, Delhi, 1973.

Smith, Wilfred Cantwell, *Modern Islam in India*, Lahore, 1943.

Trivedi, Rajkumar, *The Critical Triangle: India, Britain and Turkey*, Jaipur, 1993.

Zurcher, Erik J., *Turkey: A Modern History*, New York, 1994.

CHAPTER 4

A Critical Review of the Biographical Literature (Sira) *of the Prophet Muhammad by Syed Ahmad Khan*

GULFISHAN KHAN

بلغ العلى بكماله   كشف الدجى بجماله

حسنت جميع خصاله   صلوا عليه وآله

He attained exaltation by his perfection.
He dispelled darkness by his beauty.
Beauteous are all his qualities,
Benediction be on him and his family.

The Gulistan (The Rose Garden) of Shaikh Saadi*

SYED AHMAD KHAN: A RELIGIOUS THINKER

The religious ideas of Syed Ahmad Khan have always fascinated as well as baffled the world of scholarship, and as such has been the subject of intellectual debates and controversies even during the lifetime of the educationist and social reformer. The reformer attempted consistent, comprehensively valid theological responses and provided single theological answers to single challenges; by going back to the sources and principles of the various Islamic religious sciences as represented in the Islamic *falsafa* (philosophy), *kalam* (theology), and *fiqh* (jurisprudence). Yet all his reformist ideas were firmly rooted in the critical researches as embodied in the writings of classical scholars of Islam.[1] Of late, a number of scholars have sought to explore the socio-religious views of the great Islamic thinker as contained in his religious writings. These various researches reinforce the view that the grand old man of the Aligarh movement, Syed Ahmad, as revealed in his learned discourses was, above all, an outstanding religious thinker and a theologian who gave a new orientation to Islamic thinking.[2] In Muhammad Umar al-Din's view, as in former intellectual movements, Islam has been presented in the form of law as witnessed by the emergence of various schools of jurisprudence, and in the form of schools of philosophy, or again in the form of a Sufi system of thought. In the same way Sir Syed, keeping in mind the scientific spirit of the modern age, presented Islam in the form of scientific theory and outlook. He presented a dynamic and progressive concept of religion. He sought to prove that Islam as a system of faith was not against reason and scientific progress. It was not antagonistic towards advancement of culture and civilization. Contrary to the popular perceptions, he argued that perhaps Islam was the only faith which could accommodate the changing spirit of the time and age.[3] In the background of this radical reassessment of Islamic religious thought were also the challenges of Western philosophy, new sciences and missionary criticism of Islam as represented in Western education, and the various facets of colonial rule. This reappraisal of inherited world-view by the latter represented a new conception of Islam and laid the foundation of a new Islamic theology (*Ilm al-Kalam*) and a new *Weltanschauung*.[4] It is worth emphasizing that for the thinker too, more than the foundation of MAO College, it was primarily his intellectual contribution in the domain of religious thought which was of paramount importance. For the philosopher-reformer viewed his discourses on Islamic theology as his ever lasting intellectual achievement and religious ideas as the most important aspect of his own life. Religious stimulation could be the decisive factor in an individual's life: 'Among all the ideas in the world religious ideas are such as to have the greatest impact on the mind of the man.'[5]

WORKS ON RELIGION

Among the major religious monographs of Syed Ahmad are the bilingual *Tabyin al-Kalam fi tafsir al taurat wa injil ala millat al-Islam*, a three-volume commentary on the Old and the New Testament; and *Tafsir al-Quran*, a seven-volume Urdu translation and commentary on the Holy Koran up to Sura 20. A prolific writer, and versatile genius who could express himself with ease and clarity on diverse subjects, Sir Syed contributed countless editorials and articles to the *Aligarh Institute Gazette* and *Tahdhîb al-akhlâq* (The Muslim Reformer), the two periodicals founded by him which still await study.[6] Another significant oeuvre of the author in the field of comparative study of religions is *Al-Khutbat al-Ahmadiya*, known as the *Life of Mohammed* in its English version, originally published in English in the form of individual essays devoted to a specific theme during the 15 months sojourn (May 1869–August 1870) of the author in the British metropolis.[7] Later, the same were published in the form of a book as the *Essays on the Life of Mohammed* with preliminary discourses called 'Preface and Introduction' and entitled as *Dibacha* in the *Khutbat*, its Urdu version.[8] This present article too, is exclusively concerned with this bilingual work of the author. It revolves around a single query, not altogether irrelevant—an examination of the various sources, Eastern as well as Western, which constituted the subject matter of the *Essays on the Life of Mohammed* and that of its Urdu version *Al-Khutbat al-Ahmadiya*. This Urdu edition is almost the same as the standard English edition yet it is different in one significant respect. It contains verses of the Holy Book and also Traditions from the Books of *Ahadith* to explain and corroborate his own arguments on various subjects discussed in this study.

Furthermore, the Urdu version contains extensive quotations in Arabic from *Hujjat Allah al-Baligha* the *magnum opus* of the celebrated eighteenth-century Islamic thinker Shah Waliullah Dehlawi (1703–62) to substantiate as well as to strengthen his own ideas on different subjects put forward in the work.[9] While in the English *The Life of Mohammed* there occurs but only one direct reference to the thoughts of Shah Waliullah and that he had been criticized for his emphasis on the use of reason and rational approach to religion.[10] There are occasional references to *Tuhfah i-Athna Ashariah*, a scholarly work of Shah Abd al-Aziz Dehlawi (1746–1823) distinguished son and successor of Shah Waliullah.[11] It is more than evident that Waliullah's ideas exercised a profound influence on our author's entire world-view, not the least on his religious thought and outlook.[12]

THE LIFE OF MOHAMMED OR *AL-KHUTBAT AL-AHMADIYA FIL ARAB WA SIRAT AL-MUHAMMADIYA*

SOME PRELIMINARY REMARKS

The essays on the life of the Prophet Mohammad, which are twelve in number, were addressed to the Western Orientalists as well as to the Western educated Indian Muslim middle classes. *Khutbat*, the Urdu version, was intended for the Urdu reading and speaking Muslim gentry of India. A careful examination of both the texts, the language employed and the subjects commented upon, shows that these were addressed to an academic audience rather than to the educated public at large. Again this voluminous yet a highly methodical work—*Khutbat al-Ahmadiya*—is thought to have been written in response to the missionary orientalist William Muir's *Life of Mahomet* but one finds that the work under consideration explored much more wide-ranging themes.[13] At least three of the essays are exclusively concerned with the Age of Ignorance (*Jahilliya*)—the pre-Islamic Arabia, its geography, tribes and tribal structure, religions and religious creeds, socio-economic condition of the peninsula on the eve of the rise of Islam. Among these the 'Essay on the Historical Geography' of Arabia is the longest of all.[14] Other essays are devoted to the early life of the Prophet, his genealogy, childhood and his early youth. Some other compositions are concerned with an examination of the religious books of Islam, books of traditions (*ahadith*), and exegesis (*tafsir*), major works on the science of jurisprudence (*fiqh*), and biographies (*sira*) of the Prophet, while one full essay is on the revelation of the Holy Koran.

Thus the actual scope of the work under consideration is comprehensive indeed—it being a nineteenth-century restatement of Islam on a very vast canvas. It would be too simplistic to assume that *The Life of Mohammed* is merely a forceful defence of Islam and its founder from the attacks of William Muir which the latter raised in his biography of the Prophet.[15] It contains a complex and influential body of discourse wherein the author displayed magical powers with analysis of documents and genius in integrating various points of views. It is an evidence of painstaking and planned scholarship from the pen of a man of imagination and initiative. It is a creative response to the criticism of not only William Muir but also of other European polemicists, controversialists, Orientalists and historians who wrote about Islam. More significantly perhaps the author became aware of the development of slow but perceptible positive view of Islam in European intellectual discourses. More specifically the author could discern an affirmative and meaningful evaluation of the achievements of the Prophet in emerging contemporary European thought. The author noted with satisfaction the Western recognition of cultural contribution of Islam in the development and progress of world civilization. This work is an evidence of the remarkable qualities of the author, namely the maturity of judgement in spite of an obvious irresistible propensity for criticism. It also exhibits philosophic composure and dignity of style as the sagacity with which the conflicting views are estimated and developed by the author. The work is concerned with a number of fundamental issues of vital importance for both religion and Islamic societies. It contains a well-articulated exposition, of the various socio-cultural practices and Islamic values. Only one of the twelve essays, 'Islam duniya ke liye rahmat hai aur ambiya ke mazahib ki pusht wa panah', i.e. 'Islam is a blessing to humanity and a support to the cause of the revealed religions', is a direct response of Muir's brief but severe criticism of some of the social practices and institutions of Islamic societies such as polygamy and divorce.[16] Muir asserted that these socio-cultural practices were based on Islamic *Shariat* and hence a manifestation of the faith itself.[17] G.F.I. Graham, the British biographer of the author, considered these essays a glowing tribute to the comparative study of religions.[18] In Graham's view, 'These essays . . . show an extraordinary depth of learning, great toleration of other religions, great veneration for the essential principles of true Christianity, and should be attentively studied by all interested in religion.'[19] Graham considered these a suitable reply to the allegations of Muir. To quote Graham, 'Our author, of course, breaks many a lance with Sir William Muir, his intimate friend, over the latter's life of Mohammed; and impartial critics will, I think, agree in giving their verdict on many points against that learned author.'[20] Graham also informs that printed copies of these essays were sent to the Ottoman Sultan Abd al-Aziz (1861–76) and Ismail Pasha (ruled 1863–79) of Egypt. In both these letters the author sought to emphasize that the prime objective for writing this volume was to demonstrate that 'the onward march of science and enlightenment is in every respect compatible with Islam,'[21] and 'that the most liberal views and opinions upon the sciences and knowledge in general are perfectly consistent with the precepts and practices of our holy religion'.[22]

GOD AND THE UNIVERSE: THEOLOGICAL EPISTEMOLOGY

The 'Preface and Introduction' (*Dibacha*) contains an exposition of the theological world-view of the author. It begins with a highly philosophical question as to what is the meaning and essence of religion. The author offers serious reflections on the existence and transcendental nature of 'all knowing and all wise Creator'.[23] Here the thinker clearly displays mystical outlook in recounting the proofs on the existence of that Supreme Being. This universe is nothing but manifestations of that Unseen Reality.[24] It contains an epistemological explanation of the powers and attributes of God of the Absolute Omnipotence and Infinite Proximity, as says a Tradition, 'I am near to the thought of My servant as he thinks about Me.'[25] Additionally, the author also delves into the complex question of God's relationship with man and universe. The author seeks to provide a highly rationalistic view of religions as the latter sought to emphasize that the underlying principles of all religions was the same, so was the purpose of all religions, to search out God the Almighty, cause of all causes, one who has Lordship over nature and over the laws of nature.[26] In this essentially universalistic view of the purpose of religion the author also included extensive quotations from the *Ethical Epistles* of Horace and the English poet Alexander Pope's 'Essay on Man': 'All are but parts of one stupendous whole, Whose body nature is, and God the soul'.[27] In the Urdu version Horace's Latin verse, 'Unde nil majus genratur ipso Nec viget quicquam simili aut secundum' is replaced and the following Persian stanza cited: 'I became jealous otherwise I would have taken off your veil, taken you by hand and shown you to the world.'[28] Similarly the citation from the essay of Alexander Pope (1688–1744) is substituted with a Persian couplet of the renowned Indo–Persian poet and prose writer Amir Khusrau Dihlawi (1253–1325), 'I have become Thou and Thou hast become Me. I have become body and Thou hast become soul. So that no longer anyone could say: I am one person and you are another.'[29] More significantly the preface contains a public profession of the author's firm faith in Islam, and an exposition of the precepts of what the latter considered true faith: 'Thus as far as I was able to investigate the truth of religions, I found only Islam to be the true religion. And I hope that those who hold the truth dear will always in candour and sincerity investigate the truth of Islam.'[30] For Syed Ahmad Islam is based upon sound principles which enable one to discriminate between right and wrong, 'a religion which offers to the world a world view not only true, but capable of being seen'.[31] The author viewed Islam a religion of perfect monotheism, *Tauhid*, and the Prophet an establisher of this pure monotheistic faith. In the establishment of pure *Tauhid*, the Prophet was the greatest reformer the world has ever seen. 'Thus this true religion and the person through whom we were taught in it, is worthy of our greatest respect and unlimited praise and, no doubt, he [the Prophet] is worthy of the following address: "You are dearer to me, O Messenger of God, than the soul within me".'[32]

The idea of writing a befitting reply to the critique of William Muir and other Western Orientalists in general was clearly conceived and conceptualized much before the author actually visited Britain. Syed had been taking notes from the relevant sources available to him while in India. Yet the work suffered from 'the want of many MSS which were indispensable for the successful accomplishment of my undertaking'.[33] But, many of the books were not available in India due to the ruin and destruction of many of the old libraries.[34] Therefore, one of the compelling motives of Syed Ahmad's visit to London was consultation of these works in the growing Oriental collections of the India Office Library. Unquestionably, Syed was acutely aware of the importance of use of source material in writing history. He had already adopted the scientific method and approach mainly based on the textual study of the original documents as evidenced from his Urdu-language topographical work on Delhi, *Asar-us Sanadid* (1846; revd. edn., 1852), a work which made him known internationally. It is not unlikely that the author had already developed a blue-print for his *Essays* before he left India. As yet, there remained two major impediments in the way of fulfilment of his mission: first, a complete lack of assistance and support from any quarter, and second, the usual mundane concern for the means of living (*fikr-i maash*).[35] Syed Ahmad acknowledged frankly that the biographies of the Prophet were many, written by the European authors as well as by Muslim scholars. These works are known as the *Kutub i-Sira* a common designation while the same in English are called the 'Life'. The author introduced various sources of information, Eastern or Oriental and European or Western which Sir Syed used in writing the Preface of his *Essays*. Herein Sir Syed mentioned a number of European scholars mainly British, German and also French who had contributed significantly to the Western discourses on Islam but admitted his inability to access many of those works directly due to his lack of linguistic expertise in those languages. Even for the English work, Sir Syed frankly confessed indebtedness to others: 'being myself wholly ignorant of that splendid tongue so as to be unable to construct a single sentence in it I hereby publicly and sincerely express my deep obligations to those friends by whose literary assistance I am now enabled to submit to the attention of an indulgent and intelligent public this first volume in its complete and digested form'.[36]

However it must be appreciated that Syed Ahmad despite all self-confessed ignorance of English language, had very early in his life become familiar with Western scientific and philosophical ideas because of his close association with the Western academic institutions as represented by the English-styled colleges at Agra and Delhi, learned societies like the Vernacular Translation Society of the Delhi College, and the Archaeological Society of Delhi. He was actively involved with the academic activities of these reputed institutions and societies. Evidently *Tazkirah i-ahl i-Dehli*, originally the fourth chapter of the splendid archaeological treat, *Athar al-Sanadid* is full of delightful reminiscences of colleagues and friends, many of whom were associated with the Delhi College as students and some as teachers such as Maulavi Mamluk Ali (d. 1851), and the classicist Imam Bakhsh Sahbai (d. 1857).[37] He was fully aware of the use of modern printing presses for dissemination of ideas and the spread of journalism in the great cultural centres of north India. One of his earliest works, namely the *Qaul-i matin dar ibtal-i harkat-i zamin*, a scientific treatise, was written in response to the teachings of modern astronomy as taught in Delhi College.[38] While working as the Naib Munshi at the Commissioner's office at Agra, he was closely associated with the academic activities of Agra College and adapted a short scientific treatise of his maternal grandfather Khwaja Farid entitled *Tashil fi Jarr i-saqil* (Introduction to the art of mechanics) which was published from the Sikandara Orphan Press in 1844 for the Agra School Book Society.[39] Again *Fawaid al-Afkar fi amal al-farjar* on the use of compasses was published under the auspices of the Vernacular Translation Society in 1846, when Dr Alois Sprenger was the principal of Delhi College from 1845–51, and when Syed Ahmad Khan was a Munsif (judge) in Delhi (1846–55) before his transfer to Bijnore as Sadr Amin.[40] Evidently the references to a wide variety of European texts in the *Essays/Khutbat* became possible as many of these were taught in English while others were translated into Urdu for the curriculum of Delhi College, such as *Paradise Lost* by John Milton (1608–74), *History of Great Britain* by David Hume (1711–76), *History of Scotland and History of the Reign of Charles V* of William Robertson (1721–93), Pope Gregory's essays and the *Natural Theology* of William Paley (1743–1805). Edward Gibbon (1737–94) was also taught in Delhi College. The curriculum of Delhi College included many of these works cited by the author.[41]

SOURCES OF THE *AL-KHUTBAT*

THE EASTERN SOURCES

In his discourses on the 'Religious books of Muslims' the author enumerated almost all major biographical works on the life of the Prophet. Moreover, in the same essay the author expressed dissatisfaction with the existing books of *Sira* and questioned their authenticity as compared to the books of *Ahadith*, given the differences in the methodology of collection and compilation of the two historical sources, the *Hadith* and *Sira*. Consequently, the author sought to argue, that the Prophetic traditions were more reliable, and more authentic as source of information for the purposes of a biography of the Prophet than the extant biographical literature on the subject.[42]

Our author's list of the main biographical works included *Tarikh-i Muhammad Ismail Bukhari, Tarikh-i Muhammad Jarir Tabari, Sirat-i Shami, Sirat-i Hishami, Sirat ibn Sad Katib al-Waqidi.* There were other noteworthy works—such as *Madarij al-Nubuwwa*, *Qisas al-Anbiya*, *Mirajnama*, *Shahadatnama* and *Mauludnama* of reputed scholars.[43] Again in the Preface and Introduction, the *dibacha*, Syed Ahmad re-enumerated the extant biographical compositions. Among the major biographical works are *Ibn Ishaq, Ibn Hisham*, *Tabkat-i-Kabeer* generally called *Katib-ul Waqidi, Tabari, Sirat-i Shami, Abul Fida*; *Masudi Mawahib al-Laduniyah*. Of these, the first four are of very ancient date, while the rest are considerably later.'[44] However, Sir Syed pointed out that it is difficult to separate facts from fables in almost all these books of *Sira*. Moreover, he suspected that many of the stories which would have been current amongst the Jews in those days crept into the text of these compilations. Therefore, he stressed the fact that none of the above-mentioned works should be utilized uncritically. All these works should be subjected to an objective, careful and searching examination and dispassionate research. In this sense *Sira* works should not be treated as an independent historical source. Much of the *Sira* literature consists of *Hadith* material arranged in biographical order. Therefore, for an analysis of the *Sira, Ahadith*, biographical interest as contained in the books of biography should be analysed in the perspective of the *Hadith*.[45] *Hadith*, the utterances and deeds of the Prophet, was an important source and more reliable than the existing biographies to reconstruct the life of the Prophet. Many of the *Hadith* have a direct bearing on the personality of the Apostle of God. Unlike the biographers, the *muhaddithun* followed strict methodological rules in collection of the sayings and doings of the Prophet. The emergence of authoritative collection of *Hadith* was an outcome of the emergence of the *Hadith* sciences. Even this second source, reiterated the author, like the biographical literature should be assessed critically. The rules for establishing the reliability and authenticity of *Hadith* had been laid down in a separate chapter of the work under consideration.[46]

Given the greater reliability of *Hadith* literature, in view of the critique *Shamail-i Tirmizi* of Muhammad al-Isa bin Saurah al-Tirmizi this was an important work to reconstruct a biography of the Prophet. Though, Tirmizi, the author (b. AH 209/AD 824; d. AH 279/AD 892 at Tirmiz) is better known for his other work, namely, the *Jami al-Tirmizi* which is a standard work on *Hadith* and one among the six canonical collections of Traditions, the sayings and doings of the Prophet.[47] His work *Shamail-i Tirmizi* Syed Ahmed clarified, is not a full biography in the traditional sense of the term, but its importance lay in the fact that it contains most valuable data on the person and personal life of the Prophet—his noble disposition, mode of living, manner of speech, deportment, likes and dislikes, daily routine—not found in the other better known books of *Sira*.[48] In his view *Tarikh-i Abul Fida*, i.e. *al-Mukhtasar fi-Akhbar al-Bashar* a universal history going down to 1329 of the historian Abul Fida (1273–1331) was also a trustworthy source to be relied upon as this historian was careful in selection of biographical *Ahadith*.[49] Syed Ahmad refers to the Latin version also as he specifically mentions that this history, together with its Latin translation, was reprinted in 1831, with the title *Abul Fedae Historia Anteislamica Arabice* and edited by Henricus Orthobius, an obvious reference to the German scholar Henricus Orthobius Fleischer (1801–88).[50] Historian Abul Fida remained a prime source of information in Europe until the knowledge of the earlier and more authentic biographical works on the subject in the nineteenth century reached Europe via India. For instance, he was the main source in George Sale's *Preliminary Discourse* through the edition of J. Gagnier. During the time when Gibbon wrote, and for long after, historians mainly relied for their knowledge of the life of Mohammed on the biography of Abul Fida who died in the year AH 722/AD 1322, of whose work Gagnier produced.[51] In India this work was translated and published by Maulavi Karimuddin, a student and later a teacher of Delhi College, with the press of the same institution.[52] So was the medieval geographer Masudi.[53]

The other authorities Syed Ahmed referred to are the earliest biographers of the Prophet, Muhammad ibn Ishaq (AD 704–67), author of *Sirat al-Rasul Allah* and its editor Abd al-Malik Ibn Hisham (d. AD 833 or 828) through whose recension the *Sira* reached us. The first standard edition of the Arabic text *Sirat Rasul Allah*, a life of the Prophet by Muhammad Ibn Ishaq in the annotated rescension of Abd al-Malik Ibn Hisham is that of Ferdinand Wustenfeld, 1858–60, and translated into German by Gustav Weil, 1864. Syed Ahmad had a copy of this printed edition. 'We have in our possession this published edition of Hishami's book printed and published at Gottingen in 1858, under the care and supervision of Dr Ferdinand Wustenfeld.'[54] The other authority is the traditionist Katib al-Waqidi Muhammad Ibn Sad (b. AH 168 /AD 784; d. AH 230/AD 845), author of the work *Kitab al-Tabaqat al-Kabir* (Book of Classes). The other important works on the subject consulted by the author are al-Tabari (d. AH 310/AD 922) author of *Tarikh*. *Sirat-i Shami* and *Mawahib al-Leduniya* of Shaikh Ibrahim al-Bejuri a later authority.[55]

Almost all the above historical and biographical works mentioned by Syed Ahmad were available in India in the pre-Mutiny period. Alois Sprenger (1813–93) and Muir both could obtain their desired books on Islam and its founder from these Indian libraries and also directly from the personal collections of the educated Indian Muslim elite.[56] Both Islamicists were intimately acquainted with each other and perused their respective works with scholarly interest and curiosity. Both were known to Syed Ahmad Khan, Sprenger as the Principal of the Delhi College was aware of Syed Ahmad's gentlemanly scholarly interests. William Muir was also known to Syed Ahmad since the former was posted in Agra from 1847–54, and the official Graham attested to their mutual friendship. The sources on which William Muir and Alois Sprenger based their biographies of the Prophet were procured from Delhi, Lucknow and Kanpur. Delhi having long been the capital was also the hub of all such intellectual activities. The Mughal nobility and gentry maintained their personal collections and private libraries. It seemed innumerable libraries, personal as well as public, along with the mosques and *madrasas* dotted the landscape of the Mughal capital. Delhi, the former Shahjahanabad, it seemed was the centre of the Islamic East and its scholars the depositories of Islamic knowledge. In the eighteenth century, decline and disintegration of the Mughal Empire forced many scholars and the erstwhile bureaucracy to leave their beloved city along with their highly treasured collections. Some of these books mostly in manuscript form found their way to the regional capitals such as Lucknow and Hyderabad and ultimately in the state libraries of these regional potentates. Even the library of Tipu Sultan in Srirangapatnam contained many valuable collections of Arabic and Persian manuscripts and also books in the regional languages. Many rare Indian treasures reached European libraries mainly through British officials who got these from their Indian clients as special presents. The library of the Fort William College was another source through which these rich Indian collections reached Europe, mainly London, where these are still preserved in the fabulous Oriental Collections of the British Library.[57] Many such collections were destroyed during the Mutiny, an unfortunate fact to which Syed Ahmad alluded to though indirectly.[58]

Muir observed that although 'It should be recollected, too, that the facilities for consulting works of occidental learning are, in these remote parts of India, rare and imperfect.'[59] But as to what Muir would have termed Oriental, 'The facilities for the study are, probably, greater here than any other part of the world, . . . '[60] As this was the land which preserved what the British Orientalist called the 'treasures purchased from the West [Asia] at some remote period by the riches of Indian conquerors and Ameers, being still extant in the land'.[61]

Evidently, one of the earliest extant biographies of the Prophet by Ibn Ishaq in the recension of Ibn Hisham was borrowed from the personal library of poet and jurist, Sadr al-Din Azurdah of Delhi,[62] as acknowledged by William Muir. This particular copy of *Sira*, 'An abridgement of Ibn Hisham's work was made at Damascus in AH 707/AD 1307, by one Ahmad ibn Ibrahim. A beautiful manuscript, in the handwriting of the abbreviator himself, is in the possession of Muhammad Sadr-ood-Deen, the Principal Sadr Ameen of

Delhi. It is the copy which has been used by Dr Sprenger (vide Sprenger's *Mohammad*, p. 70, n. 2) and the same to which (the author also having had access to it), reference is made throughout this work. A valuable manuscript of the entire work is in the library of the Asiatic Society in Calcutta.'[63]

So was the first volume out of the fifteen, of *Kitab al-tabaqat al-kabir* of Muhammad Ibn Sad al-Zuhri (d. AH 230/AD 844–5) that contains the Prophet's biography and was also available in India in the personal collections of Muzaffar Husain of Kanpur.[64]

In the fifteen volumes here noticed, the Secretary is supposed to have embodied the researches of his master, Al Wackidi, together with the fruits of his own independent labour. The first volume has, fortunately in the interests of literature and of truth, been preserved to us in an undoubtedly genuine form. It contains the Sirat or 'Biography of Mahomet,' with detailed accounts of the early learned men of Medina, and of all the Companions of the Prophet who were present at Badr. For a copy of this invaluable volume we are indebted to the indefatigable research of Dr Sprenger, who discovered it in the library of Mozuffer Husain Khan at Cawnpore. This manuscript is written in an ancient but very distinct character and is in excellent preservation. It was executed at Damascus, AH 718 (AD 1318) by a scholar named al-Hakkari, who traces up, link by link, from the pupil to the master (by whom it was successively taught, or by whom copied), the guarantee of the authenticity of the volume, till the chain reaches to the Secretary, Muhammad ibn Sad himself.[65]

In all of the subsequent editions of the *Life of Mahomet* Muir provided the same information except that the name of Muzaffar Husain is omitted![66]

Another invaluable work is the universal history, *Tarikh i-Rusul wal Muluk* (The History of Messengers and Kings) of Abu Jafar Muhammad bin Jarir bin Yazid al-Tabari (839–923), the historian and exegete, too was preserved in India in the magnificent state libraries of the Awadh Nawabs at Lucknow and it was utilized in preparation of the Leiden edition.

Here again the literary world is indebted to Dr Sprenger, who having been deputed by the enlightened policy of the India government to examine the native libraries of Lucknow, succeeded in tracing from amongst heaps of neglected manuscripts, a portion of a long lost volume. It begins with the birth of Mahomet; but it terminates with the siege of Medina, that is, five years before the Prophet's death. The remainder of the work is in all probability extant in India, and may yet reward the search of some future collector of manuscripts.[67]

Thus Muir acknowledged intellectual debt to Sprenger. Furthermore, Muir also quoted the opinion of the German Orientalist work entitled 'Notice of the 4th volume of Tabari' published in the *Asiatic Journal*, no. CCXII, p. 108.

One of the most important books, which it was my good luck to find during my late mission to Lucknow, is the fourth volume of the history of Tabari (who died in AH 310), of which I believe no other copy is known to exist. It is a volume in a small quarto of 451 pages, fifteen lines in a page. Ten pages are wanting. The writing is ancient and bold, and though not without errors, generally very correct. I should say, from the appearance, the copy is five hundred years old. The intrinsic merits of the work are not so great as might be expected. Two-thirds of the book consist of extracts from Ibn Ishac and Wackidi, and only one-third or thereabouts contains original traditions. Some of these are very valuable, inasmuch as they contain information not to be found anywhere else.[68]

Muir expressed satisfaction thus: 'The discovery of this portion of Tabari in its original language is, after that of Wackidi and his Secretary, the most important event affecting the biography of Mahomet which has occurred for many years. It has a marked bearing on the sufficiency and completeness of our other authorities, Ibn Ishac (as known to us from Ibn Hisham) and Wackidi'.[69] Muir confirmed later that 'I have been fortunate enough to secure this MS also, and have placed it with that of Al-Wackidi and Ibn Hisham in the India Office Library. It has been used in editing the complete works of At-Tabari now been printed at Leyden.'[70]

Another indispensable work the *Kitab al-Maghazi*, a chronicle of the Prophet's campaigns, by Muhammad bin Umar al-Wackidi (AH 130/747–8–AH 207/823) popularly known as Al-Waqidi, reached India from Syria owing again to the efforts of Sprenger. As Muir noted 'Notwithstanding the extraordinary fertility of his pen, none of the works of Wackidi have reached us in the original form, with the exception of the *Maghazi*, or *History of the Wars of the Prophet*, a copy of which was recently discovered in Syria.'[71] This work reached India via Syria through the efforts of 'The enthusiastic and unwearied Sprenger, to whom we owe all the late discoveries of MSS bearing on the biography of Mahomet.'[72] Thereafter Muir quoted a long passage from an article of Sprenger:

I have met with a work of the veritable Waqidy; I do not mean Ibn Sad, the secretary of Waqidy, who died in 230, but Muhammad ibn Omar ibn Waqid who was born in 130 and died AH 207. Yes, my eyes have seen it, and my fingers have touched it, and what is more I secured it for the Bibliotheca Indica. The work is the *Maghazi*. It has 392 pp. of 19 lines. The copy was written about AH 525, or sooner. It belongs to H. von Kremer, dragoman of the Austrian Consulate of Alexandria. He bought it at Damascus. The wars of Mohammed appear to be treated in it at three times as great a length as they are in any other known work. He gives always his authorities, and among them it would appear in some instances written ones, as for instance, Abu Mahsar' (Abu Mashar?). *Proceedings of the Asiatic Society*, no. 4 of 1854, p. 407.[73]

William Muir also added: 'The work is now being published in the Bibliotheca Indica of the Asiatic Society. I have not been able yet to take advantage of it, but as the present volume extends only to the Hegira, after which the *Maghazi* of Wackidi opens, the want of it has not been seriously felt.'[74]

WESTERN SOURCES

The Western sources of the *Essays on the Life of Mohammed* could be divided into two broad but overlapping categories from the perspective of the commentator: those European authors who viewed Islam and the teachings of its founder in a positive light and those who representated the Prophet and Islam in a negative light. In the first category Syed Ahmad warmly acknowledged the names of famous historians Edward Gibbon (1737–94), Godfrey Higgins, essayist and historian, Thomas Carlyle, and writer and social scientist John Davenport 'as those able and learned English writers who have taken a correct view of the subject'.[75] These being the European scholars 'for whose talents I shall ever cherish high esteem and respect, are Edward Gibbon, the celebrated historian, Godfrey Higgins, Thomas Carlyle and John Davenport'.[76] He quoted extensively from their writings on Islam and the Prophet in support of his views on diverse subjects discussed throughout the book. Foremost among the writers frequently quoted by the author was Edward Gibbon, whose views on the subject would have been known to the author as Gibbon's classic was taught in Delhi College. Chapter 50 of Gibbon's *Decline and Fall of the Roman Empire* is devoted to Mohammed (PBUH) and the rise of Islam. It is a work of remarkable learning, based on wide reading of the works of European scholars and also the works of such travellers as Chardin, Volney and Niebuhr. To Gibbon, Mohammed appeared in as favourable a light as any religious leader could and confessed that Mohammed the Prophet of

Islam, had 'an original and superior genius', formed in solitude, as it must be: 'conversation enriches the understanding, but solitude the school of genius'. The product of that solitude was the Koran, 'a glorious testimony to the unity of God.'[77] Syed Ahmad quoted Gibbon's views on the civilizing role of Islam, social and moral virtues inculcated by the faith, and the latter's views that Islam was a religion of toleration, and peace, which allowed full religious freedom to other religious communities. 'The disciples of Abraham, of Moses, and of Jesus were solemnly invited to accept the more perfect revelation of Mahomet; but if they preferred the payment of a moderate tribute, they were entitled to the freedom of conscience and religious worship.'[78]

The other two British authors consistently cited appreciatively by Syed Ahmad are Higgins and Davenport. Davenport was an admirer of the historical role of the Prophet as is evident from *An Apology for Mohammed and the Koran* (London: 1869) and his articles in the *Edinburgh Review*.[79] For Davenport the Prophet was a 'Restorer of the Worship of the UNITY' [80] for entire mankind. The Prophet of Islam was the 'most transcendent genius the world itself ever produced'.[81] The purpose of the work under consideration was 'to free the history of Mohammed from false accusations and illiberal imputations, and to vindicate his just claim to be regarded as one of the greatest benefactors of mankind.'[82] The Prophet was born within full light of history: 'It may be truly affirmed that of all known legislators and conquerors, not one can be named, the history of whose life has been written with greater authenticity and fuller detail, than that of Mohammed.'[83] In the same work the author sought to provide a historical review of the growth and progress of learning under the patronage of different Muslim rulers beginning with the seventh century down to the early modern period including that of the great Mughal emperors in India. The author observed: 'It is well known that arts and sciences flourished among the Arabians for almost six hundred years; whilst amongst us, rude barbarism reigned and literature became almost extinct.'[84] Similar seems to have been the approach of another British scholar, a historian and archaeologist, Godfrey Higgins (1773–1833) whose *An Apology for the Life and Character of the Celebrated Prophet of Arabia, called Mohamed or the Illustrious* (London: 1829) is cited approvingly on many issues raised and discussed in the *Essays*. Godfrey Higgins, a Member of the British Association for the Advancement of Sciences, a philosopher with an active social conscience, was educated at Cambridge and later studied law in London. Higgins, essentially an archaeologist of religion, was a true admirer of Islam, 'a religion destined to sweep like a tornado over the face of the earth, to carry before it empires, kingdoms, and systems, and to scatter them like dust before the wind.'[85] He appreciated the historical role of the Prophet. 'In a word, he may justly be said to have lived like a hero, and to have died like a philosopher.'[86] Both Davenport and Higgins, shared one more common characteristic, apart from the respectful attitude towards the Prophet and that was their concern and sympathy for the people of India, and which is evident in their strong critique of the British colonial rule in India. More especially, Davenport sought to highlight the negative impact of British economic, political and administrative policies in India. The judicious writer sought to sensitize these issues through his writings. He sought to describe the miserable plight of the people of Bengal following the establishment of British political ascendancy in the region, the ruin of arts, crafts and agriculture, and the drain of wealth of the nation. Davenport opined that the take-over of Awadh and other independent indigenous powers was an open violation of the treaties entered with the Indian princes.[87]

Among all these writers Thomas Carlyle was unique as Syed Ahmad had the rare opportunity of meeting the English philosopher. He had an interview with Carlyle, and the British biographer Graham tells us that the 'Chelsea Sage was unusually gracious to him.'[88] And a long conversation followed. 'They talked long and earnestly over "Heroes and Hero-worship" especially about Mohammed, of whom Carlyle expresses a very high opinion in that work; and also about Syed Ahmad's "Essays on the Life of Mohammed" then in the press.'[89] This is an explicit reference to Thomas Carlyle's lecture on 'The Hero as Prophet', in *On Heroes, Hero-Worship and Heroic in History*, published in 1841, which came to have a great and lasting influence in the English speaking world. In it Carlyle argued that Islam is an authentic expression of human need to believe in a God. Further, pantheistic Carlyle accepted Prophet Muhammad as an inspired prophet, 'a silent great soul: one of those who cannot but be in earnest.' He was alive to 'the great mysteries of existence . . . the unspeakable fact, "Here am I" '.[90] More than the above psychological portrait of the Prophet, it were Carlyle's observations on the rise and expansion of great majestic civilization of Islam which are highlighted:

To the Arab nation it (Islam) was a birth from darkness to light; Arabia first became alive by means of it . . . a Hero-Prophet was sent down to them with a word they could believe: see the unnoticed become world-notable, the small has grown world-great; within one century afterwards Arabia is at Granada on this land and Delhi on that; glancing in valour and splendour and the light of genius, Arabia shines through long ages over a great section of the world. Belief is great, life-giving. The history of nation becomes fruitful, soul elevating, great, so soon as it believes. These Arabs, the men Mahomet, and that one century, is it not as if a spark had fallen, one spark, on a world of what seemed black unnoticeable sand; but lo! The sand proves explosive powder, blazes heaven-high, from Delhi to Granada![91]

Syed Ahmad was also aware of changing perceptions of Islam in the works of some nineteenth-century eminent Orientalists such as the Leiden Orientalist Reinhart Dozy (1820–83), an anti-clerical liberal historian whose four-volume *Histoire des Mussulmans d'Espagne, jusqua la conquete de l'Andalousie par les Almoravides* was published in 1861, and Michele Amari, the investigator of Muslim Sicily. The names of German scholars like Theodore Noldeke (1836–1930), and Johann Wolfgang von Goethe were also known albeit only through other sources. As the commentator elaborated, 'Goethe, Amari, Noldike, and Dozy have also written up much upon the above subjects.'[92] The author also quoted from the *Quarterly Review* that these scholars are regarded to, 'have taught the world at large that Islamism is a thing of vitality, fraught with a thousand fruitful germs; and that Mohammed, whatever view of his character (to use that vague word for once) be held, has earned a place in the golden book of humanity.'

While the writers who were thought to have made just representations of the Prophet and whose scholarly productions were accessible to the author were mostly British scholars, paradoxically, the second category is far more numerous than the first one as it also included writers from non-English speaking parts of the continent. Our author recognized that the British Orientalists shared this antipathy for Islam and its Prophet with their continental colleagues. The author regretfully noted that the European scholars lacked moderation and patience, which this exalted subject deserved, and their attitude showed deep-seated bias and prejudice in writing the biography of our Prophet. More disappointing was the fact that the European scholars had committed blunders in the interpretation of the available sources. This responsible undertaking is being treated unconscientiously.[93]

Syed recounted:

In addition to the Oriental I have enumerated above, there are many European authors who have written works upon Islam and its founder. Unfortunately, I could not avail myself of many of the early works upon these subjects such as those of Daniel, Luther, Melancthon, Spanheim, De Herbelot; but from what I learn of them from other sources, I find that they contain little else that mere abuse, and harsh and uncharitable expressions. To these names may be added that of Maracci who appears never to have been able to satiate himself with malignant and disgusting vituperations.[94]

Obviously the author was referring to Martin Luther, Philip Melancthon (1497–1560) and the seventeenth-century polemicist Ludovico Marracci, author of the *Refutatio*.[95] Given the polemical attitude of Marracci's remarks such as 'Mohammedanism and Lutheranism not very dissimilar–witness the iconoclastic tendencies of both', as quoted in a contemporary journal *The Quarterly Review* and attributed to him, were somewhat puzzling for our commentator.[96] Syed Ahmad regretted further that 'Dean Prideaux is another of these uncompromising and intolerant writers'.[97] His writings on Islam are characterized by deep-seated bias, prejudice and ignorance. 'When any Mohammedans happened to dip into his book, he cannot repress a smile at the extreme ignorance of his subject which this Christian author displays in almost every page of his work.'[98] Perhaps Syed Ahmad's remarks about Humphrey Prideaux (1648-1724) were not inaccurate as his work was largely distorted due to polemical bias. The title of Prideaux's work clearly announces its polemical purpose: *The True Nature of Imposture Fully Displayed in the Life of Mahomet: With a Discourse Annexed for the Vindication of Christianity from this Charge, Offered to the Consideration of the Deists of the Present Age* (1697). As pointed out by Edward Said also, the subtitle of this famous seventeenth-century biography of Muhammad (and for a time most influential work), itself suggested the biased image generalized since the Renaissance, a phrase canonized in d'Herblots's *Bibliotheque* and dramatized by Dante.[99] The list of biased writers is not exhausted yet as the author continued to enumerate: 'Besides these writers Hottinger, Gagnier, Reland, and Ockley have also written upon subjects relative to Islam and Mohammed, but I am sorry to have to state that I could not avail myself of the labours of these writers.'[100] Syed Ahmad was referring to the Cambridge scholar Simon Ockley (1678–1720) whose *History of Saracens* (1708, 1718) was considered the first major work of Oriental scholarship after that of the Bibliotheque Orientale of Barthelemy d'Herbelot's *Bibliotheque Orientale* published posthumously in 1697, with a Preface by Antoine Galland (1646–1715).[101] Similarly the English Orientalist George Sale's (1697–1736) *Preliminary Discourse* to his English translation of the Koran (1734) is not referred in the Introduction under discussion but *Preliminary Discourse* is more frequently quoted in the text of the *Essays* than Ockley's work.[102] Similar is the case with Charles Foster (1787–1871), a graduate of Trinity College (Dublin) and author of *Mahometanism Unveiled* (1822) whose work *Historical Geography of Arabia* (1844) is cited as a reliable work throughout the *Essays* on pre-Islamic Arabia.[103] Similarly John Milton's views on the issue of polygamy as contained in his work 'A Treatise on Christian Doctrine' is cited passionately. Other seventeenth-century writers such as the Swiss scholar Johann H. Hottinger author of the *Historia Orientalis* (Zurich 1651 and 1660), Adrianus Reland (*De religione Mohammedica libri II*, Utrecht 1705) and the French cleric and Lord Almoner's Professor of Arabic at Oxford, Jean Gagnier author of *Vie de Mohamet*, (two volumes, Amsterdam: 1732), are also mentioned but their works are not quoted. It seems that apart from Alois Sprenger, Syed Ahmad's list of European writers included works from the German-speaking area of Europe. More was known about Martin Luther and the latter's role in the Protestant Reformation.

Syed Ahmad was aware that until the early medieval ages the Christian world had nothing but hatred and ignorance for Islam. It was in the early modern period, just prior to the Reformation that a positive view of the faith began to emerge, when Christians studied about Islam not simply to refute the rival faith, or under the impulse of curiosity, but rather to employ this knowledge as a veiled critique of their own society and religion, and more significantly to reassess their own ideas and beliefs. In the view of the author the greatest contribution of Islam to mankind is the establishment of pure monotheism, *Tauhid*, the belief in the oneness of God. It was Islam which clarified and completed the whole conception of the Unity of God (*wahdaniyat i-Khuda*) in all the three respects, the Unity of Person, Unity of Attributes, and finally the Unity of Lordship. This completion strengthened both Christianity as well as Judaism. Nonetheless, among all the revealed faiths, it was Christianity that owed an enormous debt to Islam. First, Islam defended Christianity against the attacks of the Jews. As against the accusations of the followers of Moses, the

Koran declared that John the Baptist was a true apostle of God and that the Jesus Christ was the Word of God (*Kalamat Allah*) and Spirit of God (*Ruh Allah*) and above all His Creature (*Abd Allah*). The Koran also declared in unequivocal terms that Christ preached pure monotheism and the doctrine of Trinity was a later innovation rather a corruption of the original teachings of Christ. The present day Unitarian Christians are the living example of the impact that the monotheistic teachings of the Koran had made on the mind of its followers. But the greatest of all the blessings conferred by Islam upon Christianity is the spirit of resistance infused by the Koran against the authority of the Pope. The commentator cited the following verses of the Koran and emphasized that these verses reprimanded the Christians for their servility, and exhorted them to throw off so ignominious a yoke of the popes and lords who had usurped the authority of God and thereby became His partners. The Holy Koran declared: 'Come to common terms as between us and you: that we worship none but God that we associate no partners with Him; that we make not from among ourselves lords and patrons other than God.' (Holy Koran 3: 64). It was precisely this call of Islam which inspired John Calvin and Martin Luther, the leaders of the grand reform movement known as Protestantism or the Reformation which was a resolution to purify Christianity of its lords and popes.[104]

Coming to the nineteenth century, his own times, Syed Ahmad noted that in recent times, 'One of the most eminent European writers of the life of Mohammed is Dr Sprenger, who has written a biography of the Prophet in English, printed at Allahabad in 1851.'[105] Syed Ahmad regretted deeply that 'The author falls into a great number of mistakes as to the subject matter, but besides this, what is still worse is, he has adopted so exaggerated a style, and his mind is so much preoccupied and warped by prejudice and bigotry as ill becomes any writer, but more especially a historian.'[106] In this respect, Syed Ahmad was aware of Muir's opinion on the works of the Austrian scholar that in view of the British Orientalist Sprenger's biography was based 'upon erroneous assumptions, both as to the state of Arabia prior to Mahomet, and the character of the Prophet himself'.[107] Syed Ahmad also knew of another work of the sarcastic Austrian though it was inaccessible to the author as it was in German.[108] Perhaps this work also suffered from similar weaknesses 'wanting in dispassionate research and candid investigation',[109] conjectured the author. However, 'The best of all the biographies of Mohammed from the pen of foreign authors, and the one which is executed in the most learned and masterly manner, is the *Life of Mahomet* by Sir William Muir.'[110] Syed noted that the work had received wide acclamations throughout Europe for knowledge as well as meticulous use of original sources of Islamic history. The latter acknowledged that Muir possessed unrivalled attainments in the field of knowledge, Oriental as well as the Occidental. The author is equally versed in the Western sciences (*maghribi ulum*) as well as Oriental learning (*mashriqi ilm*). In the words of the critic 'The extensive and intimate acquaintance of this talented author with Oriental literature is highly esteemed and justly appreciated by all educated Europeans.'[111]

William Muir seemed to have committed the same mistake for which the latter criticized Sprenger, the uncritical use of *Kitab al-Maghazi* of Waqidi. Syed Ahmad wrote emphatically that both these writers overvalued Waqidi who as a matter of fact is considered an unreliable authority, in fact the worst of all the authors. 'Sir William Muir himself seems to have preferred Wackedee to all others, as almost all his materials for the life of Mohammed rest upon the authority of, and are derived from, that book.'[112] There was no flaw with the hypothesis yet the fundamental problem with the works of William Muir lay somewhere else, the very objective and motive was to comply with the wishes of Carl Gottlieb Pfander as the work was actuated by a strong motive to promote the cause of Christianity, in a sense the evangelical fervour being the source of inspiration behind all his scholarly endeavours rather than pure academic research.[113] Muir took little trouble to conceal the missionary motives which prompted his interest in Islamic history as the latter openly confessed that 'Rev. C.G. Pfander, D.D., so well known as a Christian apologist in the controversy with the Mahometans', advised him to explore the sources of the early history of Islam. Pfander urged the British Administrator-Orientalist 'that a biography of the Prophet of Islam, suitable for the perusal of its followers, should be compiled in the Hindoostani language from the early sources acknowledged by themselves to be authentic and authoritative.'[114] Syed Ahmad had to conclude in cautious language, 'But it is with much regret, I have to state that this motive, notwithstanding the high ability and talents of Sir William Muir, exercised upon his mind the same influence which it would naturally have exerted over any other person under the same circumstances; so much so indeed, that the interesting and beautiful features of Islam appeared to him as deformed and repulsive. . . '.[115]

The reviewer added that due to the uninhibited prejudice 'the simplest and plainest facts connected with Islam and Mohammed had been strained and twisted.'[116] Syed Ahmad accredited Muir and also Sprenger for the vast researches, unfailing accuracy in the use of the source material yet the work of these writers lacked dispassionate judgement. It seems that for our author the works of Western Orientalists, William Muir and Sprenger both were a big dilemma, as on the one hand lay the enormous labours that went into the production of these scholarly works, and on the other hand he felt that both the scholars committed the same mistake—they had denigrated their favourite subject-matter and consequently, in essence their learned works conveyed the same antipathy for Islam and its Apostle.

CONCLUSION

In the medieval period, European representations of Islam were almost negative. The Western views of Prophet Muhammad were intolerant and pejorative. So was the conclusion of Syed Ahmad that it was the prejudice and lack of justice which characterized European writings on Islam and Prophet Muhammad (PBUH), the last and greatest of the Prophets. The portrayal and assessment of Islam in the Western historiography, as historical phenomena, was far removed from the reality. Ironically, the birth of serious non-Muslim scholarship of Islam begins with the Renaissance. Yet, until the early modern times, denigration of Islam and anti-Islamic tendencies continued to persist.[117] In Europe, Islamic history as a discipline grew out of the theological preoccupations of the polemicists, mainly clergymen. As late as the eighteenth century it was still impossible to draw a hard and fast line between a controversialist and a scholar. However, in the nineteenth century new approaches based on better scholarship of sources and primary texts known as the source criticism method were developed. Western scholars began to apply methodology of Biblical criticism to the primary sources of Islam as well. Thus it was the beginning of the application of scientific historiography in Europe. Also Islamic studies were greatly promoted during this era especially in British universities. As Muir observed:

> Within the last ten or twenty years, the mind of Christian Europe has been directed, with more studious earnestness and dispassionate inquiry, towards the rise of Islam, than in any preceding period: and the progress made in searching out the truths of that crisis in the world's history, characterized by

corresponding success. Indeed, the amount of facts carefully collected, and of data philosophically weighed, within this short term is, perhaps, of greater value than all the labours of Christian writers during the twelve preceding centuries.[118]

There was a distinct shift in attitudes towards Islam in this period. It seems that scholars like Thomas Carlyle who wrote from outside the Christian orthodoxy were not exceptions in Victorian Britain. Perhaps more unique were the liberals. Higgins and Davenport both had rejected traditional formulations of Christianity. The late-eighteenth and nineteenth-century thinkers and scholars' views of Islam and Islamic culture reflected dominant philosophical and historical ideas of their age also.[119] For instance, Edward Gibbon like Voltaire represented in quasi historical terms the anti-clericalism of the Enlightenment.

Muir's biography of the Prophet was directed against the mid-nineteenth century changing views of Islam. Sir William Muir's life spanned the then closely related worlds of colonialism, increasing missionary activities and Oriental scholarship, moreover, in case of Muir, 'Evangelical Orientalism'. Though his scholarship, based on original sources, was judged by Albert Hourani to be 'still not quite superseded'. Muir believed that if missionaries were successful in refuting Islam (which those missionaries he supported aimed to do), they would need more accurate information than what had been available to their predecessors. Muslims could look with 'contemptuous incredulity' on the works of Maracci and Prideaux, but now, Muir wrote, Christians could use Islam's own 'best sources' to prove to Muslims 'that they are deceived and superstitious in many important points'.[120]

Officially the British Indian government continued to profess religious 'neutrality', but in practice evangelical agendas were greatly assisted, especially in the north-west, by the increase in likeminded recruits to the service of the East India Company from the 1830s onwards.[121] More recently in an important comparative study of Victorian images of Islam, Bennett argued that Muir's criticisms of Muslims and Islam were due to his colonial experiences rather than academic research, a conclusion not very different from that of Syed Ahmad. And for this purpose Muir adopted 'confrontational tactics' in his approach to Muslims as his was motivated by his support for the missionary cause.[122] Muir saw the Christian–Muslim encounter as a battle for world supremacy and for the purpose Indian Muslims the most fertile field.[123]

Most of the British writers selected by Syed Ahmad belonged to what Bennett called the conciliatory school of thought as opposed to Muir who represented the confrontational school. Muir combined the technique of scientific historiography with unsympathetic attitude to his subject-matter; combination of scholarship and prejudice reminiscent of Marracci in the seventeenth century. Similar was the judgement of Margoliouth (1858–1940), Professor of Arabic at Oxford, who placed both Muir and Sprenger along with the well-known Orientalists such as G. Weil, Caussin de Percevel, F Wustenfeld, and accredited both for 'the merit of discovering and utilising these ancient works',[124] and that 'the lives of Mohammed by the last two of these writers are likely to be regarded as classical so long as there are students of Oriental history in Europe; notwithstanding the fact that Muir's *Life* is written with a confessedly Christian bias, and that Sprenger's is defaced by some slipshod scholarship and untrustworthy archaeology.'[125]

It goes to the credit of Syed Ahmad that the latter rose to the occasion and responded to these assertions of European writers creatively and persuasively. He chose not to simply dismiss them as hostile missionary propaganda. Neither was it expected from this rational thinking man of vision and imagination. He was the sensitive intellectual and a keen observer who had been witness to the not so imperceptible process of the transformation of the *munazara*, a dialogue and debate, an intellectual exercise in the domain of religion, a legacy of the great Abbasid Empire, what the noted historian Arnold Toynbee called universal empire of Islam and that of the Mughal Empire into *mujadala* bitter dispute and controversy. With the arrival of the evangelical missionaries after 1813 in Agra and Delhi, the heartland of the Mughal Empire was to become the scene of intense missionary activities. Syed considered it imperative to take this criticism seriously and to apply knowledge and intellectual faculties in creatively responding to the criticism. The result is a work of high intellectual calibre and creativity. It remains a convincing reply of Western Orientalist criticism of Islam. In the critical use of *Sira* literature, that it need not be treated as an independent historical source, perhaps the author foreshadowed the researches of the Jesuit Henri Lammens and C.H. Becker. In the suggestion that the *Sira* itself is *Hadith*—material arranged in biographical order—and therefore should be analysed in the perspective of *Hadith*, Syed Ahmad anticipated the Lammens-Becker thesis. We also delineated the complex nexus through which archives of knowledge passed from the dominated to the predominant culture as signified in the position of William Muir and Sprenger on the one hand, and lesser known men like Muzaffar Husain and Sadr al-Din Azurda on the other, who still largely remained resource persons. On the credit side, the author of *Khutbat al-Ahmadiya* emerges not only as a historian of calibre and an accomplished biographer, but also an excellent traditionist *Muhaddith*, and *faqih*, a gifted interpreter of law, and a specialist in the science of jurisprudence, a *mufassir*, an expert exegete, above all an Islamicist in the real sense of the term. We only explored the prologue, the 'Preface and Introduction' (*Dibacha*) of the author's tour de force, *Al-Khutbat al-Ahmadiya fil Arab wa Sirat al-Muhammadiya*. A critical study of the text of the essays as contained in the *Life of Mohammed* will definitely open new vistas of intellectual horizons.

NOTES

* Quoted by Syed Ahmad Khan on the title page of *The Life of Mohammed*. For the above cited English translation, see Edward Rehatsek (tr.), W.G. Archer, ed., *The Gulistan or Rose Garden of Saadi*, London: George Allen & Unwin Ltd., 1964, p. 58.

1. This is the assessment of Altaf Husain Hali (1837–1914) put forward in *Hayat i-Jawed*, the most comprehensive and substantial biography of Syed Ahmad Khan. The first more strictly biographical part of it has been translated from the Urdu original into English by K.H. Qadiri and David J. Matthews as *Hayat-i Jawed: A Biographical Account of Sir Syed Ahmad Khan*, Delhi, 1980.
2. Cf. Bashir Ahmad Dar, *Religious Thought of Syed Ahmad Khân*, 1957; rpt., Lahore, 1961. Bashir Ahmad analysed Sir Syed's contribution in the sphere of religious thought in the context of the political, cultural, and religious situation in colonial India. J.M.S. Baljon's pioneering study, *The Reforms and Religious Ideas of Sir Syed Ahmad Khan*, Leiden: Brill, 1949, 3rd revd. edn., Lahore, 1964, presents an overall picture of the man, subordinating Sir Syed's religious quest to his educational and socio-cultural concerns.

3. Muhammad Umar al-Din, Professor of Philosophy at the Aligarh Muslim University, presented seminal ideas in a long essay entitled 'Sir Syed ka naya mazhabi tarz i-fikr', wherein the latter argued persuasively that Sir Syed was the first and last a religious man. In fact it was the broad concept of religion he had and its true spirit that motivated him to undertake work for the community and to exalt the knowledge of public good. See, Muhammad Umar al-Din, 'Sir Syed ka naya mazhabi tarz fikr' (Sir Syed's New Mode of Religious Thought) in Naseem Qureshi, ed., *Aligarh Tahrik: Aghaz Ta Imroz*, Aligarh: Aligarh Muslim University, 1969, pp. 103–67 [hereafter: 'Sir Syed ka naya mazhabi tarz i-fikr']. For an exposition of a similar line of argument see, Christian W. Troll, *Syed Ahmad Khan: A Reinterpretation of Muslim Theology*, Delhi: Vikas, 1978 [hereafter, Troll, *A Reinterpretation of Muslim Theology*].
4. Muhammad Umar al-Din, 'Sir Syed ka naya mazhabi tarz i-fikr', pp. 125–6 ff.
5. See the Preface of the edition of collected works of Syed Ahmad Khan, *Tasanif i-Ahmadiya*, vol. I, part I, Aligarh Institute Press, AD 1883/AH 1313, p. 2.
6. Syed Ahmad Khan, *Tabyîn al-kalâm, The Mahomedan Commentary on the Holy Bible, Genesis,* Syud Ahmud, part I, printed and published by the author at his private press, AD 1862 (AH 1278); The Mahomeden Commentary on the Holy Bible Genesis I–XI; part II, Allygurh: printed and published by the author at his private press, AD 1865 (AH 1281); part III was published in the *Tasanif Ahmadiya*, vol. I, part II, Aligarh Institute Press, 1887, pp. 2–129; *Tafsir al-Koran*, the seven-volume Urdu translation and commentary on the Koran up to surah 20, 1880–1904), Aligarh Institute Press, 6 vols., AH 1257 (AD 1880–95), vol. 7, Agra: Mufid-i-am Press, 1905. Most of these articles and tracts, including important parts of his Koran commentary, have been re-edited in sixteen volumes by M. Ismail Panipati, ed., *Maqalat-i Sir Syed*, Lahore: Majlis-i taraqqi-i adab, 1962–5.
7. The titles of some of the essays were as follows: Essay on the Prophecies Respecting Mohammed as contained in both the Old and the New Testament; Essay on the Pedigree of Mohammed; Essay on the Birth and Childhood of Mohammed; Essay on Shakki-Sadar and Meraj that is the Splitting (open) of the Chest of Mohammed; and His Night Journey; Essay on the Holy Koran; Essay on Mohammedan Traditions; Essay on the Question Whether Islam has been Beneficial or Injurious to Human Society in General; and To the Mosaic and Christian Dispensations. All the above essays carried the following information: 'The original English of the Essay has been revised and corrected by a friend.' Syed Ahmed Khan Bahador, C.S.I., Author of the 'Mohammedan Commentary on the Holy Bible', Honorary Member of the Royal Asiatic Society, and Life

Honorary Secretary to the Allygurh Scientific Society. London: Trubner & Co., 1869–70.

8. Syed Ahmad Khan Bahadur, *Essays on the Life of Mohammed and Subjects Subsidiary Thereto* (collection of twelve essays of the life of Mohammed), vol. 1, London: Trubner & Co., 1870; title page gives the title in Arabic: *Khutubat al-Ahmadiyah 'ala al-'Arab wa'l-sirah al-Muhammadiyah (allafaha al-muftaqir ila Allah al-samad Syed Ahmad 'afa Allah anhu)*, and adds, 'The original English text of these essays has been revised and corrected by a friend.' By Syed Ahmed Khan Bahador, C.S.I., Author of the 'Mohammedan Commentary on the Holy Bible' Honorary Member of the Royal Asiatic Society, and Life Honorary Secretary to the Allygurh Scientific Society. An Urdu version of the work was published later by the learned author. This original Urdu text was published first in Sir Syed's edition of *Tasanif-i Ahmadiyah*, vol. 1, part 2, pp. 182–639, Aligarh Institute Press, 1887; Reprint in Muhammad Ismail Panipati, ed., *Maqalat-i Sir Syed*, vol. XI, Lahore: Majlis-i taraqqi-i adab, 1962–5); As to the genesis of the work see Muhammad Ismail Panipati, *Maktubat-i Sir Syed*, Lahore: Majlis-i taraqqi-i adab, 1959 [hereafter: *Maktubat-i Sir Syed*], pp. 52, 59–60, 81–2, 62. See Altaf Husain Hali, *Hayat-i Jawed*, lith. printing, Lahore: Ainah-i adab, 1966, p. 172. In this article the references are made to Sir Syed Ahmad Khan, *Life of Mohammed*, New Delhi: Cosmos Books, 2002 edn. [hereafter: *Life of Mohammed*]. The Urdu version *Khutubat al-Ahmadiyah* has been published from a number of places: Lahore: Fadl-i Din, 1870; Karachi: Nafees Academy, 1961; Aligarh: Sir Syed Academy, 2003 [hereafter: *Khutbat*]. It is to the Aligarh edition that references are being made in this article. We shall, throughout, follow the English edition, and references to the Urdu version are also made especially where new information is added by the author.
9. *Khutbat*, pp. 5–6.
10. *Life of Mohammed*, p. 281.
11. *Khutbat*, pp. 8–9. Chapters ten and twelve of the *Tuhfah-i Ithna Ashariyah*, wherein the author Shah Abd al-Aziz sought to clarify differences between the Sunnis and Shias by researching upon the origins of the dispute, were translated by Syed Ahmad Khan into Urdu on the advice of his teacher and mentor Maulana Nurul Hasan Kandhalawi (d.1868). See, *A Reinterpretation of Muslim Theology*, pp. 33, 39–40.
12. *Life of Mohammed*, p. 281; *Khutbat*, pp. 2–7, ff.
13. Sir William Muir (1819–1905), British administrator and scholar, arrived in north India in 1837, at the age of eighteen, to serve the Company and the Raj for almost forty years. He was head of the Intelligence Department at Agra during the Great Revolt in 1857; in 1865 he became Foreign Secretary to the Indian government; Lieutenant-Governor of the North Western Provinces (1868–74), Member of

Council of India in London (1876–85) and from 1885–1902 he was Principal of the Edinburgh University. He helped found and endow Muir College and University at Allahabad. William Muir, *The Life of Mahomet and the History of Islam to the Era of Hegira*, 4 vols., London: Smith Elder & Co., 1861; vols. 1 and 2, 1858; vols. 3 and 4, 1861; Other editions followed soon: *The Life of Mahomet with introductory chapter on the original sources for the biography of Mahomet, and on the Pre Islamite History of Arabia* by William Muir Esq., Bengal Civil Service, 4 vols., London: Smith Elder & Co., 1861 [hereafter: *Life of Mahomet*]. *The Life of Mahomet* from Original Sources by Sir William Muir L.L.D., New Edition Abridged from the 1st edn. in four volumes, London: Smith Elder & Co., 1877 [hereafter: *Life of Mahomet*, 1877 edn.]. *The Life of Mohammad* from Original Sources, a new and revised edition by T.H. Weir, Edinburgh, J. Grant, 1923 [hereafter: Edinburgh edn.]. However, in this article all the citations are from the 1861 edition. References to the other editions are made to show the omissions. William Muir, apart from *The Life of Mahomet*, also wrote a classical work on the Orthodox Caliphate *The Caliphate: Its Rise, Decline and Fall from Original Source* (1891; new edn. 1915). *The Coran* (1878); *The Mameluke or Slave Dynasty of Egypt* AD *1260–1517 to the End of Caliphate*, London: Smith Elder & Co., 1896 are his other works in the field of Islamic studies.

14. *Khutbat*, pp. 19–120; *Life of Mohammed*, pp. 1–118.
15. Christian W. Troll viewed the *Khutbat* as a defensive response to Sir William Muir and other Western scholars' critical studies of the Prophet's biography and of classical Islam. In his opinion these Western critiques of Islam and the Prophet compelled Syed Ahmad to evolve ever more severe canons of external and internal *Hadith* criticism. Taking into account the long period of oral transmission preceding the codification of the *Hadith*, along with the laws of the rise and growth of legends, Sir Syed accepted the results of post-Newtonian natural science as established truth and used them to justify the need for metaphorical interpretation (*tawil*) of Biblical and Quranic texts. The credibility of the Koran (as of any revealed scripture) is based not on miracles but on the intrinsic value of its content, in the same way that the unsurpassed and unsurpassable greatness of Muhammad is due to the essential nature of his teaching and to his unparalleled moral effort to spread it. See Troll, *A Reinterpretation of Muslim Theology*, pp. 112–43.
16. *Khutbat*, pp. 152–204. In the English edition of the *Essays* it figures last, 'Whether Islam has been beneficial or injurious to human society in general'. *Life of Mohammed*, pp. 405–44.
17. *Life of Mahomet*, vol. IV, pp. 321–2.
18. G.F.I. Graham's, *Life and Works of Syed Ahmad Khan, K.C.S.I.*,

Edinburgh: W. Blackwood, 1885, rpt., Delhi: Idarah-i Adabiyat-i Delhi, 1974 [hereafter: Graham, *The Life and Work*].

19. Graham, *The Life and Works*, p. 106.
20. Ibid., p. 107. Graham also reproduced a long passage from the last essay which is a reply of Muir's allegation 'Toleration is unknown in Islamism' as an example of this remarkable piece of writing. Ibid., pp. 107–14.
21. Ibid., p. 114.
22. Ibid., p. 115. Copies of the texts of the letters are reproduced by Graham. See Graham, *The Life and Works*, pp. 114–15.
23. *Khutbat*, p. 5.
24. *Khutbat*, pp. 2–4; *Life of Mohammed*, pp. xiii–xv. In chapter 3 of his edited work, *The Rose and the Rock: Mystical and Rational Elements in the Intellectual History of South Asian Islam*, Durham, N.C., 1979. Bruce B. Lawrence throws new light on Sir Syed's early phase of religious practice and thought. He detects there rational elements and mystical components important enough to merit serious attention in any critical assessment of Syed Ahmad Khan's later contributions.
25. *Khutbat*, p. 3. For expression of similar ideas, *Life of Mohammed*, p. xiv.
26. *Khutbat*, pp. 4–5; *Life of Mohammed*, pp. xvi–xviii.
27. *Life of Mohammed*, p. xiv.
28. Ibid., *Khutbat*, p. 5.
29. Ibid., p. 3. For a complete text of the above cited *ghazal*, see Syed Ghulam Samdani, *Amir Khusrau*, Delhi: National Book Trust, 1985. See *Selections*, p. 112.
30. *Life of Mohammed*, p. xvii; *Khutbat*, p. 6. The first part of the *Dibacha*, i.e. 'Preface and Introduction' has been translated by Troll. See *A Reinterpretation of Muslim Theology*, pp. 242–51. However, there seems to be one error in the translation, the Perso-Urdu term *dahriyon*, i.e. the atheists has been rendered as Darwin. See Troll, *A Reinterpretation of Muslim Theology*, p. 247. Compare the text *Khutbat*, p. 5. Perhaps Charles Darwin's *Origin of the Species* which appeared in 1859 was not known to Syed Ahmad Khan.
31. For a detailed discussion of Syed Ahmad's ideas see Troll, *A Reinterpretation of Muslim Theology*, pp. 194–222. Also see, Muhammad Umar al-Din, *Sir Syed ka naya mazhabi tarz i-fikr*, pp. 128–34, 136–9.
32. *Khutbat*, p. 7.
33. *Life of Mohammed*, p. xxvi.
34. *Khutbat*, pp. 14–15. This seems to be an implicit reference to the destruction and dispersal of libraries of the imperial city in the wake of British retribution of the capital, after the Revolt of 1857, an irreparable loss which Ghalib bewailed. See S.M. Ikram, *Muslim Rule in India and Pakistan 711–1858: A Political and Cultural History* (originally

published as *History of Muslim Civilization in India and Pakistan*), revised and enlarged (Lahore, 1961, 2nd edn., 1966), pp. 463–4.

35. *Khutbat*, p. 14.
36. *Life of Mohammed*, p. xxvi. This particular passage is not found in the Urdu version.
37. *Tazkira i-Ahl Dihli* (Biography of the People of Delhi), contained in the fourth chapter of the first edition of *Athar al-Sanadid*, 1846.
38. Reprint, *Maqalat-i Sir Syed*, vol. XVI, pp. 485–500.
39. Ibid., pp. 75–94.
40. Ibid., pp. 97–206. For Syed's interaction with the British institutions and the latter's relations with the British administrator-scholars, see Gulfishan Khan, 'Syed Ahmad Khan: Some Early Influences', in Abdul Ali S. Ahsan, ed., *Contribution of Sir Syed Ahmad Khan to Islamic Studies*, Seminar Papers, Aligarh: Institute of Islamic Studies, 2005, pp. 43–61; Troll, *A Reinterpretation*, pp. 58–70, 144–70.
41. See Maulawi Abdul Haq, *Marhum Dehli Kalej*, Delhi: Anjuman Taraqqi Urdu Hind, 1989, pp. 83–104, 129–55.
42. See *Khutbat*, pp. 8–9, 210–11 for his insightful remarks on the comparative value of *Hadith* and *Sira*. *Life of Mohammed*, pp. 275–6, and p. xix.
43. *Khutbat*, p. 211; *Life of Mohammed*, pp. 276–7. For the details of the authorship of the above-mentioned biographies of the Prophet see, C.A. Storey, *Persian Literature: A Bio-Bibliographical Survey*, vol. I, part I, Quranic Literature; History and Biography, Quranic Literature; History, London: Royal Asiatic Society, 1970, pp. 194–5 [hereafter: *Persian Literature*]. *Madarij al-nubuwwah* a detailed biography of the Prophet by Abd al-Haq Muhaddith Dehlawi (1551–1642), pp. 11–12, 179–80, 187–9, 204–7.
44. *Life of Mohammed*, p. xix. For similar statement, see *Khutbat*, p. 9. 'The extant works of Siyar are *Ibn Ishaq*, *Ibn Hisham*, *Tabaqat-i Kabeer*, known as *Katib al-Waqidi*, *Tabari*, *Sirat-i Shami*, *Abul Fida*, *Masudi Mawahib al-Leduniya*.'
45. *Khutbat*, pp. 210–11.
46. Ibid., pp. 8–9. For a detailed analysis of the author's views on this subject see Troll, *Sayyid Ahmad Khan: A Reinterpretation of Muslim Theology*, pp. 136–43.
47. *Khutbat*, pp. 8–9. This work was translated into Urdu and also published from the press of the Delhi College. See Abdul Haq, *Marhum Dehli Kalej*, p. 155. *Life of Mohammed*, p. xviii.
48. *Khutbat*, p. 8. For the various editions of the *Shamail al-Nabi*, see *Persian Literature*, pp. 172–5.
49. *Life of Mohammed*, pp. xx–xxi. Vol. 1 of *Tarikh-i Abul Fida* entitled '*Zikr-i Maulud-i Rasul*' contains a biography of the Prophet.

See *Tarikh-i Abul Fida*, Constantinople: Shahaniya, AH 1386 pp. 115–62. *History of Abul Fida* is frequently quoted in the text.

50. See *Life of Mohammed*, p. 35.
51. D.S. Margoliouth, *Mohammed and the Rise of Islam*, 3rd edn., London & New York, G.P. Putnam's Sons, 1906; new edn., 1923, p. iii [hereafter: *The Rise of Islam*]. J. Gagnier, *Ismael Abul-Feda, de vita et rebus gestis Mohammedis*, Oxford, 1723. Only the portion dealing with the biography of the Prophet was translated.
52. See *The History of Abul Fida from Creation to AD 1328*, translated from Arabic by Maulavi Karimuddin, Matba-ul Ulum Madrasah Delhi, Delhi, 1847.
53. The greatest of medieval geographers, Masudi (d. 956) and his historio-geographical work *Muruj az zahab wa madain al jawahir* was translated into English by Sprenger and published from London in 1841 and the English translation was followed by a complete French translation. Barbier de Meynard and Pavet de Courteille edited and translated the entire text in French, Paris, 1861–77; 2nd edn. 1913–30. See *Encyclopaedia of Islam*, new edn., E.J. Brill, 1991, vol. VI, pp. 784–9.
54. *Life of Mohammed*, p. 197.
55. Shaikh Ibrahim al-Bejuri, *Mawahib al-Leduniya*, Dar al-Tabat al-Misriya, Bulaq, AH 1280. Its commentary entitled *Sharh al-Mawahib al-Leduniya* was written by Imam Muhammad bin Abdul Baqi al Azraqani al-Maliki, published from Egypt in eight volumes (al-Azhariya al-Misriya: AH 1325–8).
56. William Muir discussed the not-so-easy process of obtaining these rare Islamic works from Indian libraries in the introductory chapter entitled 'Introduction Chapter First Sources for the Biography of Mahomet—The Coran, and Traditions', *Life of Mahomet*, vol. I, pp. i–cv. In the 1877 edition this chapter with the same title 'Sources for the Biography of Mahomet—The Coran and Traditions' forms Appendix *Life of Mahomet*, pp. 549–613. Again the same chapter, 'Sources for the Biography of Mohammad, The Quran and Tradition and early biographies' now forms the first chapter of his *Life of Muhammad*, Edinburgh edition, pp. xii–lxxxvii.
57. See, Charles Stewart, *A Descriptive Catalogue of the Oriental Library of Tippoo Sultan of Mysore*, etc., Cambridge, 1809. These manuscripts are now described partly as MSS of Tippu and partly as MSS of the College of Fort William, and all these formed part of the Mohammedan MSS of the East India House. See Preface, Otto Loth, *A Catalogue of the Arabic Manuscripts in the Library of the India Office*, printed by order of the Secretary of State for India in Council, London, 1877.
58. *Khutbat*, pp. 14–15.
59. *Life of Mahomet*, vol. I, p. v.
60. William Muir, 'Biographies of Mohammed for India; and The Moham-

medan Controversy from the "Calcutta Review" 1852', in Sir William Muir, *The Mohammedan Controversy and other Indian Articles*, 1st edn., 1897, rept., Allahabad: R.S. Publishing House, 1979, p. 66. [Hereafter: *The Mohammedan Controversy and other Indian Articles.*]

61. Ibid.
62. Sadr al-Din Khan Azurdah, was an accomplished scholar who had studied the traditional sciences from Shah Abd al-Aziz and Shah Abd al-Qadir, and the rational sciences from Fazl-i Imam Khayrabadi. Before the Mutiny his house in Matya Mahall, Delhi, was the meeting point of scholars and poets. During the pre-Mutiny period, he served as Mufti and Sadr al-Sudur of Delhi and was also associated as examiner of Arabic language in Delhi College and as such he had direct contacts with some of the prominent officials of the East India Company. Suspected of complicity in the Mutiny of 1857, his property, including his large private library, was confiscated and auctioned. After his release, his property, but not his library, was restored to him. For a brief and informative biography by A.S. Bazmee Ansari see, *Encyclopaedia of Islam*, under Azurda, vol. I, 1960, pp. 827–8. Also see n. 34 above. Syed Ahmad and Azurda enjoyed close scholarly rapport as Azurda also wrote a review (*taqriz*) of *Athar al-Sanadid*. Some specimens of his Persian and Arabic prose and poetical compositions including Urdu verses were produced by Syed Ahmad Khan in the *Athar al-Sanadid*, along with a biography of the poet and writer. *Athar al-Sanadid*, Delhi, 1846, pp. 72–114.
63. *Life of Mahomet*, vol. I, p. xcv. William Muir clarified 'The abridgement consists chiefly in the omission of the authorities, i.e. of the series of witnesses leading up to the Companion who first given forth the tradition.' Ibid., p. xcv. There is a similar acknowledgement in the 1877 edition but the name of the owner Sadr al-Din Azurdah has been omitted. 'A beautiful manuscript in the handwriting of the abbreviator himself, was met with by Dr Sprenger in Delhi; and has been used as an authoritative copy both by Dr. Sprenger and myself.' *The Life of Mahomet from Original Sources* by Sir William Muir L.L.D., New edn., abridged from the 1st edn. in four volumes, London: Smith Elder & Co., 1877, p. 607. The introductory chapter forms an Appendix in this edition, pp. 549–613. In the 1923 edition this vital information has been relegated to a mere note 'An abridged edition of Ibn Hisham was made at Damascus AH 707 (AD 1307) by one Ahmad Ibn Ibrahim. A beautiful manuscript in the handwriting of the abbreviator himself was met with by Dr Sprenger in Delhi, and has been used both by Dr Sprenger and myself. I have placed a portion of this valuable MS, with an English abstract of its content in the India Office Library.' *Life of Mohammad*, Edinburgh edition, p. lxxx, fn. 1.
64. Muhammad Ibn Sad, *Kitab al-Tabaqat al-Kabir*, S. Moinul Haq (trans)

assisted by H. K. Ghazanfar, Karachi: Pakistan Historical Society, 1967; for an earlier trans. see E. Sachau et al., 9 vols. Leiden, 1904–21.

65. *Life of Mahomet*, vol. I, pp. xcvii–xcviii.
66. *Life of Mahomet*, 1877 edn., p. 609, n. 1. In the same edition the author confirmed, 'This rare manuscript is now in my possession and I propose depositing it in the India Office. There is but one other copy believed to be extant which is in the Library of Gotha. Further, 'For a copy of this invaluable volume we are indebted to the indefatigable research of Sprenger, who discovered it in a library at Cawnpore. This manuscript is written in an ancient but very distinct character, and is in excellent preservation. It was transcribed at Ḍamascus, AH 718 (AD 1318), by a scholar named al-Hakkari, who traces up, link by link, from the pupil to the master (by whom it was successively taught, or by whom copied) the guarantee of the authenticity of the volume, till the chain reaches to the Secretary, Muhammad Ibn Sad himself. This rare MS having come into my possession was presented (with a careful digest of its contents in English) to the India Office Library. A beautiful transcript, made for my own use at Delhi, I propose depositing in the Library of the University of Edinburgh, where it may readily be consulted.' *Life of Mohammad*, Edinburgh edn., pp. lxxxii–lxxxiii, note 2.
67. *Life of Mahomet*, vol. 1, p. ci. Later Muir restated 'Here again the literary world is indebted to Dr Sprenger: who, having been before the Mutiny deputed by the Indian government to examine the libraries of Lucknow, succeeded in tracing, from amongst a heap of neglected manuscripts, a portion of the long-lost volume.' *Life of Mohammad*, Edinburgh edn., p. lxxxiv.
68. *Life of Mahomet*, vol. 1, pp. ci–cii; *Life of Mohammad*, Edinburgh edn., pp. lxxxiv–lxxxv, n. 2a. Sprenger, *Report of the Researches into the Muhammaden Libraries of Lucknow*, Calcutta, 1896. (Selection from records of Government of India), Foreign Department, no. CCXXXIV, serial no. 32. A. Sprenger, *A Catalogue of the Arabic, Persian and Hindustany MSS of the Libraries of the King of Oudh*, vol. 1, Calcutta, 1854.
69. *Life of Mahomet*, vol. I, p. cii.
70. *Life of Mohammad*, Edinburgh edn., p. lxxxv. The Leiden edn. of the *Tarikh al-Rasul wa almuluk*, was prepared from this manuscript. This is a reference to the Leiden edn. under the general editorship of M.J. de Goeje (1836–1909), trans., Annales . . . al-Tabari, *Tarikh al-Rusul wal muluk*, 15 vols., Leiden, 1879–1901. *Tarikh al-Rasul* contains material on the life of Muhammad (PBUH) notably reports from Urva bin al-Zubayr (d. 94/812–13) a very early source.
71. *Life of Mahomet*, vol. I, p. xcvi.
72. Ibid., see note on p. xcvi.
73. Ibid. This is an obvious reference to the Austrian Diplomat-Orientalist,

Alfred von Kremer (1828–89), author of *Kulturgeschichte des Orients under den Chalifen*, 2 vols., Vienna, 1875–7; English tr., S. Khuda Bakhsh, *The Orient Under the Caliphs*, Calcutta, 1920.

74. *Life of Mahomet*, see note on p. xcvi. This work was published by the Bibliotheca Indica under the title *History of Muhammad's Campaigns*, by Aboo Abd Ollah Mohammad bin Omar al-Wackidi, Alfred von Kromer, ed., Calcutta: Bibliotheca Indica, 1856. The edition was prepared from a manuscript discovered by the editor in Damascus in 1851. Muir noted in the 1877 edn. that it has been published in the Bibliotheca Indica. *Life of Mahomet*, 1877 edn., p. 608. The Arabic text of this voluminous work was published at Leiden by E. Sachau, et al. in 1924–8. For a recent standard edition of al-Waqidi is *Kitab al-Maghazi*, 3 vols., J. Marsden Jones, ed., London, 1966. (This same copy of Wackidi was given to me by its possessor after the Mutiny. It was transcribed at Damascus AH 713 (AD 1318); the chain of copyist attesting its accuracy runs up to the Secretary of Wackidi himself. I have placed it in the India Office Library. It is worth inspecting for the beauty of its antique writing. A beautiful copy of the same has also been deposited in the Edinburgh University Library) see, *The Mohammedan Controversy and other Indian Articles*. This seems to be a certain confusion, a deliberate one perhaps with *Sirat Ibn Ishaq* or *Kitab al-tabaqat* that the high British officials would have obtained from Sadr al-Din or Muzaffar Husain.
75. *Life of Mohammed*, pp. xxvi–xxvii; *Khutbat*, p. 15.
76. Ibid., p. xxvii. For a similar respectable reference see *Khutbat*, p. 15.
77. For Edward Gibbon, see, *Dictionary of National Biography*, ed. Leslie Stephen, Sydney Lee, London: Smith Elder & Co., 1908, vol. VII, pp. 1129–35 (hereafter: *DNB*).
78. *Life of Mohammed*, pp. 438, also see 406–7, 442.
79. See John Davenport, *An Apology for Mohammed and the Koran* printed for the author, by J. Davy and Sons, 137, London: Long Acre, 1869 [hereafter: *An Apology*]. The work is divided into four parts: I Mohammed: A Biography; II The Koran and its Morality; III Charges against Mohammed Refuted; IV Beauties of the Koran. The title page also carried reference to the other works of the author: 'Author of the "Life of Ali Pacha of Janina"'; 'Oude Vindicated'; 'Koorg and its Rajahs'; 'Aide Memoire to the History of India'; 'Historical Class Book', and various educational works. The work has been reprinted from Ghum, Iran: 1971. Herein the references are to this edition.
80. Davenport, *An Apology*, see Preface.
81. Ibid.
82. Ibid.
83. Ibid., Chapter I, 'Life of Mohammed', p. 1.
84. Ibid., Chapter II, 'The Koran', pp. 89–130.

85. Godfrey Higgins, *An Apology for Mohamed*, Mirza Abul Fazl (ed.), *Mr Godfrey Higgins' Apology For Mohamed* (A Verbatim Reprint) edited with Introduction, Critical Notes, Appendices, and a Chapter on Islam. Reform Society, Daryabad, Allahabad, 1929 [hereafter Higgins, *Apology for Mohamed*]. For the above remark, see, the 'Preamble', ibid., p. 2. For a life-sketch and writings of Higgins see, 'Memoir of the author', ibid., pp. viii–xiii.
86. Higgins, *Apology for Mohamed*, p. 44.
87. Davenport, *An Apology*, pp. 114–20.
88. Graham, *The Life and Work*, p. 98.
89. Ibid., pp. 98–9.
90. Thomas Carlyle, 'On Heroes, Hero-Worship, and the Heroic in History' (lecture 2). 'The Hero as Prophet', London: J. Fraser, 1841, and various other editions. For Carlyle see, *DNB*, vol. III, pp. 1020–36.
91. *Life of Mohammed*, p. 411; *Khutbat*, pp. 159–60.
92. Ibid., pp. xxi–xxii; ibid., p. 11.
93. See *Khutbat*, pp. 211–12; *Life of Mohammed*, p. 277.
94. *Life of Mohammed*, p. xxi; *Khutbat*, p. 11.
95. L. Marracci, *Prodromus ad Refutationem Alcorani*, 4 pts, Rome, 1691.
96. *Life of Mohammed*, p. 444, n. 1.
97. Ibid., p. xxi.
98. Ibid.; *Khutbat*, p. 11.
99. See Edward W. Said, *Orientalism*, Middlesex: Penguin Books, 1978, p. 72.
100. *Life of Mohammed*, p. xxi; *Khutbat*, p. 11.
101. Antoine Galland, prefatory 'Discourse' to Barthelemy d'Herbelot, *Bibliotheque orientale, ou Dictionnaire universale contenant tout ce qui fait connaitre les peuples de l'Orient*, The Hague: Neaulme & van Daalen, 1777.
102. George Sale, *The Koran: Commonly Called the Alcoran of Mohammed . . . to Which is Prefixed a Preliminary Discourse* (1st edn., London, 1734; new edn. in 2 vols., London, 1801. George Sale (1697–1736) made the first accurate English translation of the Koran.
103. Charles Foster, *Mahometanism Unveiled*, 2 vols., London: Duncan and Cochran, 1822.
104. *Khutbat*, pp. 201–4; *Life of Mohammed*, pp. 441–4. B.A. Dar looked upon these discourses contained in this essay as a contribution of author to the Christian controversy of the day. And as such the latter had discussed these particular ideas embodied in the fourth essay in the context of the nineteenth-century Muslim–Christian debates between Rahmat Allah Kairanawi and Carl Gottlieb Pfander. See B.A. Dar, *Religious Thought of Syed Ahmad Khan*, Chapters 5 and 6 both entitled 'Christian Controversy', pp. 86–132.

105. *Life of Mohammed*, p. xxii. Aloys Sprenger, *The Life of Mohammad from Original Sources*, Allahabad: Presbyterian Mission Press, 1851.
106. *Life of Mohammed*, p. xxii; *Khutbat*, pp. 11–12.
107. *Life of Mohammed*, p. xxii; *Khutbat*, p. 12; *Life of Mahomet*, vol. I, p. iv.
108. *Khutbat*, p. 12. Syed Ahmad was referring to Sprenger's *Das Laben und die Lehre des Muhammad*, 2nd edn., Berlin, 1869.
109. *Life of Mohammed*, p. xxiii. For a similar view of Sprenger's approach see, Ann Marie Schimmel, *Deciphering the Signs of God: A Phenomenological approach to Islam*, Albany, 1994, p. 87.
110. *Life of Mohammed*, p. xxiii; *Khutbat*, p. 13.
111. Ibid.
112. Ibid.
113. *Khutbat*, p. 13. Syed Ahmad was referring to the famous German Pietist missionary Carl Gottlieb Pfander (1803–68) who is seen as a paradigm of 'Evangelical Orientalism', and the catalyst whose writings and activities created the high colonial interface with the world of Islam. See Avril Ann Powell, *Muslims and Missionaries in Pre-Mutiny India*, Surrey: Curzon Press, 1993, pp. 132–57.
114. See the Preface, *Life of Mahomet*, vol. I, p. iii; *Khutbat*, p. 13.
115. *Life of Mohammed*, pp. xxiv; *Khutbat*, pp. 13–14.
116. Ibid., p. xxv; ibid., p. 14.
117. Historians of medieval Europe have shown that the Western images of Islam in the Middle Ages (AD 800–1400) were full of ignorance but very complex and refined ignorance. 'The popular version of the life of Mahomet and the principles of his religion which became current among Christian writers from the time of the First Crusade naturally, were not very edifying or instructive: but alongside these there are traces of some serious attempts to understand the rival faith.' R.W. Southern, *The Making of the Middle Ages*, London: Hutchinson's University Library, 1953, pp. 38–9; R.W. Southern, *Western Views of Islam in the Middle Ages*, Cambridge, Maas.: Harvard University Press, 1962, p. 72.
118. Muir, *The Mohammedan Controversy and other Indian Articles*, p. 65.
119. See Albert Habib Hourani, *Islam in European Thought*, Cambridge: Cambridge University Press, 1991. This brilliant collection of essays examines the relations between European and Islamic thought and culture from the late eighteenth century to the twentieth century. Especially the long first essay, 'Islam in European thought', where the author provides a synoptic view of the development of ideas about Islam in European thought and scholarship, ibid., pp. 1–60.
120. William Muir, *The Mahomedan Controversy*, Edinburgh: T&T Clark, 1897, p. 66.

121. See Powell, *Muslims and Missionaries.*
122. Clinton Bennett, *Victorian Images of Islam*, London: Grey Seal, 1992.
123. Albert Habib Hourani, *Europe and the Middle East*, London: Macmillan, 1980, p. 34.
124. *The Rise of Islam*, p. iv.
125. Ibid., Similar was the opinion of J.W. Fuck that Muir's books reveal 'in an indiscreet fashion the author's Christian bias'. Fuck, 'Islam as an Historical Problem in European Historiography since 1800', B. Lewis, P.M. Holt, eds., *Historians of the Middle East*, London: Oxford University Press, 1962; rpt., 1964, p. 305.

CHAPTER 5

Sir Syed's Exegetical Vision

SANAULLAH MIR

Sir Syed was a multidimensional personality, a creative thinker, a philosophical theologian, a community leader, an educationist and a liberal modernist. He had an unflinching faith in the eternal truth of Islam. However, the scientific progress and consequent optimism in nineteenth-century Europe deeply impacted Sir Syed's thinking and approach to Islamic *Weltanschauung*. The stimulating events of 1857 shifted the very paradigm of his thought and this can never be overemphasized. Consequently, Sir Syed adopted a two-pronged strategy with a view to bringing about Muslim Renaissance both at the subcontinental and at the international level.

He became convinced that the only way of rehabilitating the subcontinental Muslims post-1857 devastation, was through the cultivation of natural sciences in English language. Accordingly, he established MAO College with a view to introducing Muslims to the latest scientific research.

The impact of Western science not only stimulated Sir Syed to practically impart modern scientific education to Muslims, it also inspired him to undertake the far more arduous task of reinterpreting Islam in the light of the latest historical scholarship and scientific research. It gave him a new perspective on religion. He not only reignited the need for *ijtihad* already underlined by Shah Waliullah but tried to work out a new *Ilm-al-Kalam*, in fact, a new conceptual framework with a view to restoring the relevance, significance and meaningfulness of Islam in post-Enlightenment times and climes. He reconceptualized a new role and function for Islam in our age. It is this reconceptualization or exegetical vision which should constitute the contemporary relevance of Sir Syed as his nineteenth-century interpretation of Islam, is essentially unacceptable to large sections of twenty-first-century Muslims across the globe.

RELIGION AND SCIENCE

Sir Syed realized that religion is inevitable and science is unavoidable. Civilizational march requires both the blessings of religion and the investigations of science. Therefore, religion and science cannot be mutually contradictory. If we think them to be so there must be something fundamentally wrong with our understanding of both religion and science. In view of the same, Sir Syed tried to work out a reconciliation between religion and science.

Working out a reconciliation between modern scientific cosmology and Semitic creationistic world-view is not the easiest of intellectual projects. The insuperable methodological limitations of such a project notwithstanding, Sir Syed made it his life-long intellectual mission to rationally demonstrate the truth of both scriptural revelations and scientific propositions. He became convinced that scientific cosmology is perfectly compatible with scriptural discourse. There can be no real contradiction between the injunctions of the Koran and the laws of nature. However, apparent contradictions, if any, must be ironed out by recourse to interpretation. Accordingly, Sir Syed proceeded to work out an exegesis of the Koran which is in accord with the naturalistic cosmology. Sir Syed started with the assumption that the divinely revealed Koranic discourse or the 'word of God' and scientific discourse objectively describing the physical world or 'work of God' cannot be incompatible. The assumption of the essential harmony between the 'word of God' and the 'work of God' led Sir Syed to a radical reinterpretation of the classical formulations of Islamic beliefs.[1]

Sir Syed denied all the miracles attributed to all the prophets throughout the history of Semitic religions. He denied the literal truth of the Koranic verses pertaining to *jin, Satan,* angels, creation of Adam, antichrist, immaculate birth of Jesus, ascension of the prophet of Islam to the divine *sanctum sanctorum*, paradise, hell, hand of God, seat of God, etc. Thus Sir Syed tried to project a version of Islam which is in accord with the Western Scientific rationality or criteria of justification.

Sir Syed even offered a naturalistic explanation of the prophetic revelation, the bedrock of the Semitic *Weltanschauung*. He did not accept the classical view that scriptural revelations were delivered to the prophets through the archangel Gabriel. For Sir Syed, Gabriel signifies the natural potential for prophethood or what Christian Troll calls 'Habitus of Prophethood'.[2] The prophet's inner potential when fully realized delivers messages which are perfectly divinely ordained. The prophet in his revelatory experience is in perfect attunement with God who speaks through the supremely developed consciousness of the prophet. The prophet delivers divine injunctions and promulgates divinely ordained *Shariah* through the depths of his revelatory experience.

Sir Syed's vociferous advocacy of complete compatibility between religion and science is fraught with serious methodological difficulties. In post-Enlightenment predominant European attitude towards religion is perfectly understandable. It is perfectly methodologically justifiable to go in for wholesale repudiation of a religious perspective of the universe. One can go in for a scientific approach and offer cogent and coherent arguments against the very possibility of religion. How-ever, to strive for complete or perfect compatibility of religion and science is to be asking for the moon.

Now, how can ongoing, changing and revocable scientific research be compatible with the perennial beliefs and values of Islam? How can the reconciliation worked out by classical and medieval theologians and interpreters between Islam and Ptolemiac cosmology be justified in a post-Copernican heliocentric era? Now when we are anchored on pro-heliocentric and antigeocentric cosmological predilections what should be our understanding and interpretation of the verses of the Koran with implicit and explicit cosmological, astronomical and scientific import? Should we design our interpretations in accord with the heliocentric account or not ? And, what is the guarantee of the perennial truth of the heliocentric cosmology? May be a future paradigmatic breakthrough divests the heliocentric framework of its meaning and relevance and then we shall be appropriating the essentials and principles of the post-paradigmatic cosmology whatsoever. And should we then again fashion our interpretation of the relevant Koranic verses in keeping with those post-paradigmatic scientific or cosmological assumptions and so on *ad finitum*. How long can interpreters of religion go on playing to the gallery of scientific opinions masquerading as final and ultimate key to the *mysterium tremendum* of the universe? Should we not stop somewhere and cry 'enough is enough', for scientific opinions may come and scientific opinions may go but the Koranic vision and mission will go on forever.

Sir Syed responded to this dilemma with plausible hermeneutical creativity and ingenuity. He did not maintain that the verses of the Koran are multisemic and the fixing of the signification of these verses is indefinitely vortexed into the realm of undecidability till all possible meanings evaporate through an endless play of differences and deferrals. He rather optimistically pointed out that the divinely ordained and inspired Koranic prepositional gestalt as 'word of God' is perfectly in accord with the universe as the 'work of God' is supremely and miraculously invested with multi-layered, multi-dimensional and multi-purpose semantic pelenitude, which is amenable to interpretation cross-culturally and cross-historically and in every age with its scientific and cosmological baggage will discern and discover appropriate meanings in this gestalt in the light of its respective postulates and presuppositions. The Koran provides us exact guidance and enlightenment at every stage of our scientific progress.

The words of the Koran have been so miraculously revealed that whatever the extent of the progress of our sciences and whatever our considered opinions in the light of these developed sciences, we shall find that its words are still in accordance with reality. Our earlier meanings which have now been proved wrong entailed a fault in our knowledge and not with the words of the Koran. Thus, if our sciences so develop in times to come that the then established laws are no longer held, we shall again return to the Koran and again definitely find it in accordance with reality. And we shall find that our earlier meanings emanated from our faulty knowledge and the Koran was innocent of every fault.[3]

Scientific research will unavoidably register progress or negotiate paradigm shifts and the Koranic exegesis will inevitably respond to such progressive or shifting nature of scientific discourse. The Koranic exegesis will definitely respond to scientific developments as hundreds of the Koranic verses seem to be referring to cosmological, astronomical, chemical, biological, geological and geographical phenomena or features. These verses may be proto-scientific or quasi-scientific or fully-fledged scientific propositions. Accordingly, the Koranic exegesis will try to interpret such verses in the light of the latest scientific discourse. The Koranic verses are immutably anchored to their textual structure while our understanding and interpretation of these verses will always operate within the given parameters of the scholarship or research of an age or era. While our understanding and interpretation of the Koran will always be susceptible to mistakes and ever-revocable and changeable in the light of ongoing scientific research, the Koranic propositional gestalt will perennially remain immune to change or innocent of limitations and faults. For example, in pre-Copernican times our understanding and interpretation of the Koran led us to believe that the Sun moved around the Earth. The Koran refers to the movement of the Sun only parenthetically, i.e. as believed by the people at large and not as a statement of fact. Now, when in post-Copernican times we know the Sun is stationary and the Earth moves round the Sun, we realize that our previous understanding and interpretation of the Koran was faulty. The perennial revocability of our understanding and the miraculous quality of the Koranic verses to perennially accord with latest scientific findings only establishes or proves the perfection of the Koran.[4] Thus, while the textual perfection of the Koran, according to Sir Syed, is demonstrable; our faulty understanding of the Koran is also understandable. However, such proneness to faulty interpretation does not absolve us of our perennial interpretative responsibilities.

EXEGETICAL VISION

For Sir Syed, interpretation of the Koranic propositional gestalt entailed profundity of understanding as well as methodological, hermeneutical and exegetical skills of highest sophistication. One must be well-versed in Islamic and Koranic sciences and subtleties of Arabic lexicography, grammar, morphology, syntax, semantics, styles and other features of language and literature. Besides, one must be aware of the history of exegetical literature and fully cognizant of the dynamics of exegetical disagreement. Additionally, one must be aware of the sources of misinterpretation of the injunctions and propositions of the Koran.

The misinterpretation of the Koranic verses can emanate or originate from several sources. The interpreters can misunderstand the function and purpose of the revelations of the Koran if they try to historicize, culturalize or scientificize the essentially transcendental character of Koranic discourse. Any historical or cultural or scientific analysis of the transcendental character of the Koranic verses can serve some of our immediate situational purposes or cater to some contemporary intellectual or methodological concerns. However, we must be cognizant of the fact that all situational reductions are amenable to revocation at any point of time and space. Nevertheless, any situational reduction of an essentially transcendental verse of the Koran can lead to its misinterpretation. Furthermore, if several interpreters of the Koran resort to such a reductive fallacy from several vantage points, we shall be ending up in an irresolvable theological disagreement and all of us will be simply parading our respective misinterpretations.

The interpreter of the Koran has to be well-versed in the styles of the Koran. He must understand the multifunctional character of the Koranic verses. Koranic language is comprised of diverse types of statements. For example, the entire Koranic propositional gestalt cannot be deemed to be descriptive in function or meaning. One of the commonest and most widely prevalent sources of misinterpretation can be our natural propensity for literal translation. If we go in for wholesale literal translation of the Koran and deem every verse of the Koran to be descriptive of some empirical or transempirical state of affairs, we shall be knotting ourselves into irresolvable difficulties. As it happens, the Koran is comprised of thousands of verses, multifunctional in character. Its verses are: descriptive, assertive, informative, declarative, expressive, interpretative, symbolic, allegorical, metaphorical, analogical; metaphysical, transcendental, ontological, cosmological, axiological, epistemological, ontogenetic, axiogenetic, epistemogenetic, methodogenetic, semiogenetic, hermeneugenetic, etc. A mature, judicious and methodologically balanced interpretation of the Koran requires that the exegete be well-versed in understanding the complex logic of the Koranic discourse.

The classical exegeses of the Koran need to be revisited in the light of contemporary historical research and methodological advancement. Most of these time-honoured and sanctified multivoluminous contributions have been worked out on faulty grounds. The conceptual frameworks within which the classical exegetes were operating have turned out to be bristling with grave methodological fault lines.

The classical exegetes based their exegetical contributions either on the reported sayings of the prophet or on biblical/Israelogical stories or on Greek philosophical speculations. All the three grounds are too shaky to be acceptable as sound and authentic bases for working out the exegetical formulations of the Koranic vision and mission.

Firstly, the reported traditions of the Prophet, even when authenticated through a gruelling process of methodological analysis, historical scholarship and hermeneutical deductions, cannot be accepted as unimpeachable and incorruptible reported sayings of the prophet.[5] These reported sayings were collected and compiled 200 years after his demise. For 200 years most of the reported traditions of the prophet were oral transmissions and therefore amenable to all additive, subtractive, multiplicative and divisive manipulations which all oral transmissions have suffered across the multiple periodizations of the historical continuum. Furthermore, these manipulations were powerfully accelerated on account of sectarian motivations, denominational ambitions, personal predilections and professional considerations. The post-Muhammad(s) times were politically and socially unstable and therefore fertile enough to lead to endless proliferations of the so-called traditions of the prophet. Such proliferations might even have been inspired by the best of intentions. Nevertheless, proliferations these were and repeated transmissions subjected their truth increasingly to the law of diminishing returns.

Secondly, the biblical or Israelogical stories too cannot be deemed to be an authentic or reliable source on which to anchor the interpretation of the Koranic verses pertaining to ancient prophets. The Koran has advanced the narratives of shorter or longer length profiling the life and times of numerous Israelite prophets. The narratives of the ancient prophets have been outlined in ancient books as well. The Israelite scholars had written detailed narratives with regard to the life and times of ancient prophets. Those were the times when miracle-mongering was at its highest. Therefore, these narratives are full of mythological accounts violating both rational justification and natural laws. These mythological accounts were part of the Semitic Historical Collective Unconscious, so to say. They were part of the conceptual milieu within which the classical doctors of Islam were operating. So, when the Koran outlined these narratives, their interpretations were worked out by the doctors of Islam, in keeping with their conceptual milieu in which mythological accounts and miraculous elements predominated. In view of the fact that the mythological and miraculous accounts pertaining to ancient prophets were fully known to our classical interpreters and the Koranic outlines with regard to these very ancient prophets were partially similar, the classical interpreters felt genuinely free to interpret these Koranic outlines in consonance with their biblically oriented and directed mindsets.

The Koranic outlines of the ancient prophets were no doubt similar to their historically evolved and crystallized biblical versions or renderings. However, the Koranic accounts, according to Sir Syed, are so worded or phrased that irrational, unnatural and mythological elements explicitly preponderant in biblical narratives are rendered without any justification. The classical Islamic scholars could not appreciate this fine distinction and construed the meanings of the Koranic words *mutatis mutandis* on biblical narratives. They did so because the biblical narratives since pre-Koranic times were so popular and so famous that they just could not liberate themselves from their preconceptions or just could not summon sufficient critical acumen to question the biblically oriented accounts violative both of human rationality and natural law. Furthermore all mythological and miraculous components of bibliological cosmogony were easily interpreted by classical Islamic scholars as indicative of the supreme and absolute power of Allah. Accordingly, they did not feel called upon to ponder over the real import of the words and phrases employed in the Koranic outlines pertaining to ancient prophets. Besides, there was no standardized progress of experimental sciences which could serve as a criterion of distinction between fact and fiction and attract their attention towards understanding natural laws.[6]

The miraculous components and mythological dimensions inserted into the exegetical literature of the Koran emanated not from the verses of the Koran but from the collective conceptual milieu within which our classical doctors of Islam were inspired. For example, it was not proved those days that the spread of a storm or tornado across the entire globe and the rise of water above the highest mountain-tops was simply impossible of occurrence. Therefore, the exegetes felt free to imaginatively widen the scope of the storm of Noah referred to in the Koran as hyperbolically as possible.

Long before the emergence of post-Copernican experimental scientific revolution, Islamic beliefs and values negotiated a major challenge posed by Greek philosophy. The methodological assumptions and ontocosmological tenets of Socrates, Plato, Aristotle and Plotinus impacted powerfully Muslim intellectuals during the Abbasid Caliphate. The foremost Muslim philosophers who responded to this challenge with remarkable intellectual daring were al-Kindi (801–73), al-Farabi (870–950), Ibn Sina (980–1037) and Ibn Rushd (1126–98). They tried to reconcile the theocentric or creationistic ontocosmological account of the Koran with the supposedly rationalist metaphysical interpretations worked out by Greek philosophers. These philosophers were essentially field-integrationists and grand reconciliationists. To them the rationalist interpretations worked out by Greeks and the revelatory tenets of Islam were perfectly compatible. They did not see any contradiction between Islam and Greek philosophical rationalism. However, the quest for compatibility did not remain confined to working out a reconciliation between Islamic beliefs and Greek philosophy. Muslim interpreters, exegetes and scholars, in course of time, tried to reconcile the Koranic cosmological tenets with the then established principles of Greek cosmology, physics and astronomy. They appreciatively highlighted the verses of the Koran apparently in accord with Greek sciences. They also interpretatively managed to adjust the verses apparently inconsistent with Greek scientific assumptions.

Sir Syed gave certain broad hermeneutical principles with a view to providing the prospective interpreters or exegetes a guideline as to how to carry out a methodologically informed analysis of the Koranic propositions and injunctions:

1. The interpreter will have to grasp and appreciate the nuances, the mood and the style of the Koranic use of words.
2. The interpreter will have to seek help from one verse to simplify or explain the meaning of another verse.
3. The interpreter must understand that the stipulation of a word and its designated meaning are mutually strictly correlative.
4. The interpreter must understand as to whether a word, under consideration, in a particular context, is not used in a meaning other than the designated one.
5. The interpreter must ensure as to in what sense an equivocal world is used.
6. The interpreter must ensure as to whether a word has been used literally or figuratively.
7. The interpreter must ensure as to whether a particular discourse is amenable to allegorical interpretation or not.
8. The interpreter must determine as to whether the designated meaning of a word is or is not context-specific.[7]

The interpreter must be cognizant as to whether the designated meaning of a word does or does not carry a rational or what may be stipulated an interpretative rider. This stipulation or consideration has been practised by almost all classical and medieval doctors of Islam or interpreters of the Koran. For example, the Koranic phrase of Gods' sitting on the throne has not been taken literally by the interpreters or exegetes of the Koran. The literal or originally designated meaning of such Koranic phrases as 'face of God', 'hand of God', etc., has not been espoused by interpreters of the Koran in view of several considerations. According to Sir Syed, such phrases cannot be taken literally because they are either impossible of rational consideration or violative of divinely promulgated natural laws or contrary to what is ordinarily experienced by man. In view of the same, whether we are interpreting divinely revealed discourse or human speech or writing, we cannot fix the meanings of words literally or referentially or designatively unless we abide by the interpretative rider with a view to ascertaining as to whether words under consideration are univocal, monosemic and monoreferential or polysemic, polyvocal and polyreferential or whether they are used literally or figuratively.

With regard to the exegesis of the Koranic discourse, Sir Syed propounded a crucial distinction between what he called intended speech (*kalam-i-maqsood*) and unintended speech (*kalam-i-ghair maqsud*). This distinction brings out the role of idiomatic, figurative, metaphorical, allegorical and symbolic expressions both in the context of human speech and divinely ordained or revealed discourse. According to Sir Syed, the Koranic discourse is repeatedly employing, what can be said to be unintended speech (*kalam-i-ghair maqsud*) in the form of idiomatic, figurative, metaphorical, allegorical and symbolic expressions. He cited the following Koranic verse with a view to illustrating the distinction between intended speech and unintended speech:

> To those who reject
> Our signs and treat them
> With arrogance, no opening
> Will there be of the gates
> Of heaven, nor will they
> Enter the Garden, until
> The camel can pass
> Through the eye of the needle.
> Such is our reward
> For those who sin.[8]

Sir Syed writes:

> From this we cannot conclude that at some time the camel will pass through the eye of the needle, for it is unintended speech (*kalam-i-ghair maqsood*). Its function is to stress on the impossibility of admission to paradise of those people who rejected the signs of God. Similarly, on the basis of this verse, we cannot argue on the possibility of gates of heaven out there, as it is unintended speech; its purpose being to stress on the inadmissibility of the rejector to the mercy of God. Various similar instances of unintended speech can be cited from the Koran and we cannot argue on the basis of their literal meanings.[9]

The Supreme wonder of the Koran is the style in which it has been revealed. The greatest of scholars and philosophers as well as the illiterate and ignorant masses can equally benefit from its revelations. Whether we try to understand it from the viewpoint of commoners or from the perspective of philosophers and scholars, we all arrive at the same conclusions. It is specifically a special feature of the Koranic discourse that an ignorant and illiterate person can arrive at the same inductions or derive the same deductions from it which a scholar or philosopher can bring out after extensive investigations and intensive interpretations. In fact, each one of us can benefit from the Koran according to one's knowledge and potential for understanding.

Sir Syed carried out his intellectual endeavours in a East-West civilizational crossfire of nineteenth-century India. As a sincere and enlightened intellectual leader and social reformer of his times he negotiated this dilemma with exceptional hermeneutical skills and methodological sophistication. His culture and upbringing pulled him to the majesty of Islamic beliefs and values. However, the long-term communitarian interests pushed him to the irresistible attractions of Western science. Sir Syed realized the inevitability of a religious world-view and value-system and the unavoidability of scientific research. The civilizational march required both the blessings of religion and investigations of science. Therefore, religion and science cannot be mutually contradictory. If we think them to be so there must be something fundamentally wrong with our understanding of both religion and science. In view of the same, Sir Syed tried to work out a reconciliation between Islam and science, the insuperable methodological limitations of such a project notwithstanding. It became the life-long intellectual mission of Sir Syed to rationally demonstrate the truth both of the Quranic revelations and scientific propositions. He became convinced that scientific cosmology is perfectly compatible with scriptural discourse. There can be no real contradiction between the injunctions of the Koran and the laws of nature. However, apparent contradictions, if any, must be ironed out by recourse to interpretation.

Sir Syed also qualified the formalistic account of Islam, Koran and *Sunnah*. He sincerely believed in the perfection *of Din* (religion) and finality of the prophethood of Muhammad. However, he does not accept the finality of *Shariah* as it is nowhere referred to in the Koran. The perfection of *Din* needs to be categorically distinguished from the alleged finality of *Shariah*, which, in fact, is an ongoing and evolving legal mechanism of socio-political, economic and inter-personal crisis management and changes in keeping with the shifting conditions of human culture. The vertical claim of perfection of *Din* should not be horizontally applied to mean complete guidance in the spheres of culture, science, politics, economy, etc.

For Sir Syed religion who essentially the cultivation of personal relationship of man with God. He does not accept the totalist version of religion. He does not deem religion to be a complete code of conduct. Religion has been unwarrantedly stipulated to be capable of guiding in all worldly matters. Muslims have lost their initiative because of this totalist interpretation of Islam. They have wrongly come to believe that they can do nothing to resolve their social, political and economic problems without seeking permission from theologians and jurists who obviously are supposed to be in possession of a complete list of prescriptions and proscriptions for all times to come.

As Sir Syed saw it, the totalist version of religion arose out of methodological field-confusion. When we are not clear about different segments of a cultural gestalt and jumble them up, our confusions are worse confounded. In view of the same Sir Syed emphasized on clearly demarcating the jurisdiction of religion from other spheres of analysis as well as operation. For example, the nuclear core of Islam needs to be separated from the historical, geographical and cultural conditions of the Islamic world. It also needs to be separated from social, political and economic imperatives of Muslim struggle for survival or expansion. It also needs to be categorically delineated from scientific or experimental fields of investigation.

Sir Syed maintained that theological systematization of any religion like other intellectual responses is not over and above the operation of cultural conditioning or situational determination. The nuclear core of Islam or the Koran, in the process of expansion and propagation got culturally or situationally concretized. Any interpretation of the Koranic discourse is the function of concrete cultural and situational dynamics of a particular society at a particular point of history. Sir Syed underscored that while the nuclear core of Islam, i.e. its moral and spiritual perspective on human-life, is perennially and universally valid, no concrete interpretation of Islam can lay any claim to finality. All interpretations of Islam are situationally evoked and culturally directed.

The final authority of various schools of Islamic jurisprudence was also radically contested by Sir Syed. The juristic inductions and deductions of various doctors of Islam cannot be identified with the mandatory beliefs, values and principles enshrined in the fundamental propositions of the Koran. At best these juristic derivations can have recommendatory significance or relevance in our times and climes. In fact, they were individual opinions expressed within the context of their space and time and were never meant to be eternally applicable. In view of the fact that the *Shariah* can never be conclusively or definitively formulated, it is obligatory upon Muslims of every age to resolve their social, political, economic, administrative, cultural and educational problems within the framework of the moral and spiritual tenets of Islam. Every age demands a new framework of interpretation. The doors of *ijtihad* or reinterpretation, so to say, can never be closed. The interpretation of the Koranic discourse is to be accomplished by every age in the light of its specific historical and situational requirements.

In his quest for harmonization of reason and revelation, Sir Syed's hermeneutical and exegetical endeavours invited the severest possible criticism from votaries of religious orthodoxy and theological establishment. They accused him of being a naturalist. He was not a naturalist masquerading as a Muslim. He was a philosophical theologian or an enlightened apologist for Islam. However, the underlying assumption of Sir Syed was to adjust the Korantic doctrines to the norms and criteria of Western scientific rationality.

Sir Syed's was a monumental task to resolve a universal and profound dilemma—the conflict between science and religion. The conflict is too deep, too profound and too powerful to allow any easy reconciliation between these competing paradigms of interpretation or perspectives upon the cosmos. Whether Sir Syed succeeded in this endeavour or not is besides the point. Plato, Aristotle, Shankara, Ramanuja, Ibn Arabi, Sirhindi, Descartes, Locke, Hume, Kant, Hegel and many more before him, and, Dilthey, Husserl, Aurobindo, Iqbal, Heidegger, Wittgenstein and many more after him too did not. What is crucial is that Sir Syed amongst all modern Muslim thinkers attempted to resolve the central dilemma of 'religion or science' facing human civilization.

Sir Syed's views deserve to be thoroughly debated. His methodological framework lacks some essential elements of perennial value and significance. For example, Sir Syed almost ignores the mystical dimension of human consciousness and its moral and spiritual role in the ongoing march of human civilization. He is also blissfully unaware of an existentialist perspective on religion. It is in this respect that the philosophically more brilliant and the creatively profound Sir Iqbal of Lahore scores over the methodologically far more advanced and analytically sharper Sir Syed of Aligarh.

Sir Syed was an outstanding Muslim modernist and reformer of nineteenth-century India. He was the first modern Muslim thinker. He was captivated by the amazing progress registered in multiple fields by European people. He wanted similar scientific and technological sophistication and material progress for Muslims as well. Galvanized by a vision and inspired by a dream, a determined Sir Syed established MAO College, presently the Aligarh Muslim University, for the modernization of Indian Muslims by recourse to English education and scientific research. Whether he succeeded in this endeavour or not is besides the point. What needs to be underscored is that armed with the courage of his convictions, he tried to weave his dream into the fabric of reality. Indian Muslims missed a Sir Syed of the twentieth century. Let us pray and hope they do not miss a Sir Syed of the twenty-first century.

NOTES

1. K.A. Nizami, *Sayyid Ahmad Khan*, Delhi: Publications Division, Ministry of Information and Broadcasting, Govt. of India, 1980, pp. 113–14.

2. C.W. Troll, *Syed Ahmad Khan: A Reinterpretation of Muslim Theology*, Delhi: Vikas, 1978, pp. 190–3.
3. J. Khwaja, ed., *Sir Syed ki Islami Basirat* (Urdu), Aligarh: New Aligarh Movement, 1987, p. 86.
4. Ibid.
5. Ibid., p. 26.
6. Ibid., p. 84.
7. Troll, pp. 160–70.
8. *Al-Kor'an,* 7: 38.
9. Khwaja, p. 82.

CHAPTER 6

Sir Syed's Scheme of Education

ALI AHMAD

Sir Syed Ahmad Khan was one of those dynamic and revolutionary figures of history who have moulded the destinies of nations and changed the course of time. He was a great saviour of Indian Muslims and possessed a multi-faceted personality. He was a social reformer, theologian, political and educational thinker. The impact of his views on all spheres of our national life has been profound. The real greatness of Sir Syed lies in his stressing a scientific attitude of mind and adopting a secular approach in all matters of human relationship. He believed in the supremacy of reason in all matters, spiritual or temporal. Throughout his life he fought against fanaticism, conservatism, and traditionalism. A great crusader against ignorance, Sir Syed advocated a system of education which laid equal emphasis on training the minds and morals of the pupils. He stood for liberty of conscience and freedom of expression. 'Sir Syed Ahmad had inaugurated a revolution in Muslim thought. His endeavour was to reform the Muslims individually and collectively.'[1]

Brought up as an oriental scholar, he rose to be the apostle of modern education amongst his co-religionists. In fact, Sir Syed stood for dynamic movement of society according to the needs of the time, supremacy of 'reason' in all matters, hard work and incessant struggle for the betterment of society and a concept of 'nation' which overrode all parochial considerations. He contributed many essential elements to the development of modern Indian society and is certainly one of its most distinguished architects.

Sir Syed was the first Muslim in modern India to catch a glimpse of the dynamic character of the emerging age and he dedicated his whole life to what he thought to be the supreme need of the hour—the upliftment of Indians by apprising them of the problems of the modern world. He ignored all the hurdles in his way and strove, patiently and incessantly, to bring about a reorientation in the outlook and behaviour of Indians, particularly the Muslims who were more backward in education than any other Indian community. He thus became a social and moral force which accelerated the processes of transition from the medieval period to the modern age.

Among the galaxy of great men of India in second half of the nineteenth century, Sir Syed was one of the most prominent. His greatness is to be measured by his impression made on society and transformatory effect on thought and action. He believed that Muslims would not get their due place in the changed situation unless they learned to adjust themselves to the new situations. He asked the Muslims to imbibe the liberal ideas and exhorted them to eschew politics and to devote themselves to education. He was convinced that the Muslim community in India could not regain its rightful position in the national life of the country unless it imbibed modern ideas and gave up its traditional mode of thinking. He tried to guide the Muslims in the most dismal period of their history.

Sir Syed had a very scientific and practical view about the planning of the new system of education. He forbade people to think only in the present and urged them to look forward and start a new system of education for future generations. He visualized the future requirements of a rising generation. Sir Syed wanted to use modern education as an instrument of reconstructing the society. He believed that education was a strong means of socio-economic and cultural change. He was much perturbed by the prevailing condition of Indians, specially Muslims, after the 1857 Revolt. He was an eyewitness to the deteriorating condition of Muslims who were upset, frustrated, confused and uncertain about their lives and culture. There seemed to be no way to meet the problems and the challenges before the Muslim community. Sir Syed came on the scene and advocated that social and cultural reforms may be made with the help of modern education. He was criticized and opposed by many. But in spite of oppositions from various corners, he stood fast in his mission to provide modern education to Muslims. One very remarkable thing about Sir Syed was that he was educated in traditional education but he stood up with a mission to provide modern education to Indian society, particularly the Muslims.

Eminent writers and scholars have written on the various aspects of the life of Sir Syed. In their writings, we find his biography, social, political, literary and religious contributions. They also made attempts on his educational contributions for Indians as a whole and specially for Muslims. However, there is a need for systematic efforts to identify his educational scheme which has not attracted much attention of scholars.

Sir Syed wrote many books and articles through which he expressed his ideas. In his writings, we find ideas about different aspects of educational schemes but he is not regarded as an educationist though a sound system of education was developed in Mohammedan Anglo-Oriental College (MAO College) established by him.

His educational scheme was a bit different from the schemes prevailing in Western countries. Western education was materialistic in nature and there was very little emphasis on morality and traditional education. In the case of Sir Syed's scheme, there was a synthesis between Western education and traditional education. He said once, that he wanted the products of his college to carry on in the one hand the degree of sciences and in the other hand the degree of philosophy and the crown of the sacred Kalmah of Islam to adorn their heads.

This paper is a humble effort to present Sir Syed's three important components of his scheme of education—aims of education, curriculum and method of teaching.

SIR SYED'S SCHEME OF EDUCATION

Sir Syed Ahmad Khan was not satisfied with the British policy of education in India as it was against the interest of Indians as a whole, and particularly for the Muslims. He paid much attention to introduce and provide modern education to Muslims for their upliftment. He expressed his views on various aspects of education to bring about changes in the prevailing system. It is beyond the scope of the present study to cover and analyse the whole of his educational scheme. I have therefore focused on the following aspects of his scheme of education for a brief discussion:

1. Need and importance of education.
2. Aims of education.
3. Curriculum.
4. Method of teaching.

NEED AND IMPORTANCE OF EDUCATION

Sir Syed held the view that education was essential for an all-round development of human personality. Emphasizing the importance of education, Sir Syed said, 'The human soul without education is like a rough piece of marble, and unless the sculptor works on it and removes its roughness . . . its good qualities remain hidden in it, and its fascinating shades, beautiful view . . . do not appear.' However gentle-hearted a man may be, unless he is educated, all the good qualities and graces that are latent in him cannot emerge without the assistance of education.[2]

Sir Syed maintained that 'Muslims could not progress without sound religious education combined with the arts and sciences of the west.'[3] He applied English education as a socio-political catalyst, and by synthesizing Western knowledge with traditional Islamic modes he created a new model of progress which stimulated national life on a large scale. Despite opposition from some Muslim quarters Sir Syed's educational experiment gained wide support amongst the Muslims of the subcontinent.

Emphasizing the importance of education in one of his speeches, Sir Syed said, 'It appeared to me that nothing could remove the obstacles to progress of Musalmans but education. And education, in its fullest sense, has been the object in furthering which I have spent the most earnest moments of my life, and employed the best energies that lay within my humble power.'[4] Delivering a speech on self-reliance in education, Sir Syed said, 'It is regrettable as both the nations whose ancestors had been so enlightened and educated, defame the ancestors by their ignorance. Education is becoming widely popular these days. We have to think in the realm of education as to what subjects we should study and what is that the learning of which will not be useful to us.'[5]

He said there was no reason why we should not avail the educational opportunities provided by the government with gratitude. He was of the opinion that no government could take the responsibility of education of the whole nation, and he firmly believed that it was not possible for government to meet out fully the educational requirements of its subjects. Even more than this, he strongly held the view that the nation wishing for the betterment of education of its young boys, could not do so unless it provided itself for their education. Sir Syed made it clear that Indians would progress only when they themselves without the interference of the government arranged for the education of their young boys out of their voluntary contribution, and themselves administered and controlled these schools and colleges.

It is quite clear from the writings and speeches of Sir Syed that he emphasized the importance of education:

> Oh, my friends, reflect on this—that each time has its own colour, and unless you adapt yourselves to the circumstances of the time your work can not prosper. In the time of Akbar, men of learning, poets and historians were respected, people then tried to acquire learning and science and this was the cause of their glory and honour. That time has gone. And now we have the British Government, and we have to consider in what way we can now attain honour. I believe that without higher education it is impossible now to acquire honour.[6]

Although Sir Syed's efforts for the upliftment of the Muslim community covered the whole gamut of religious, social, political and economic life of the community, its main thrust was in the sphere of education. The reason was that Muslims had confined their education only to the traditional and religious learning through the medium of Arabic and Persian languages. They abhorred Western education because of their intense hatred for the British and the fear that learning the English language would weaken their faith. This misunderstanding about English education made them shun modern education and they were not aware the sea-changes brought by it. Sir Syed saw in this suicidal attitude, the final doom of the community. He was convinced that without Western education, Muslims could have no future.

In the words of Tara Chand, Sir Syed Ahmad considered 'higher English education as the panacea for all the social and political ills of India'.[7]

Stressing the need and importance of education, the Indian Education Commission (1964–6) reports as: 'In a world based on science and technology, it is education that determines the level of prosperity, welfare and security of the people. On the quality and number of persons coming out of our schools and colleges will depend our success in the great enterprise of national reconstruction whose principal objective is to raise the standard of living of our people.'[8]

From the above discussion, it is derived that Sir Syed's ideas on education got its due place in the Indian Education Commission report and other educational documents.

AIMS OF EDUCATION

Aim provides direction to a certain activity and motivates human behaviour. An aim is essential to guide and make all the activities of an individual successful in all spheres of life. Education without aim is like a ship without a destination. Raging controversy has been going on in connection with the aims of education. The nature of education itself has been a subject of debate. In different periods, it carried different meanings and aims. Some educationists say that education must have definite aims, while others say that the aims should be as diffused as possible. Some say that education should have only an ultimate aim while others say that it should have only immediate aims and should not run after the mirage of an ultimate aim, as there can never be any such aim. Some educationists emphasize individual aims and some others social aims. We find different aims of education because it is correlated to the ideals of life. Since people and societies differ in ideals and values, there have been different aims of education in different periods. However, all the aims can be broadly categorized into individual and social aims. The controversy between the individual and social aims can be removed by making a synthesis of social and individual aims.

Though educationists differ on aims of education, on one point they all agree that it should have certain aims of education. As far as Sir Syed's aims of education are concerned, he held the view that education was a means of fostering and cultivating the inherent potentialities of the child. He said that through education mankind individually and collectively, marched towards progressive development.

Defining the meaning of education, Sir Syed said,

> Human spirit is just like a mountain of marbles having several black spots on it, and unless the sculpture touches it, removes its dimness and roughness, turns it into a model, polishes and shines it, its beautiful nerves, charming colour and nice designs remain hidden. Similar is the condition of human spirit. A human being may be pious from the very core of his heart, but unless he is subjected to education, his piety and other noble qualities lie hidden in him. They can be brought into prominence only by means of education.[9]

In an article contributed to *Tahzib-ul Akhlaq* a magazine edited by Sir Syed, in 1289 Hijra, in which he defined education in the following words, 'To educate a human being is to bring out what is hidden in him. . . . For example God has bestowed upon man several capacities and capabilities. To stimulate them and to infuse life into them, so that they can blossom, is to educate human beings.'[10]

Formulating the aim Sir Syed said, 'The greatest aim of education and training was to engender piety, morality and humanness in human beings.'[11] In his opinion, for the harmonious growth of child's personality both these qualities were necessary. Sir Syed was totally against the teaching of theoretical knowledge only. He did not support the theory that the aim of education is merely the acquisition of knowledge. He opined that education should aim at the harmonious cultivation of the physical, moral, intellectual and aesthetic sides of human nature. Training along with education was an important component of his scheme of education. According to Bertrand Russel the 'purpose of education has always been related to social thinking and has been viewed differently by different people in different ages. However, there is a fair amount of concensus among educationists, and thinkers that education is the most effective instrument to realize the inner potentialities and talents of an individual and to pave the way for the full development of his personality.'[12] The University Education Commission (1948–9) observed: 'The purpose of all education, it is admitted by thinkers of East and West, is to provide a coherent picture of the universe and an integrated way of life.'[13]

The thinking of Sir Syed on the subject is in broad concurrence with the Commission's view. In a pamphlet criticizing the government system of education, he wrote, 'The purpose of education has always been to enable a man to develop his intellectual powers to the full so that he may grasp the significance of any situation that arises, that he may know the differences between right and wrong and gain ability to contemplate the divine mysteries of nature. Education should strengthen the character on the life to come.'[14] He added, 'Education was not the putting into a person of something from outside. It was the releasing of the capabilities, talent in a human being.'

Graham said that Sir Syed's educational aims, found full manifestation in the ideals of the MAO College—'free enquiry, large-hearted tolerance and of pure morality'.[15]

Tara Chand identified the following aims of Sir Syed's educational scheme:

1. The strengthening of faith which required the knowledge of religious truths, and the reconciliation of reason and tradition;
2. The training of character through the establishment of residential institution and promotion of healthy activities;
3. Teaching of modern science up to the highest level and creating a national outlook among students.[16]

These aims indicate that Sir Syed tried to develop a synthesis between Western and traditional education. He said, 'Philosophy will be in our right hand and natural science in our left, and the crown of there is no god but Allah and Prophet Muhammad (PBUH), is his prophet, will adorn our heads.[17]

Explaining the aims of education, Sir Syed stated that

> The purpose of education has always been to create an awareness in man by which he may distinguish between good and bad, may give thought to the natural phenomena spread out before him, by acquiring knowledge he may become more refined in his manners, may earn his livelihood in a better way and may give his thought to life hereafter. The plea of government that they are not concerned with the discipline and training of mind to this extent, but want that much education which may enable a man to earn his bread and which may remain confined merely to the teaching of geography, arithmetic and digits, is unwarranted.[18]

Sir Syed found the solution to political, social, economic, spiritual and ethical ills prevailing in India in education. He held the faith that education would remove all the ills of society. On 29 January 1884, while addressing a general meeting in Amritsar, he said, 'Even if the government does not care for some of our proper rights till now, for which we have been complaining, still higher education is such a powerful tool which will enable us to attain these rights.'[19]

It is evident from the above discussion that the educational aims formulated by Sir Syed have become part of educational literature of the world. His aims of education are still very much relevant in present-day Indian education.

CURRICULUM

Curriculum plays a very important role in realizing the aims of education. It reflects the curricular and co-curricular activities carried on in educational institutions. The curriculum must respond to the needs of society and must help the individuals in developing their potentialities to the fullest possible extent.

Curriculum has been defined by Secondary Education Commission (1952–3) in these words:

> It must be clearly understood that, according to the best educational thought, curriculum does not mean only the academic subjects traditionally taught in the school but it includes totality of experiences that a child receives at school. In this sense, the whole life of school becomes the curriculum which can touch the life of students at all points and help in the evolution of a balanced personality.[20]

From this definition it becomes evident that any study of curriculum should concern itself both with the needs and the interests of the individual and the society.

As far as the curriculum proposed by Sir Syed is concerned, it was to bring about the socio-economic, educational and cultural change. He believed that education was a strong tool for transforming society. Therefore, after the 1857 Revolt he became busy with his educational activities. He had little hope that his educational scheme, prepared in England, would be appreciated by his co-religionists. The reason was that his new educational scheme differed much from the prevailing scheme of education.

Sir Syed held the view that traditional curriculum was insufficient against the new emerging curriculum which was more scientific and appropriate to meet the challenges of the time. But Muslims were against to any kind of subject which was out of their traditional curriculum. They had genuine reasons for it. Oriental languages were not properly taught and books, containing matters hostile to Islam, had been introduced in the government schools and colleges. There were other objections too like the use of Hindi in most of the government schools as the medium of instruction, inadequate staffing, the general failure to adopt instruction to the national inclination and capacities of the children, a method of examination which did not secure a thorough knowledge of a subject, but did encourage cramming. Some subjects were held to be superfluous. Moreover, the use of English in the teaching of sciences only enhanced the difficulties of the pupils. Therefore the MAO College curriculum was prepared to meet the needs of the Muslim community. Sir Syed had a very broad concept of curriculum. His curriculum included traditional as well as modern education so that it may fulfil the present and the future needs of Muslims. Apart from this, a very rich programme of co-curricular activities was an integral part of Sir Syed's curriculum. Consequently, Sir Syed's curriculum was flexible and not static.

It may be noted that Sir Syed had no special consideration either for the English language or for Western education. He wanted his countrymen, specially the Muslims, who were much more backward educationally than other communities of India, should progress and develop in education and keep pace with the advanced nations of the West. To him, this was possible only through the acquisition of modern education along with traditional education. In those days, the West represented all that was latest in the realm of knowledge and the east offered only the old and obsolete knowledge which had outlived its utility and was totally incapable of meeting the demands and urges of a changing and growing society. While rapid strides had taken place in all branches of human knowledge in the West, the traditional disciplines of the East had turned into stagnant pools in the absence of any research for many centuries. Sir Syed believed that in isolation with the advanced nation the upliftment of Muslims was not possible. He was, however, in favour of a synthesis between the two curricula— that is the curriculum of traditional education for Muslims and the modern curriculum of the West.

Sir Syed wanted to remove the faults in the curriculum of the Muslim institutions and the weaknesses in teaching methods. Thus, in both system and curriculum the new system would depart from traditional lines and would adopt Western methods and western curricula. Taking into account the various types of curricula, he proposed two different kinds of schools for Muslims. First, secondary schools based on Western models but also providing religious instructions as well. This would fulfil both secular and religious needs of the Muslims. Second, that schools should be affiliated with the government schools and colleges to provide the religious instruction for which there was no provision.

Sir Syed's Proposed Curriculum

After considering the various needs and requirements of the Muslim community, Sir Syed presented the details of his curriculum which can be categorized into two:

1. General education curriculum,
2. Special education curriculum.

The general education curriculum was to meet the needs of Muslims—secular as well as spiritual. The special education curriculum was to enable the Muslims to benefit by the education system adopted by the government. The course content of general as well as special education is given below:

1. Religion—*Fiqha* (Muslim jurisprudence), *Hadith* (Traditions of the Prophet), *Tafsir* (Commentaries on the Holy Koran), *Siar* (Ecclesiastical histories), and general principles of religious belief.
2. Moral Sciences—literature and language, history, geography, logic, philosophy, politics and political economy.
3. Mathematics—arithmetic, algebra, eucludian geometry and other branches of mathematics.
4. Natural Sciences—statistics, hydrostatics, dynamics, pneumatics, optics, electricity and magnetism, astronomy, heat, acoustics natural philosophy, etc.

Special Education Curriculum

In addition to the above subjects there was to be a special course of study which included such subjects as engineering, physiology, zoology, botany, geology, mineralogy and chemistry.

Distribution of the above subjects into different classes of schools and colleges, and quantity to be taught in each class were fixed.[21]

Sir Syed expressed his views about curriculum in following words:

> the only means to achieve the goal was by changing the old system of education pursued hitherto in all Muslim institutions. Its curriculum consisted of completely fossilized studies. Linguistics, grammar, scholasticism, logic were the main subjects of study; some history, geography, astronomy and medicine were thrown in but they had made no advance during the last five hundred years. Minds had become static, rigid, hidebound.[22]

To conclude, the curriculum proposed by Sir Syed was flexible, dynamic and progressive in nature. He adopted the curriculum being followed in Oxford and Cambridge Universities of Britain with certain modifications which were essential for the Muslim community. The curriculum recommended by various Indian Education Commissions, Committees, and educational documents are in agreement with the curriculum formulated by Sir Syed.

METHOD OF TEACHING

A curriculum is framed, keeping in view, the aims of education. Similarly, the methods of teaching are determined in accordance with the curriculum and aims already framed and formulated. Thus, the aims and the curriculum both depend for their effectiveness on the methods by which they are communicated to the students. Whatever the aims and curriculum may be, it is the method of teaching which makes them effective or ineffective, significant or insignificant.

The different methods of teaching are followed for different subjects. Some of the important methods of teaching are: lecture method, demonstration method, question–answer method, problem-solving method, scientific method, project method, etc.

A far as the method of teaching is concerned, Sir Syed was not satisfied with the traditional method of teaching because it encouraged rote learning and failed to prepare the child for real life. Being a pragmatic thinker, he held the view that the scientific method of teaching should be followed. But he did not deny the importance of other methods of teaching since a lesson can be taught effectively by applying different methods and techniques of teaching. However, the effectiveness of teaching, to a greater extent, depends on the competence of teachers, though he did not write or speak about any specific method of teaching to be followed in MAO College. However, the curriculum recommended by him for different levels of education was such that a particular method of teaching would not be enough as far as its effectiveness was concerned. According to Sir Syed, learning by doing, observation, playing and freedom of expression played an important role in the methods of teaching. It made the students creative and constructive.

Sir Syed also recommended Experimental Method of teaching. He said: 'In old times, theories could be propounded and rebutted sitting in the sequestrated places, now it is the experimental age. To prove or disprove anything you have to be in the laboratories.'[23]

One can identify these methods of teaching in his writings, speeches and the methods followed in the MAO College. Since he wanted to develop scientific thinking in Indians, especially Muslims, the scientific method of teaching was more useful and effective in this regard.

Thus, it can be said that any method of teaching which is best suited to the situation, may be applied to make the teaching effective in order to link education with life.

As far as Sir Syed's scheme of education is concerned, it is still very relevant today. If we analyse his educational scheme, we find that there is much stress on the synthesis between modern and traditional education which is the need of the present time. He was very clear about the role played by education in building a dynamic nation. He emphasized the vocational, technical and professional education which are also being emphasized today.

His scheme of education was open for all and there was no discrimination on the basis of caste, creed, colour, religion and region. It was the result of his secular policy of education that the first graduate and the first postgraduate of MOA College was a non-Muslim.

Sir Syed emphasized the training of character which is the gravest challenge before society today.

It is unfortunate that we cannot properly maintain the infrastructure which Sir Syed has left behind for the educational upliftment of Muslims. The All India Muslim Educational Conference and the Scientific Society, the two important institutional organs of Aligarh movement, are defunct and virtually dead organizations today. The need to revive them can hardly be over-emphasized in the present context.

NOTES

1. Tara Chand, *History of the Freedom Movement*, vol. 2, Delhi: Ministry of Information and Broadcasting, 1967, p. 359.
2. Shan Muhammad, *Sir Syed Ahmad Khan: A Political Biography*, Meerut: Meenakshi Publication, 1969, p. 210.
3. Mohammad Yusuf Abbasi, *Genesis of Muslim Fundamentalism in British India*, New Delhi: Indian Institute of Applied Political Research, 1987, p. 59.
4. Shan Muhammad, *Sir Syed Ahmad: Writings and Speeches*, Bombay: Nachiketa Pubs., 1972, p. 129.
5. Ibid. , p. 171.
6. Malik Hafeez, *Political Profile of Sir Syed Ahmad*, Islamabad: Institute of Islamic History, Culture and Civilization, Islamia University, p. 380.
7. Tara Chand, p. 361.
8. Govt. of India, *Indian Education Commission Report* (1964–6), New Delhi, p. 1.
9. Maulana Ismail Panipati, *Maqalat-i-Sir Syed*, p. 12.

10. Ibid.
11. Muhammad Imamuddin Gujrati, *Mukammal Majmu-i-Lectures and Speeches*, p. 533.
12. Ishrat Ali Qureshi, *Aligarh: Past and Present*, Aligarh: AMU, 1992.
13. Govt. of India, *University Education Commision (1948–9)*, Delhi, p. 34.
14. Altaf Husain Hali, *Hayat-i-Javed*, tr. K.H. Qadri and D.J. Mathews, Delhi: Idarah-i-Adabiyat-i-Delhi, 1979, p. 59.
15. G.F.I. Graham, *The Life and Work of Syed Ahmad Khan*, Delhi: Idarah-i-Adabiyat-i-Delhi, 1974, p. 275.
16. Tara Chand, p. 30.
17. Shan Muhammad, *The Aligarh Movement: A Concise Study*, Aligarh: Educational Book House, 1999, p. 49.
18. Hali, p. 85.
19. K.A. Nizami, *Sir Syed Ahmad*, Delhi: Ministry of Information and Broadcasting, 1966, p. 185.
20. Govt. of India, *Secondary Education Commission Report (1952–3)*, Delhi.
21. Syed Ahmad Khan, *Report of the Committee for Better Diffusion and Advancement of Learning Among the Mohammadans of India* (English version), Aligarh: Medical Hall Press, 1872, pp. 57–9.
22. Shan Muhammad, *Sir Syed Ahmad Khan*, op. cit.
23. Ishrat Ali Qureshi, *Present Day Relevance of Sir Syed's Educational Philosophy*, reference taken from Sir Syed: *Bazyaft*, ed. Ateeq Ahmad Siddique, Aligarh: Sir Syed Academy, AMU, 1990, p. 308.

CHAPTER 7

Sir Syed Ahmad Khan: A Visionary of Modern Scientific Education

HASSAN IMAM

The nineteenth century forms a watershed in the annals of history of the modern world. The progressive nations of Europe, and Muslim societies all over the world were facing obscurantism, inertia and frustration. Several centuries ago Baghdad, had been a centre for excellence in learning and the *Baitul Hikmat* (the House of Wisdom), the repository of knowledge from where scientific knowledge was transmitted to the whole world, had gone into the limbo of history. At the debris of Muslim intellectual empire, Europeans raised their head and posed intellectual threat to Muslim Societies all over the world. Macaulay had remarked about European science and literature that 'a single shelf of a good European Library was worth the whole native literature of India and Arabia'.[1] It was really a great challenge posed by scientific development of the West. In response to these challenges, a number of social and educational reformers all over the world launched movements for moral and intellectual rejuvenation of Muslim society.

The question before the social reformers were how to raise Muslim society to the level of European society. Some social thinkers realized that the evils from Muslim society could be removed only through socio-political change in accordance with the tradition of early Islam. Others thought that the remedy did not lie in religious revival but could be achieved only through the acceptance of Western values and concepts. The third school of reformers followed a middle path between the two extreme approaches and advocated acceptance of Western education and science while maintaining their religious values and intellectual identity. Sir Syed Ahmad Khan belonged to this category of thinkers. He tried to maintain a balance, i.e. modern

European education without compromising with the religious values. In other words Sir Syed tried to bring a rapprochement between science and religion.

The task of reforming Indian society, particularly Muslim society, was undertaken by Sir Syed Ahmad Khan, who occupies the position of a major thinker of the nineteenth century, and who wished to reach a conciliation between Islam and modern science.

He was born in Delhi on 17 October 1817[2] and received his early education at home. He studied *Gulistan* and *Bostan* of Shaikh Saadi and also went through a number of books on astronomy and medicine (tibb).[3] In his youth he was fond of music and picnic parties[4] and was noted for his sense of humour.[5]

When we analyse Syed Ahmad Khan's writings on various scientific developments in the pre-Mutiny era. We know that he wanted to prove through his writings that modern scientific discoveries were not in opposition to the teaching of the Holy Koran when properly interpreted. Sir Syed's early works include, *Jilal-ul qutub bizikr-ul Mahbub* (1839). This small booklet deals with the birth, death, miracles and other events relating to the life of the Holy Prophet. Sir Syed in this work confined himself to all those practices which were held to be correct in accordance with the thinking of the time.[6]

Tuhfa-i Hasan (1839), the Urdu translation of a few chapters of the Persian work, *Tuhfa-i Isna Ashna Ashariya* was the only work of Syed Ahmad in which he had some disagreement with the Shia community regarding the four caliphs of Islam. He also translated a Persian work, *Miyar-ul Uqul* of Abu Ali which contains the five principles of mechanics. In this work pictures of many mechnical devices were shown along with their description and how these devices could be used for lifting heavy objects. It was argued that through the use of such mechanical devices one could save much labour and give more output.[7]

Besides the *Asar-us-Sanadid*,[8] Syed Ahmad Khan wrote a number of scientific articles which were based on discoveries. Since the dawn of history many questions relating to the universe ingaged the human mind and philosophers sought the answer to these questions through deep thinking and observation. It was Aristotle, a Greek philosopher, who believed that the Earth was the centre of universe and that the Sun, stars and planets revolved round it. The Aristotelian-Ptolemaic helio-centric view of the universe, held sway until the rejection of this theory by Copernicus (1473–1543). Thus began the debate and a true scientific revolution. Copernicus came to the conclusion that the Sun was the centre of universe, and the planets (including Earth) revolved round it in a fixed orbit. Copernicus published his famous book *On the Revolution of Heavenly Bodies* in which he explained that the Sun and stars are motionless; that the Sun lies at the centre and the stars at the circumference of the universe; that the Earth rotates about its axis taking twenty-four hours to complete one revolution; that the Earth and all the planets revolve round the Sun. His work created a great stir, as it contradicted existing religious beliefs.

In his early life, Syed Ahmad Khan was not willing to accept the Ptolemaic view, which seemed to suit one's normal observations, the language of the scripture, and the conclusions of Islamic scientists. In 1848, he published a tract entitled *Qaul-i Matin dar Ibtal-i Harakat-i Zamin* (Powerful Arguments in Showing of the Falseness of Attribution of Motion to the Earth') in refutation of the Copernican theory. Here Syed Ahmad seems to have been inspired by the Holy Koran while discussing the rotation of earth. Syed Ahmad asserted that the Earth was the centre of universe and that the sun rotated around the Earth. He tried to prove his arguments rationally. His arguments were: (i) When we throw a stone upward it comes down at the same place from where it was thrown. This proves that there is no movement of the Earth[9] (ii) If the Earth rotates, then everything on Earth rotates accordingly. Then there was a chance that Delhi would be in Agra (Akbarabad), Akbarabad in Allahabad, the Jama Masjid of Delhi in Mathura, etc. Since that did not happen, it proved that the Earth does not rotate.[10] (iii) If we consider that the Earth rotates on its axis, then everything on the earth would be in motion. In actual fact, however, we see that all things are at rest, unless they move or are moved by forces. Syed Ahmad further argued that if Earth rotates then there must be some force behind it which puts it in motion. But there is no force behind the movement of the Earth so the Earth cannot rotate.[11] (iv) For the movement of anything, two things are required (a) *zati* (personal force), (b) *arzi* (natural force). Further *zati* has been classified in three parts (1) *qisra* (force) (2) *iradi* (intentional), and (3) *tabai* (natural).[12]

At one place Syed Ahmad quotes Maulvi Shah Rafiuddin and Shah Abdul Aziz that they have given 110 different possible forms of the rotation of the Earth and have proved so far that the Earth does not rotate. But these profound examples had not been traced, he wrote.[13]

Later on Syed Ahmad modified his views and withdrew his statements written in the pamphlet in refutation of the Copernican theory. Syed Ahmad wrote that the said pamphlet was written at the insistence of his friends.

During the later half of nineteenth century. Darwin put forth his concept of organic evolution (1859), in which species evolved through natural selection. Syed Ahmad Khan did not agree with the 'Evolution' theory of Darwin and put forth his arguments, against Darwin that the creation of human being was from 'dust or clay' and then from a drop of seed.[14] In support of his argument, he quoted many verses of the Holy Koran, where the creation of human being had been mentioned:

1. . . . Disbelievest thou in his created thee of dust, then of a drop (of seed) and then fashioned thee, a man?[15]
2. O mankind! . . . We have created you from dust, then from a drop of seed, then from a clot, then from a little lump of flesh shapely and shapeless, that we may make (it) clear for you. And we cause what we will to remain in the Womb for an appointed time and afterwards we bring you forth as infant, then (give you growth) that ye attain your full strength.[16]
3. He it is who created you from dust, then from a drop (of seed), then from a clot, then bringeth you forth as a child, then (ordained) that ye attain full strength and afterwards that ye became old man—though some among you die before—and that ye reach an appointed term that happy ye may understand.[17]
4. Was he not a drop of fluid which gushed forth? Then he became a clot; then (Allah) shaped and fashioned.[18]
5. So let man consider from what he is created. He is created from a gushing fluid.[19]
6. He began the creation of man from clay; then he made his seed from a draught of despised fluid; then He fashioned him and breathed into him of His spirit; and appointed for you hearing and sight and hearts.[20]

Anxieties to defend traditional learning gradually began to disappear in Syed Ahmad and he sought a reconciliation between science and Islam. His celebrated belief was the word of God could not be in conflict with the 'work of God'.

He argued that 'no interpretation of the Koran was valid which went against the established law of nature'. Earlier it was interpretated under the influence of Greek learning but now it must be interpreted in the light of modern science; so that the sense of the Koran in our comprehension would keep changing as our scientific knowledge grew.

Syed Ahmad devoted himself to any idea or scheme which could be beneficial to the country and its people. He supported homeopathic treatment for he found it to be reliable and effective for the cure of diseases though its basis was totally different from Greek–Islamic medicine. In 1867 he formed a committee to spread the idea of homeopathic treatment to people and persuade them of its benefits. This committee decided to open a homeopathic clinic in Benaras to be known as the Homeopathic Dispensary and Hospital. Syed Ahmad used every means to convince the people to use homeopathic medicines for chronic disease, and sometimes he sent medicine to those who were unable to come to Benaras.[21]

In December 1867 Syed Ahmad delivered a lecture at the meeting of the committee 'On the History and Practice of Homeopathy Treatment' and argued that it was the most effective and least dangerous of treatments and later wrote a small pamphlet 'On the Treatment of Cholera by Homeopathic Method'.[22]

Syed Ahmad during his membership in the Legislative Council proposed a bill making the small pox vaccination compulsory in the North West Provinces, Awadh and Central Provinces (UP), British Burma, Assam, Ajmer, and in all military contonments.[23] In the post-Mutiny era, Sir Syed tried to give a practical shape to his thought and ideas—principally the upliftment of Indians in general and Muslims in particular. He thought that the best way to prepare Muslims for modern education was through translations of modern European works into vernacular language. Muslims regarded English education sinful and that it was employed to convert Muslims to Christianity, while the Hindus looked upon English education as a means of obtaining employment. Therefore Sir Syed decided that the historical and learned works should be translated from English to Urdu, so that Indians would develop a sense of respect for Western literature and scholarship.[24]

In 1863 Sir Syed published a pamphlet, *Iltamas ba Khidmat-i Shkinan-i Hind dar Bab-i Taraqqi-Tahim-i ahl-i Hind*[25] (A Petition to the People of India Concerning the Development of their Education). The pamphlet urged that the progress and spread of modern education in India would greatly strengthen the foundation of Indian society.

The outcome of his positive endeavour to spread modern scientific education was the foundation of the Translation Society which he established at Ghazipur in 1863.[26] On his transfer to Aligarh, the Society was also transferred to Aligarh under a new name, 'Scientific Society'. The purpose of the Society was to translate the best works of ancient Indian literature and the most useful English works. By 1875 the society had translated and published 27 standard works on various subjects from English into Urdu which included Elphinston's *History of India*, Malcolm's *History of Persia*, Max Müller's works on Sanskrit, Mills *Political Economy*, Leipzig's *Agricultural Chemistry* and Darwin's works.[27]

Moreover, Sir Syed believed that the Muslim needed some special attention and required special arrangements because the Hindus had already accepted Western education due to the efforts of Raja Rammohun Roy, Keshav Chandra Sen and others who had opened the doors for them to Government services. But the Muslims were far behind in Western education because of their false notion of conservatism, religious fanaticism and hatred for the British.[28] Moreover, the confiscation of Muslim property after the Revolt of 1857 had crippled their economy and reduced them to penury. Syed Ahmad had come round to the idea that higher English education was the panacea for all the social and political ills of India particularly for Indian Muslims.[29]

On the occasion of laying the foundation stone of the Mohammedan Anglo-Oriental College (MAO) on 8 January 1877, Sir Syed in his address to Lord Lytton, the then Viceroy, stated the position of Muslims in these words: 'so different in many respects our educational wants from those of the rest of the population of India, that the best measures the Government can adopt, consistency with its polity'. Sir Syed's thinking about Muslims education may be summed up in these words, 'Philosophy may be in our right hand and Natural Science in our left; and the crown of "There is no God but Allah" will adorn our head.' Sir Syed believed that knowledge based on the senses gave man immense power but that it should be subordinate to religion. If it is not subordinate to religion, then it is a satanic force. He wanted Muslim youths to gain excellence in different disciplines and at the same time become true practicing Muslims with all virtues and attributes which Islam seeks to cultivate among its followers—large heartedness, broadmindedness, truthfulness, honestly, integrity and universal brotherhood.

To achieve all these objectives Sir Syed enunciated his education policy: religious knowledge must be in consonance with reason; promote healthy activities through residential institutions; modern science to be taught up to the highest level and a rational outlook cultivated among students. To implement his education policy Sir Syed established the Scientific Society; MAO College and Mohammedan Educational Conference (1886). The MAO College formed the nucleus of his movement.

In order to keep Muslims well informed about national and international affairs Sir Syed started his famous weekly, the *Aligarh Institute Gazette* in 1866. On his return from England he started *Tahzib-ul Akhlaq* to bring the news of scientific developments that were taking place all over the world to the Muslim masses.

NOTES

1. C.H. Philip, ed., *Correspondence of Lord William C. Bentick*, vol. 2, London: Oxford University Press, 1977, p. 1405.
2. Altaf Husain Hali, *Hayat-i Javed*, tr. K.H. Qadri and D.J. Mathews, Delhi: Idarah-i-Adabiyat-i-Delhi, 1979, p. 1.
3. Ibid., pp. 23–4.
4. Ibid., p. 25.
5. For instance, there was a dancing girl, called Shirin Jan, who was renowned for her beauty, while her mother was a dark-skinned lady. When Syed's friend remarked about her mother, Sir Syed replied 'Indeed she is sour, but has borne the sweetest fruit'. Hali, *Hayat-i Javed,* p. 26.
6. Ibid., pp. 31–2.
7. Originally this was published in Arabic. Abu Ali translated it into Persian.
8. *Asar-us-Sanadid* was published by Syed Ahmad Khan which deals with the monument of Delhi. Besides there is a large collection of archaeological material available in the Archaeology Section, Department of AMU, Aligarh. In his collection there are a number sculptures of Hindu deities. By going through these collections one realizes that Sir Syed Ahmad Khan was a true Indian with a deep affection and love for his motherland and therefore, tried to preserve the cultural heritage of India.
9. Syed Ahmad Khan, '*Qaul-i Matin-dar Ibtal-i Harkat-i Zamin*, Delhi: Sayyid-ul Akhbar, 1948, p. 4.
10. Ibid., p. 9. Here Syed Ahmad was ignoring the eastward momentum of the Earth's movement.

11. Ibid., p. 12. Syed Ahmad Khan here not only forgets the eastward momentum, but also that objects on Earth without such movement would move eastwards, not northwards or southwards.
12. Ibid., p. 13.
13. Ibid., p. 11.
14. Syed Ahmad Khan, *Khalaqal Insan Mafil Koran.*
15. *Surah*, Al-Kahf (Holy Koran), 18: 37.
16. *Surah*, Al-Hajj (The Pilgrimage), the Holy Koran, 22: 5.
17. *Surah*, Al-Mumin (The Believer), the Holy Koran, 40: 67.
18. *Surah*, Al-Qiyamah (The Rising of the Dead), the Holy Koran, 75: 34 and 38.
19. *Surah*, Al-Tariq (The Holy Koran), 86: 5, 6 and 7.
20. *Surah*, Al-Sajdah (The Prostration), the Holy Koran, 32: 7, 8, 9.
21. *Hayat-i Javed* (tr.), pp. 98–9.
22. Ibid., p. 99.
23. Ibid., p. 177.
24. Ibid., p. 85.
25. Ibid., p. 85.
26. Ibid., pp. 86–8, see also Ishrat Ali Qureshi, *Aligarh Past and Present*, Aligarh: AMU, 1992, p. 29.
27. Qureshi, pp. 29–30.
28. Tara Chand, *History of Freedom Movement*, Delhi, 1967, p. 361.
29. G.F.I. Graham, *The Life and Works of Sir Syed Ahmad Khan*, London, 1885, p. 268.

CHAPTER 8

Sir Syed's Movement for Modern Education in Muzaffarpur (Bihar)

M. SAJJAD

It has assumed a proportion of truism, and rightly so, that Sir Syed Ahmad was the first and foremost person to have persuaded the north Indian Muslims to obtain modern education. From Lahore to Calcutta, many places witnessed the emergence of various associations, societies, educational institutions to spread modern education and obtain government jobs in the colonial administration of India.[1] The entire movement is known in India's history as the Aligarh movement, simply because the town of Aligarh happened to have become the centre of Sir Syed's unforgettable efforts towards modern education for the Indian Muslims. Moreover, his efforts fructified (in 1920) into the most enduring and ever expanding institution called the Aligarh Muslim University (AMU).

However, there were other places too, where significant impact and replication of the Aligarh movement took place. Muzaffarpur,[2] in northern Bihar, was one such place, where probably the strongest impact of the Aligarh movement could be seen.[3]

The moving spirit behind this movement in Muzaffarpur was Syed Imdad Ali (d. August 1886). Quite a lot of details about him have been given by Dr B.K. Sinha[4] and Ashfaq Ahmad Arfi.[5] Yet, there are many significant aspects which remain unexplored. It has been said that there is 'no direct evidence of the fact that Syed Imdad Ali of Muzaffarpur had any connection with Sir Syed Ahmad Khan'.[6] But way back in 1960, the great Urdu scholar and freedom fighter of Patna, Qazi Abdul Wadood, had published an essay giving evidence of correspondence between Sir Syed Ahmad Khan and Syed Imdad Ali.[7] Moreover, the French Professor, Garcien de Tassey, provides us with a lot of detailed information about the accomplishments of Syed Imdad Ali's Bihar Scientific Society of Muzaffarpur.[8]

Syed Imdad Ali had started his career as an employee in the revenue department in 1829 and rose to the post of the Deputy Collector.[9] He subsequently switched over to the judicial services and became *Munsif* in 1848, rose to the post of Subordinate Judge (*Sadar Amin*) and retired as such in 1875. Like Sir Syed Ahmad, Imdad Ali was also an eye witness to the upsurge of 1857 when he was posted at Arrah in Bihar.

In 1863, the then Sub-Judge of Ghazipur, Sir Syed Ahmad established his Scientific Society with the objective of disseminating European knowledge and modern education. Similarly Syed Imdad Ali also founded the 'Bihar Scientific Society' at Muzaffarpur, on 24 May 1868. He was then posted there as Sub-Judge. He advocated that European sciences should be taught to the Indians in their own language. His tremendous faith in the efficacy of the vernacular languages is testified by his letter to S.W. Fallon (Inspector of Schools, North-West Division, Dinapore, Patna). He wrote: England, France and Germany would never have attained that exalted degree of Civilization which they now enjoy if the works of sciences originally imported from Rome and Greece, in Latin and Greek, were not disseminated among the people by means of their own vernacular.'[10]

He expressed his enthusiasm to welcome the Government of India's Resolution (No. 2296 dated 31 March 1870) aimed at diffusion of general education in the languages of the people throughout British India.

Thus, to actualize the spreading of European scientific knowledge through Indian languages, Imdad Ali founded the Bihar Scientific Society. W.W. Hunter (the then Director-General, Statistics, Govt. of India) informs us:

> ... The Behar Scientific Society, is primarily made up of Mohammedans, and was founded in 1868, under the title of the, 'British Indian Association, with the object of criticizing the proceedings of the Government and defending the people from oppression by conveying their true complaint to the Government. In 1872, it assumed its present title (i.e. Bihar Scientific Society). Among its objects are spreading the knowledge of European sciences through the vernacular and the establishment of schools, printing presses, and a newspaper.... Arabic and Persian works are to be collected and lectures to be delivered. This Society, in 1871, had 511 members (8 of whom were females), contributing a monthly sum of £ 39.2s. It also supports a school at

Muzaffarpur and a smaller one at Paroo, both being funded by Syed Imdad Ali, some years ago, when he was Subordinate judge. The school at Muzaffarpur had 119 boys on the roll in March 1873, 99 being Mohammedans, 20 Hindus, the majority of the Hindus are Kayasthas. Persian, Sanskrit, Hindustani and Hindi are taught.[11]

Imdad Ali, in his letter to the Viceroy Lord Northbrook, explained,

> . . . the deplorable state of ignorance in which greater portion of my countrymen have for many years immersed excited my deepest sympathies and actuated by the desire of ameliorating as a as lay in my power their unenlightened condition, I took active and principal part in founding the Scientific Society.[12]

The Society launched its fortnightly Urdu newspaper, *Akhbar-ul Akhyar*, from September 1868. It published essays aimed at 'improving moral, intellectual and social condition of the people';[13] it was edited by Babu Ajodhya Prasad 'Bahar',[14] who was a scholar of Persian and Urdu and author of *Gulzar-e-Bahar* or *Reyaz-e-Tirhut*. The editorship was succeeded by Munshi Qurban Ali.

Qazi Abdul Wadood had read some thirty-one issues of the newspaper (from 10 April 1869 to 10 December 1870). These newspapers were sent to Patna (for an exhibition, held by Qazi Abdul Wadoods's *Idara-e-Tehqeeqaat-e-Urdu* in November 1959),[15] by Prof. Maqbool Ahmad of the Central College, Calcutta. One of these issues had reprinted a letter sent by Sir Syed Ahmad to Imdad Ali, during the former's stay in London during 1869–70. The issues of the newspaper, *Akhbar-ul Akhyar* inform us that the founding President of the Society was Nawab Syed Mohd. Taqi, the Secretary was Syed Imdad Ali and the Life Honorary Secretary was Sir Syed Ahmad.[16] The *Awadh Akhbar*, dated 10 November 1876 reports:

> The headquarters of the Behar Scientific Society is Muzaffarpur. The founder of this Society is a learned Muslim. There are 318 members of the Society, presently. Of them, 128 are Muslims, 162 are Hindus and 20 Europeans. . . . There is a proposal that the Society will open a college for the education of Western Sciences and will perform the task of publishing Western knowledges.[17]

Imdad Ali's Society, therefore, established a school at Muzaffarpur to impart scientific knowledge through the vernacular medium. The success of the school was recorded in praiseworthy words of the then officiating Joint Magistrate of Muzaffarpur, J.D. Hodgkinson. He wrote to Imdad Ali,

I visited the Bihar Scientific Society's school yesterday morning, and examined the two upper classes in Euclids, and the fourth class in Arithmetic . . . The boys seemed generally to have a clear knowledge of the propositions of Euclid which I set them and had apparently been well taught.

In appreciation of the good standard of teaching in that school, S.C. Bailey, the officiating judge, offered a silver medal for the boy who displayed the highest general efficiency in all subjects. F.M. Holliday, the officiating Collector also awarded a silver medal.[18]

The ongoing success of the ambitious efforts of Syed Imdad Ali resulted in the opening up of many vernacular schools for teaching European sciences in the vicinity of Muzaffarpur. Under his inspiration, schools were set-up in Saran, Narhan, Jaintpur, Hardi, Paroo, Sitamarhi, etc.[19] He mobilized many influential persons to collect funds and donations. Parmeshwari Prasad Narain Singh of Narhan, offered a sum of Rs. 5,000 for the construction of the school building in his village. Apart from this lump sum of money, he earmarked another Rs. 150 every month to run the school. Mahanth Raja Ram Das of Jaintpur offered Rs. 2,000 for another school to be established in his village.[20] At Paroo, Qazi Syed Abdur Rahaman and Babu Raghunandan Prasad started a school. They provided house for the school, and later it was shifted to its own building.[21] Garcien de Tassey, in his annual lecture of 1870, reports: 'The Society intends to establish a big college and also to provide agrarian and technical education and training to the poor students. Presently, as many as 5 schools are run by the Society, in which, without religious discriminations, Hindus and Muslims participate.'[22]

Garcien de Tassey was extremely surprised about this. He continues,

. . . it appears that Indians don't have any objection against letting their children obtain education together with followers of another religion. This is unlike many people in France and Ireland where many people refrain from allowing their children to have education with the children of different faith.[23]

He further informs that, 'of the 5 schools, one had made particularly greater progress, where, through Urdu medium, the students were taught not only European sciences but also religious things. With this purpose, a *Pundit* to teach Sanskrit and a *Molvi* to teach Arabic were appointed.'[24] Garcien de Tassey, in his subsequent lecture of 1872, says,

. . . the Society has established many schools in Tirhut and other districts. If the government extends its cooperation to the Society then it is expected that, very soon, it will establish few more schools. Thus far, the Society's total asset has been coming from donations provided by the *zamindars* and other rich people. The address of Imdad Ali to the Lt. Governor of Bengal contains the list of the donors.[25]

Sir Syed Ahmad, Syed Imdad Ali, Syed Amir Ali and many other people from different parts of the country were demanding that the government provide for vernacular medium education. Consequently, the Calcutta University Senate, on 12 May 1871, adopted a resolution allowing that the Middle Class Examinations could be written in vernaculars, e.g. Hindustani, Bengali, Oriya, Assamese, etc. Garcien de Tassey testifies that this was largely because of the efforts of Syed Imdad Ali that this could be provided by the University and that it paved the way for government jobs for Indians.[26] As a matter of fact, Imdad Ali had come to command great respect in the intellectual circles and was considered an expert on educational matters. Therefore the Calcutta University Senate, before taking the decision on 12 May 1871, had requested Imdad Ali to send his considered opinion on the subject.

Imdad Ali was quite grateful to the Vice-Chancellor and the Syndicate of the Calcutta University. He suggested that 'the standard prescribed for the University examination be adopted for the vernacular Examination and the science be taught in Urdu or Hindee.'[27] He further demanded that schools should be set-up in every district of Bihar; a college (for the students of the Zilla schools having passed the Entrance examination) should also be opened for higher education. He also suggested that these students be given preference over others, in matters of employment in government services, which he felt would encourage the students to acquire European education.[28]

By that time the Society had enhanced its membership to 500 and it established a college on 7 November 1871.

The foundation of the Central College of Muzaffarpur was laid by the Lt. Governor of Bengal, G. Campbell, on 7 November 1871. This college is situated in the centre of the town in a mango orchard. On the occasion, right since the morning, thousands of people had gathered.

Imdad Ali addressed the people in Hindustani, whereas Campbell and S.W. Fallon addressed in English. Campbell told that even though the government has allowed the vernaculars uptill the Middle class examinations, it would be better to learn English, so that they could obtain university degrees of higher courses.[29]

Thus we see that the movement of Syed Imdad Ali was ahead of the movement of Sir Syed Ahmad in three ways: (a) Imdad Ali's 'Central College' (or collegiate school) of Muzaffarpur was founded on 7 November 1871, i.e. six years earlier than Sir Syed's MAO College of Aligarh (in 1877); (b) Muzaffarpur's Bihar Scientific Society had several schools in different districts, including many in villages, e.g. Paroo, Jaintpur, Hardi, Narhan, etc.[30] It was less elitist in character, having relatively wider reach among the people; (c) compared to Aligarh, the participation of non-Muslims (particularly Hindus) was much more in the Society of Muzaffarpur.[31]

Imdad Ali had realized that only the introduction of vernacular medium of instruction in schools was not enough. He expressed, 'The best way and means of diffusing among the people, of this country the Western Arts and Sciences, which are treated of in works composed in English or in some other language into the native tongue, i.e. into Urdu and to publish and sell them'.[32] Therefore he started a translation department in the Society to make available books in vernacular languages:

> Trigonometry, Material Medica, Optics, Animal Physiology, Chemistry, Dyeing, Geography, Botany, Physical History, Mechanics, Algebra, History of Philosophy, Agriculture, Zoology, Arithmetic, Law of Hospitals, Mineralogy and Masonry.

For this purpose a team of translators was appointed at an expense of Rs. 200 per month.[33] The Society also had its own printing press for publications. The press was called *Chashma-e-Ilm*. Imdad Ali also established a library. Sir Syed's letter to Imdad Ali reveals that he (i.e. Imdad Ali) had sent Rs. 1,000 to Sir Syed (during his stay in London for seventeen months in 1869–70) to purchase books for the library. The text of the letter informs us that on the request of Imdad Ali, Sir Syed prepared a book list and the courses of study with the help of scholars from Oxford and Cambridge and that Sir Syed had sent the books to the library in Muzaffarpur.[34] Garcien de Tassey also corroborates this:

> . . . with the collaboration of the Aligarh Scientific Society, the Bihar Scientific Society has published 5 books and 12 more are being translated. Its library has added, two more books in Arabic, published from Egypt,

130 more books in English pertaining to different subjects. The protagonist of the Society has brought these books on the advice of the British Scholars.[35]

During his stay in London, Sir Syed Ahmad kept making queries about the developments of the Bihar Scientific Society, Muzaffarpur and kept giving advice on educational matters.[36] Meanwhile, on 1 February 1872, a general meeting of the Bihar Scientific Society was held at Muzaffarpur and about a thousand people attended the meeting. Prizes were distributed among the students of the schools managed by the Society. Afterwards, Imdad Ali delivered a brief but categorical speech, explaining about the accomplishments of the Society and its objectives were re-emphasized. In the address, he specifically told the Muslims that they should not be apprehensive that scientific knowledge was against their religion. He also insisted that Muslims acquire English education as it was the key to the treasures of modern knowledge. Then he gave the details of the books already translated or to be translated. He gave the details of the schools, managed by the Society; he admired the students who had performed well in English and in the Calcutta University Examinations. Finally, he presented the account of the income and expenses of the Society.[37] This was the last address of Imdad Ali, as after this he was transferred to the district of Gaya, where he established another branch of the Bihar Scientific Society and established a school there as well, imparting education to a number of students.[38]

The Society at Muzaffarpur had set-up another body called Anjuman-e-Tehzeeb in 1869. It established an orphanage and organized seminars, debates, conferences, educational publication, social reforms, etc., were its major objectives. Within six months of its existence, it earned the laurels of the then Deputy Inspector of Schools. He reported that 'the papers read under the auspices of the Society bore evidences of research and scientific analysis'.[39] A branch was opened at Hajipur, called Refaah-e-Aam (lit. Common welfare); its specific objective was to subscribe to the Indian newspapers for its members.[40]

In 1877, the Anjuman-e-Tehzeeb succeeded in accomplishing one of the objectives of the Bihar Scientific Society, viz., establishing a school of agricultural and technical training.[41] Accordingly, on the occasion of the visit of the Prince of Wales, the college was opened at Muzaffarpur and it was named after the Prince of Wales. Garcien de

Tassey, himself was one of the members of the managing committee of the college.[42]

In September 1873, a branch of the Anjuman-e-Tehzeeb was opened in Patna whose President was Syed Wazir Ali Khan.[43] The contributions of Imdad Ali were duly acknowledged by the Government of Bengal in its resolution dated 9 May 1873. It said, '. . . in all Behar, the most active and successful promoter of Education is a Mohammedan . . .' Bailey also noted, '. . . thanks are due to Syed Imdad Ali . . . the Lt. Governor fully believes that the society is doing a great work'.[44] In the 'Delhi Durbar' of 1878 the Government of India invited Imdad Ali as its guest and conferred upon him the title of *Khan Bahadur*. On his return from Delhi, he suffered a paralytic stroke and died of it in August 1886.[45]

In the efforts of Syed Imdad Ali, his closest companion was Nawab Syed Mohammad Taqi. He was the founding President of the Bihar Scientific Society of Muzaffarpur. Syed Mohd. Taqi's grandfather, Mir Ghulam Haidar Khan, was the *Amil* of *pargana* Baruraj (Muzaffarpur), who was murdered at Baruraj, by a member of the Phalsahi zamindar family, while performing his government duties (the dispute was probably around a temple). While imparting justice to this murder, in the form of wergeld (*Khoon-bahaa*), his two sons, (viz., Mir Yusuf Ali Khan, i.e. father of Syed Mohd. Taqi and Mir Mehdi Ali Khan, were given the zamindari of 1356 villages yielding revenue of about Rs. 1 lakh per annum.[46] Thus Taqi came to be called 'Nawab' and became the raja of Jogriara (near Darbhanga). In 1845, he donated land for the foundation of the 'Zilla School' of Muzaffarpur, and the revenue from a village was earmarked by him for running the school. He also donated land to the college or Collegiate School that was founded on 7 November 1871.[47] (Garcien de Tassey calls it 'Central College', Muzaffarpur.) Syed Md. Taqi was also the founding President of the managing committee of the Muzaffarpur Central College (Collegiate School).[48]

Syed Amir Ali (1849–1928) started the Central Mohammedan Association (CNMA) of Calcutta in 1877 and launched an all-India campaign to enhance the proportion of Muslims in the Indian Civil Services (ICS). Its branch at Muzaffarpur was opened in 1887. The first President of the branch was none but Nawab Syed Mohd. Taqi. It was one of the most vibrant branches as it had eighty-eight members, mostly barristers.[49] After Syed Imdad Ali was transferred to Gaya in 1872, it was Nawab Taqi who sustained the movement for modern education, and continued the activities of the Bihar Scientific Society, Muzaffarpur. Yet it remains to be explored as to what happened to the Bihar Scientific Society in subsequent days, i.e. after 1872. It remains intriguing that compared to the MAO College at Aligarh, the movement for modern education in Muzaffarpur went into oblivion within a rather short period. Sir Syed strengthened and consolidated his movement through an extremely strong vehicle called the All India Muslim Educational Conference (AIMEC, started in 1886). Through this agency, 'Syed Ahmad extended the scope of Aligarh's influence to Muslims throughout India'. Both Sir Syed and Morison (the Principal of the MAO College, Aligarh) insisted on the need for higher education for Muslims and to fulfil the task, and opposed the establishment of small English schools in various parts of India. They preached that all such funds should be pooled together to concentrate on development of one institution, i.e. the MAO College, Aligarh, which had to be developed into a university for Muslims. Endorsing Sir Syed's view, Morison said, '. . . the logical way out is that (the MAO College, Aligarh) be extended and efforts to establish colleges in other regions or districts would be futile. . . . We should make it attractive for all the Muslims of different provinces to receive education here. . . .'[50]

This persuasion might have been one of the reasons for abandonment of the idea of establishing and running schools in different parts of India and concentrating upon developing the Aligarh College. Small wonder then that all the important leaders of Bihar associated themselves with the AIMEC. Maulana Md. Sulaiman Phulwarwi (1857–1935) joined the AIMEC after Sir Syed's death and being a powerful orator, his speeches in the annual meetings of the AIMEC helped mobilize great funds, while campaigning for a Muslim university. One Syed Muzaffar Husain acted as the permanent *safeer*, i.e. paid agent (from 1905 to 1945) of the AIMEC's Bihar branch and Muzaffarpur was a promising centre for his campaign. Sir Ali Imam (1869–1932) and Mazharul Haq (1866–1930) joined the AIMEC's campaign for a Muslim University. Dr Syed Mahmud (1889–1971), arranged the AIMEC session at Patna in 1938, when he was the Minister of Education in the Government of Bihar during 1937–9. Such a powerful mass movement of the AIMEC (particularly in its 1895 session at Agra), the Aligarh College was projected to emerge as a University with power to affiliate the schools/colleges run by Muslims in different parts of India.[51] This mass movement of

'Muslim solidarity in British India', financed by the Muslim princely states and landed elites, put enough political pressure on the colonial state to enhance grants, provide lands and ultimately in 1920 giving it the status of a university.[52] This shift in the priority of the Muslims might have been the reason for the decline of the Bihar Scientific Society, Muzaffarpur.[53]

Nevertheless, two significant bits of informations, which could be obtained, are given below:

1. Sir Syed Ahmad visited Patna twice, on 26 May 1873 and again on 27 January 1883. It was probably in 1883 that he also visited Muzaffarpur. He was given hospitality by Hafiz Shah Rahmatuallah 'Ahqar' (d. 1927), the founder of the Madrasa Jamial Uloom (founded in the 1880s or AH 1307). This *madrasa* was meant to impart education, not only in Islamic theology but also in poetic literature, modern criticism and history. Ahqar was a good poet, used to host poetic assemblies (*mushaira*) and presented a versified welcome speech (*Sepaas Naama*) to Sir Syed. This poem (*Sepaas Naama*) is included in Ahqar's unpublished collection of ghazals (*Deewan*). Ahqar was much influenced by the anti-colonial ideology of the so-called 'Wahhabi' movement of Syed Ahmad of Rai Bareli.[54] Ahqar was one of the greatest freedom fighters of Muzaffarpur during the Non-Cooperation/Khilafat movement. He also started the Urdu Sahityik Sabha for Urdu–Hindi friendship in 1914.[55] Ahqar died in 1927, after him, the Sabha was run by Syed Shah Qari Abdul Majeed 'Muztar', a famous poet. The Sabha continued up till 1940.

Ahqar, was the grandson of Molvi Shah Ahmadullah,[56] and his great grandfather was a *qazi* in the district of Murshidabad (Bengal) from where, he was sent by his *pir* to Muzaffarpur, possibly for missionary purposes. Shah Ahmadullah constructed a mosque in the Chhaata Bazar (literally umbrella market) locality of Muzaffarpur. There he purchased some land near Chandwara, where, Ahqar established the Madarsa Jamial Uloom.

Ahqar's son Hafiz Nematullah (d. 1944), was a poet with the *nom de plume,* 'Razi'. He was one of the leading freedom fighters during the Civil Disobedience movement, of 1930–2.[57] Ahqar's grandson, Ghulam Mohammad established the Urdu Girls High School, Muzaffarpur, in 1975.

2. Another significant information about the 'movement' of the Bihar Scientific Society comes from the *Bengal District Gazetteers* of Muzaffarpur written by L.S.S. O'Malley, who says that in 1899, the

Society started a college with a 'trust fund of Rs. 50,000 contributed by the Bhumihar Brahman Sabha, affiliated to the Calcutta University'.[58]

The college was named, Bhumihar Brahman College. In 1915, it was renamed Grierson Bhumihar Brahman College and again in 1951, it was named after Langat Singh.[59] In 1952, responding to a strong public demand, the Bihar University was established (in fact, it was shifted from Patna) in the 'premises' of the L.S. College. Maghfur Ahmad Aijazi (died 1967), a valiant freedom fighter of Muzaffarpur, was one of the leaders who launched a successful campaign for the university.[60]

It is probably an irony of historic proportion that the contributions of the Bihar Scientific Society of Imdad Ali remains absolutely unacknowledged by the college and its organs. Can one hope for the retrieval of the history of the Bihar Scientific Society, Muzaffarpur? Must not we listen to the cry of Syed Imdad Ali?

Hamara naam andheron mein kho gaya lekin
Kabhi charaagh jalaaye the shahar mein ham ney

[Ameer Imam]

Acknowledgements: I am thankful to Prof. Mushirul Hasan, who advised me to write on this aspect. I am also thankful to my teacher Prof. R.K. Trivedi for his invaluable comments. Prof. Iftikhar Malik's queries also proved to be of immense help.

NOTES

1. For example, Nawab Abdul Lateef founded the Mohammedan Literary and Scientific Society in Calcutta in 1863. Syed Ameer Ali founded the Central National Mohammedan Association in Calcutta in 1877. Ghulam Md. Munshi and Md. Ali Roonje founded the Anjuman-e-Islamia in Bombay in 1876. Barkaat Ali founded the Anjuman-e-Islamia in Lahore in 1869.
2. The town/city of Muzaffarpur, is said to have been founded by Nawab Reza Khan Muzaffar Jang, the *Amil* of Chakla Nai. 'Many years before, the East India Company's accession to *Diwani* (1765)', says W.W. Hunter, 'Muzaffar Jang selected 75 *bighas* of land from the villages of Sikandarpur, on the north, Kanhauli on the east, Saiyadpura on the south, and Saraiyaganj on the west, and called the land after his own

name. In 1817, it only contained 667 houses, of which 408 paid no rent, the total assessment amounting to £391.8s. In 1871 it suffered greatly from an inundation of the Little Gandak'. (W.W. Hunter, *A Statistical Account of Bengal*, vol. XIII, London, 1877, p. 52.) In 1872, 'the total population of the town was 38,223, out of which, 10,671 were Muslims. A good deal of trade was carried through the Little Gandak (ibid., p. 51). The town is clear and streets in many cases broad and well kept'. (Also see Iqbal Husain's *Daastaan Meri*', Urdu autobiography, Patna, 1989.) A good deal of details about Nawab Reza Khan Muzaffar Jang is contained in Karam Ali's *Muzaffarnama*. (Also see Qurratulain Haidar's Urdu short story, 'Dareen Gard Sawaar-e-Baashad', in her collection, *Jugnuon ki Duniya*, Delhi, 2001.) Surprisingly, one of the most authoritative biography of the Nawab (Abdul Majed Khan, *Transition in Bengal, 1756–75: A Study of Saiyid Md. Reza Khan*, Cambridge, 1969) does not mention his role in developing the urban centre of Muzaffarpur. It is also said that the town is named after Muzaffar Khan Turbati, a General of the Mughal Emperor Akbar, who, in the 1570s, had erected a cantonment here, to take care of the Afghan rebels taking shelter in the foothills (*tarai*) of Nepal. This cantonment led to the emergence of a market which was developed into a town in the eighteenth century by the Nawab, Reza Khan Muzaffar Jung. In 1772, Muzaffar Jang was sacked by Lord Clive. His son Dildar Jang was given annual pension of Rs. 1.5 lakh and the jagir of Tirhut (Muzaffarpur) was seized by Warren Hastings in 1782. See Qurratulain Haider's autobiographical novel, *Kaar-e-Jahaan Daraaz Hai*, vol. 1, p. 180, Delhi, 2003.

In 1782, it was made the district headquarter of Tirhut, which then included the present-day districts of Muzaffarpur, Vaishali, Sitamarhi, Sheohar, Darbhanga, Madhubani, Samastipur. In 1875, the last three were separated to become Darbhanga district whereas the city of Muzaffarpur remained the headquarters of the district of Muzaffarpur. Presently it is also the headquarters of the Tirhut Division consisting of the district of East Champaran, West Champaran, Sheohar, Sitamarhi, Vaishali, and Muzaffarpur.

3. Taqi Raheem, *Tehreek-e-Aazadi Mein Bihar key Musalman ka Hissa*, Patna: KBL, 1998.
4. B.K. Sinha, 'Syed Imdad Ali: An Eminent Educationist of 19th Century Bihar', *Journal of Historical Research*, Ranchi, 1970.
5. Ashfaq Ahmad Arfi, 'Sir Syed Tehreek Aur Subah-e-Bihar', *Fikro Nazar*, Urdu quarterly, Aligarh, 1992.
6. K.K. Datta and J.S. Jha, eds., *A Comprehensive History of Bihar*, vol. III, part, II, Patna, 1976, p. 449.
7. Qazi Abdul Wadood, 'Akhbar ul Akhyaar, Muzaffarpur Aur Sir Syed', *Fikro Nazar*, Aligarh, July 1960.

8. *Maqalaat-e-Garcien de Tassey*, vol. I, Delhi: Anjuman Taraqqi Urdu, 1943.
9. Imdad Ali's ancestors had distinguished themselves for political and religious wisdom and had rendered important services to the Mughal and British rulers of India. His forefather, Syed Wajihuddin, came to India in 1468 and settled in Bihar complying with the request of Nasib Shah, the ruler of Bengal. He had a spiritual standing and was considered a *pir* over greater parts of Bengal, Bihar and what is now UP. (B.K. Sinha). The family history claims descendence from the Prophet Muhammad, on his father's side through Syed Ahmad Wali of Turkistan. He is also related to the Prophet through his mother through Syed Mohiuddin Abdul Qadir Jilani of Baghdad. Syed Ahmad Wali was said to be universally acknowledged as a ruler and a spiritual leader of Turkistan. (*A Brief History and Genealogical Tree or Pedigree of Moulvi Syed Imdad Ali, Khan Bahadur and His Descendents*, Calcutta, 1916, cited by B.K. Sinha.)
10. B.K. Sinha cites it from the Proceedings of the 3rd Annual General Meeting of the Scientific Society held at Muzaffarpur on 24 May 1871.
11. W.W. Hunter, *A Statistical Account of Bengal*, vol. 13, London, 1877, p. 164.
12. B.K. Sinha cites the letter from the Proceedings of the general meeting of the Bihar Scientific Society held at Muzaffarpur on 1 February 1872.
13. As recorded in the proceedings of its meeting held on 1 February 1872, and corroborated by Garcien de Tassey, vol. I, p. 4.
14. The ancestors of Munshi Ajodhya Prasad 'Bahaar' belonged to the qasba Maner, Patna. (Syed Badruddin Ahmed, *Haqeeqat bhi, kahaani bhi*, Urdu autobiography, Patna, 1988, 2003, p. 436.) His father, Gopal Lal Khatri was a Thanedar in Tirhut (see Bihari Lal 'Fitrat', *Aina-e Tirhut*, Lucknow, 1883, p. 193). Another Ajodhya Prasad Khatri (1857-1905) was also there in Muzaffarpur, who in the 1880s–1890s emerged as a great protagonist of the *Khari Boli*.
15. Syed Badruddin Ahmed, pp. 475–8.
16. Qazi Abdul Wadood.
17. Cited by Ashfaq Arfi, op. cit., p. 204. The membership increased to 500 in 1872 (de Tassey, p. 168).
18. B.K. Sinha, p. 3.
19. For a brief profile of Qazi Syed Abdur Rahman (d. 1889) of Paroo, see Maulana Abdul Kalam Qasmi Shamsi, *Tazkera-e-Ulema-e-Bihar*, p. 142. Also see Bihari Lal, p. 111.

    The freedom fighter, Begum Zubaida Daudi, wife of the great freedom fighter, Shafi Daudi (1875–1949), belonged to this family of Paroo. (See, Abida Samiuddin, *Tehreek-e-Azaadi mein Muslim Khwateen ka Hissa*, Patna, 1990.) Syed Sulaiman Nadvi's second marriage took place in this family of Paroo. See Syed Arshad Aslam, comp., *Mataa-e-Gum Gushta,* Paroo, Muzaffarpur, 2002. The author, Syed Arshad Aslam claims that, influenced by the movement of Shah Waliullah (1702–60) and Syed Ahmed of Rae Bareli (d. 1831), one Nadir Ali moved towards north Bihar and went up to the village Chandi Dhanki, Lalganj, Vaishali after the mutiny of 1857, when the Muslim community was full of dispair. His sons Qazi Abdul Waahid settled at Syedani, near Saraiya; Qazi Abdul Nasir settled at Churihar and Qazi Syed Abdur Rehman (d. 1889) settled at Paroo. Supposedly, they settled in the villages to help the Muslims overcome the post mutiny frustration. He was also the founder of the office of the Registrar for sale and purchase of lands at Paroo. Qazi Syed Abdur Rehman's son, Syed Abul Fateh was also the Hony. Registrar of Paroo.

20. Proceedings of the 3rd general meeting of the Society held at Muzaffarpur, on 24 May 1871, cited B.K. Sinha.
21. Hunter, *A Statistical Account of Bengal*, op. cit.
22. Garcien de Tassey, p. 5.
23. Ibid., p. 171.
24. Ibid.
25. Ibid., pp. 167–9.
26. Proceedings of the 3rd annual general meeting of the Society held at Muzaffarpur on 24 May 1871, cited by B.K. Sinha.
27. Ibid.
28. Garcien de Tassey, p. 173.
29. Ibid. It may be noted that, it was this very address of Campbell, in which, an unambiguous colonial exposition against Urdu was done for the first time, giving rise to a sharp Hindi–Urdu divide in India.
30. In these villages, schools and colleges are still running to provide a quality education to the people of the area. The high school at Hardi happens to be one of the oldest rural high schools of western Muzaffarpur. Similarly the Government Degree College at Jaintpur is one of the oldest degree colleges of rural Bihar, with relatively good infrastructure, including hostels.
31. Taqi Raheem and Muzaffar Imam, *Role of Muslims in the National Movement, Bihar, 1912–30*, Delhi, 1987, are of the view that this Hindu–Muslim cooperation was one of the few factors leading to lesser communal confrontation in Bihar compared to colonial Bengal and UP.
32. Proceedings of the general meeting of the Scientific Society Muzaffarpur, dated 24 May 1871.
33. *A Brief History and Genealogical Tree or Pedigree of Syed Imdad Ali & His Descendents*, Calcutta, 1916. Garcien de Tassey, says that the department of translation got Rs. 300 per month.
34. Qazi Abdul Wadood.
35. Garcien de Tassey, p. 170.

36. Ashfaq Arfi, p. 208. See Qazi Abdul Wadood.
37. Gacien de Tassey, pp. 267–8. See *Akhbar-e-Anjuman-e-Punjab*, 1 March 1872.
38. Gacien de Tassey, vol. 2, p. 176.
39. Datta and Jha, op. cit., p. 449.
40. Garcien de Tassey, vol. 2, p. 283.
41. Syed Badruddin Ahmed (p. 456), informs us that the Bihar Scientific Society had also wished to establish an Urdu University. The movement and the scheme, however, could not accomplish this particular objective.
42. Ibid.
43. Ibid., p. 276; Ashfaq Arfi, p. 206.
44. *A Brief History and Genealogical Tree or Pedigree of Syed Imdad Ali & His Descendents,* cited by B.K. Sinha.
45. Ibid.
46. Bihari Lal Fitrat, p. 262.
47. I owe this information to Dr. Syed Mehdi Ahmad Rizvi, Reader, Department of Urdu, LNT College, Muzaffarpur. He claims to be a descendent of Nawab Taqi. (Interview on 5 June 2005.)
48. The text of the inscription of the foundation stone of the college, now known as the Bhumihar Brahman Collegiate School, contains this information.
49. M.Yusuf Abbasi, ed., *Annals of the Central National Mohammedan Association*, Islamabad 1992. This mentions the names of all 88 members of the Muzaffarpur branch of the Association.
50. AIMEC Report, 1893, pp. 129–30, cited by Abdul Rashid Khan, *The All India Muslim Educational Conference: Its Contribution to the Cultural Development of Indian Muslims, 1886–1947*, Karachi: Oxford University Press, 2001, p. 62 . For Sir Syed's views against establishment of educational institutions in different parts of India, see Syed Ahmad Khan, *Khitab Ba Tarif Musalmanan e Hind in 1893*, Agra, 1894, pp. 4–5.
51. The Select Committee of MAO College, Aligarh, since its foundation, always nursed the ambition of emerging as a university with power to affiliate the Muslim managed schools and colleges running in different parts of India. See David Lelyveld, *Aligarh's First Generation: Muslim Solidarity in British India*, Delhi: Oxford University Press, p. 135.
52. See Abdul Rashid Khan, pp. 63–4. Also see, Gail Minault and David Lelyveld, 'Campaign for a Muslim University, 1898–1920', in *Modern Asian Studies*, vol. 8, no. 2, 1974, pp. 145–89.
53. After 1895, the AIMEC became more vocal about a Muslim University at Aligarh, with affiliating jurisdiction over the whole of India. It is interesting to note that from 1898 a vigorous campaign for a Muslim university at Aligarh started and the Bihar Scientific Society practically ceased to exist after 1899 when it established the college at Muzaffarpur,

in collaboration with the Bhumihar Brahman Sabha. It may probably be conjectured that after the campaign for Muslim University started, Muslims from all over India mainly concentrated on Aligarh rather than diverting the funds to scattered institutions. This seems more probable because with the turn of the twentieth century, Bengal emerged as one of the most popular destinations for fund raising for a Muslim University at Aligarh. In December 1899, Calcutta hosted the AIMEC, presided over by Syed Ameer Ali. After it, a number of branches of the AIMEC came up in Bengal. In 1904, at Rajshahi (in eastern Bengal), a huge meeting of the AIMEC was held for a Muslim University at Aligarh. In fact, Bengal (Bihar included) responded to this campaign only when the proposed Muslim university at Aligarh promised to obtain affiliating jurisdiction over the whole of India. Otherwise, the Bengal Muslims were not very enthusiastic about a Muslim university at Aligarh. G. Minault and D. Lelyveld, in their essay clearly show that during the entire period of campaign for Muslim university (1898–1920), whenever the prospect for affiliating authority looked bleak, the fund raising of the movement plummeted down.

54. I owe this information to Syed Ehtesham of Chandwara, Muzaffarpur (interview on 13 June 2005). He is the Social Security Officer of the district. He claims to have read the poem (*Sepaas Naama*) written by Ahqar. He also claims to be a descendent of a branch of the family of Ahqar.
55. Sita Ram Singh, 'Muzaffarpur: Itihaas ke Darpan Mein', in *Smarika*, Bihar Madhyamik Shikshak Sangh, 43rd Adhiveshan, Muzaffarpur, 1992.
56. He belonged to the tradition of Syed Ahmad Shaheed of Rae Bareli. See Bihari Lal, 'Fitrat', p. 104.
57. Muzaffar Imam, p. 223.
58. L.S.S. O'Malley, *Bengal District Gazetteers, Muzaffarpur*, Calcutta, 1907, p. 134. This is also testified by other accounts which say that the Society handed over its 'Collegiate' school to Langat Singh in 1899 to start a college there. See Muzaffar Imam, p. 21. Dr. Shamim Ahmad, 'Scientific Society, Muzaffarpur', in *4th All India Muslim Educational Conference*, Patna: Khuda Bakhsh Library, 1973, pp. 69–73.

Mr Naved Masood, IAS, has informed me that the 'Societies Registartion Act of 1860' did not allow a sectarian organization like the Bhumihar Brahman Sabha to open an educational institution. The Bhumihar Brahman Sabha, therefore, deposited Rs. 50,000 to the trust of the Bihar Scientific Society to deposit it into the Senate of the Calcutta University to open the college in 1899 at Muzaffarpur. This policy envisaged by the Act, was however, revised subsequently to grant university status to BHU in 1915 and to AMU in 1920. But by late nineteenth and early twentieth century, there started a sort of movement in favour of establishing educational institutions 'which should reflect heritage' of different communities. 'Colleges such as Annie Besant's Central Hindu College, the Arya Samaj's DAV Colleges, the Khalsa College of the Sikhs and the Aligarh Muslim College were all part of a general movement by Indians to create an education that would reflect their heritage'. (See Leah Renold, *A Hindu Education: Early Years of the Banaras Hindu University*, Delhi: Oxford University Press, 2005, p. 47.) Harcourt Butler, in 1911, persuaded the colonial government that in the face of the rise of sectarian schools, the government must increase its control and that, 'it is necessary that the government should lead the educational movement'. (See Leah Renold.)

59. The Bhumihar Brahaman Sabha was founded by the Raja of Banaras, at Patna in 1889. See Prasanna K. Chaudhry and Shrikant, *Bihar Mein Samajik Parivartan ke Kuch Aayaam*, Delhi: Vaani, 2001. Langat Singh, a railway contractor, was associated with the Sabha, and from 1899 to 1909 he remained the greatest donor of the college. (For a profile of Langat Singh, see Mark Tully, *No Full Stops in India*, Delhi: Viking, 1991). A Hindi biography of Langat Singh was published by Rambriksha Benipuri (d. 1968), no longer in print now.
60. For details, see Aijazi Papers, NMML, New Delhi, and my essay in *Tehzeeb ul-Akhlaq*, Urdu monthly, Aligarh, February 2004. Also see my forthcoming monograph, *Against Colonialism and Separatism: Muslims of Muzaffarpur Since 1857*.

CHAPTER 9

Sir Syed's Early Journalistic Endeavours: A Critical Appraisal

SHAFEY KIDWAI

Not much has been written about Sir Syed's early journalistic writings and his professional stint with the newspapers has almost escaped the attention of his biographers including Graham and Hali. Even the focused studies of his journalistic writings by Asghar Abbas (1975) and Nafees Bano (1993) hardly refer to his early journalistic endeavours. In this paper an attempt is being made to supplement and scrutinize what has been left out and the newspapers that attracted Sir Syed, who got himself associated with them in one capacity or the other.

SAYYIDUL AKHBAR

The popularity and respectability of *Urdu Akhbar*, the first Urdu weekly of Delhi had inspired Syed Mohammad Khan, elder brother of Sir Syed, to start a newspaper. Syed Mohammad launched a weekly *Sayyidul Akhbar* in 1837 which was erroneously described by Margarita Barns as the first newspaper in Urdu.[1]

Nadig Krishnamurthy too endorses Margarita by asserting that *Sayyidul Akhbar* is generally mentioned as a pioneer in the field.[2]

Margarita and Krishnamurthy's claims aside, the year of *Sayyidul Akhbar's* launch seems to be a contentious and highly debatable issue. Notwithstanding the controversy, it is generally believed that Sir Syed learnt his early professional lessons and got hands-on training at *Sayyidul Akhbar*. Since a lot of fog has been allowed to gather around *Sayyidul Akhbar*, it is essential to call attention to claims and counter-claims with objectivity. A number of historians of early Indian journalism including Dr Bhatnagar (1947), Imdad Sabri (1953),

S. Natrajan (1955), Mohammad Ateeq Siddiqui (1957), Abdus Salam Khurshid (1963), Nadig Krishnamurthy (1966) and Emmet Davis (1983) have asserted that *Sayyidul Akhbar* was started in 1837. Contrary to this, a reference in a report published by the Government Press in 1868 had put a question mark on the year of its launch.

The Government of North Western Provinces prepared an administrative report for the perusal of the Lieutenant-Governor of North Western Provinces. Mohammad Ateeq Siddiqui tracked down the report and translated the report concerning newspapers and publications of the North Western Provinces from 1848 to 1853.[3] A Shakespeare, Asistant Secretary, prepared the report for the year 1848 that states that *Sayyidul Akhbar* was started in 1841 and was said to be the organ of the Sunni sects of the Muslims and mentioned Sayyid Abdul Ghafoor as its owner and editor.

Shakespeare's claim prompted two historians of early Urdu journalism, Nadir Ali Khan (1987) and Tahir Masood (2002) to conclude that the *Sayyidul Akhbar* was started in 1841, not in 1837 as claimed by Hali and other biographers of Sir Syed and historians of Urdu journalism.

The report in question pertains to 1848, which makes a casual reference to *Sayyidul Akhbar*. It mentions the name of its proprietor, Sayyid Abdul Ghafoor but an authentic contemporary evidence makes it clear that its owner was Sayyid Mohammad Khan who had set up a lithographic press in Delhi. This evidence pertains to the first collection of Ghalib, which was printed at this press. The title page of the first edition of *Diwan-e-Ghalib* (Collection of Ghalib) carries the following line at the bottom: Printed at Sayyid Mohammad Khan's Lithographic Press in the month of Shaban 1125 Hijra, i.e. October 1841 under the supervision of Sayyid Abdul Ghafoor.

The print line makes it clear that the press was owned by Sayyid Mohammad Khan, Abdul Ghafoor was an employee; not the owner as erroneously described by the report. Further, one more contemporary evidence contradicts the assertion of the official report which says that Sayyid Abdul Ghafoor was the owner of *Sayyidul Akhbar*.

Sayyid Mohammad Khan, the owner of the *Sayyidul Akhbar* died of fever.[4]

This official report, which was used as a clinching proof by Ateeq Siddiqui, Nadir Ali Khan and Tahir Masood, made a passing reference to the year of *Sayyidul Akhbar's* launch after a gap of eleven years and it provided no concrete proof in this regard. A prolific writer and a close associate of Sir Syed, Zakaullah who lived in Delhi mentioned that *Sayyidul Akhbar* was launched between 1836 and 1837.

Hence, the official report is not correct for as other equally reliable contemporary evidences point out that *Sayyidul Akhbar* was launched in 1837, not in 1841. Needless to say, that simple assertions cannot take precedence over contemporary evidence. Therefore its looks plausible to conclude that *Sayyidul Akhbar* was started in 1837.

Some historians of Urdu journalism asserted that *Sayyidul Akhbar* was named after Sir Syed and that it shows Syed Mohammad Khan's affection for his younger brother. This assertion gained currency despite its imprecise mein. Syed is the family surname and Ahmad is the real name of Sir Syed. Had it been *Ahmadul Akhbar*, one would have accepted the argument. Syed was also very much part of the editor's name—Syed Mohammad Khan. The title of the newspaper is based on the family surname Syed.

The files of *Sayyidul Akhbar* have been consigned to oblivion but the files of some contemporary newspapers such as *Sadarul Akhbar* (Agra) and *Ahsan-ul Akhbar* (Bombay) which reproduced materials from *Sayyidul Akhbar*, are available. One could glean some pieces of information from them. Tahir Masood quoted some news items from the *Sayyidul Akhbar* that reappeared in *Sadarul Akhbar*.

Sayyidul Akhbar appeared on Wednesday and its subscription rate was Rs. 2 per month. Its editor Sayyid Abdul Ghafoor was well-versed in legal affairs as a number of editorials appeared on the Bills and Regulations enacted by the British Government. The newspaper was very popular among advocates.[5]

Since Syed Mohammad Khan was in government service, he appointed Sayyid Abdul Ghafoor its editor.

The circulation of *Sayyidul Akhbar* was, according to the official report, restricted to fifty in 1844. Eleven copies were complimentary and 39 were dispatched to its subscribers with the following break up: 'Muslims 32, Hindus 6 and the Governor-General one'.[6]

The most popular newspaper of Delhi, *Urdu Akhbar*, was edited by a well-known Shia clergy Moulvi Sayyid Mohammad Baqar and the Sunnis accused him of sectarian bias. *Sayyidul Akhbar* used to give much space to the viewpoint of the Sunnis. Generally, it was regarded as the organ of the Sunnis, as sometimes the writings published in *Sayyidul Akhbar* were partial and bordered on polemics. It usually carried eight pages and news, poems and verses formed its editorial content.

Hali made a brief reference to *Sayyidul Akhbar* and claimed that Sir Syed got hands-on training at his elder brother's newspaper and also got his early articles published in it.

'He [Sir Syed] planned to develop the newspaper *Sayyidul Akhbar*, which had been managed by his brother and published a book on the buildings of Delhi. Although the newspaper was nominally directed by someone else. It was in fact Sir Sayyid who contributed most of the articles.'[7]

Sir Abdul Qadir, a prominent Urdu writer while endorsing Hali asserts that Sir Syed laid the firm foundation of his journalism by writing articles for *Sayyidul Akhbar*.[10]

Mohammad Ateeq Siddiqui turns his attention to the title *Damul Akhwan* (the soul of brothers) that was given to *Sayyidul Akhbar* by the residents of Delhi. According to him the title reveals Sir Syed's close association with the newspaper. Tahir Masood, without marshalling any concrete evidence asserts that Sir Syed sold the newspaper to Sayyid Abdul Ghafoor in 1848.[9] It is the precise reason why the administrative report of North Western Provinces described Sayyid Abdul Ghafoor as the owner of the newspaper. He did not buttress his claim with any other reliable or concrete evidence.

One has no option but to rely on Hali and some other contemporary writers who talk about Sir Syed's association with *Sayyidul Akhbar*. As stated earlier its files are lost, hence one could not say how many articles Sir Syed contributed to it. After the death of his elder brother, how did he shape and develop it?

Though Sir Syed's articles carried by *Sayyidul Akhbar* are not known, the official report of the North Western Provinces Government for the year 1848 did make a scanty reference to its contents. It says *Sayyidul Akhbar* devoted first two pages of its last issue to news. The front page also carried an article on old buildings of Jaunpur.

The description of the content and display pattern of *Sayyidul Akhbar* is a testament to the fact that Sir Syed was instrumental in shaping it, as he retained the same news display pattern when he started his multilingual weekly—the *Aligarh Institute Gazette*—from Aligarh in 1866. In the *Gazette*, too, the first two pages usually carried news.

Similarly, Sir Syed's interest in archaeology, culture and history was well known as he wrote extensively on these topics. One could easily guess who wrote the article on the buildings of Jaunpur. Further, he published similar articles in the *Aligarh Institute Gazette* later.

Though Sir Syed's stint with *Sayyidul Akhbar* is still not well documented, the material gleaned from some contemporary newspapers and other sources pertaining to *Sayyidul Akhbar* does testify that Sir Syed learnt journalistic writing at *Sayyidul Akhbar*.

ZUBDATUL AKHBAR

Sir Syed's stint with *Sayyidul Akhbar* is mentioned by Hali and other biographers, but his association with a Persian newspaper is not covered in the extensive scholarly literature on him. Further, no historian of early Urdu journalism including Imdad Sabri Imdad (1953), Ateeq Siddiqui, Mohammad Ateeq (1957), Abdus Salam Khurshid (1963), Nadir Ali Khan (1987) and Tahir Masood (2002) made mention of Sir Syed's connection with *Zubdatul Akhbar*

Zubdatul Akhbar, a prominent Persian newspaper of North Western Province, was launched in 1833 from Agra. Nadig Krishnamurthy, asserts:

> Between 1830 and 1840, a few Persian newspapers could be found. One of the first newspapers, *Zubdatul Akhbar*, was started in 1833 by Munshi Wajid Ali Khan in Persian language. He was the editor and proprietor and commanded respect for his tact and his ability. His paper was subsidized by five rulers and rich merchants with a view to guaranteeing that the newspaper did not publish matter likely to lower the donors in the public esteem.[10]

J. Natrajan quoted the official report of the Government of the North Western Provinces, verbatim without acknowledging it explicitly while discussing *Zubdatul Akhbar* and its editor Munshi Wajid Ali Khan. He writes:

> Wajid Ali Khan was a cautious editor rarely hazarding his own opinions or in anyway laying himself open to attack. Expression of dissatisfaction was rare and when indulged clothed in flowery language. His sources were the English and other newspapers. Wajid Ali Khan did not favour the Europeanized way of life and his conservatism, subtly expressed appealed to his circle of readers. His conservatism had found its target the periodicals edited under the auspices of Government educational institutions such as *Suderul Akhbar*, the Agra College newspaper.[11]

Zubdatul Akhabar, the first Persian newspaper of the north India, was a weekly that appeared on Fridays. The English newspapers were its main sources for obtaining news and that gave it tremendous credibility. People usually held it in high esteem. It ran into four pages and its monthly subscription was one rupee. It had the distinction of being the largest circulated newspaper in north India.

Tahir Masood points out that the files of *Zubdatul Akhbar* are no longer available but its many news stories were reproduced in *Asadul Akhbar*, Agra, with proper attribution. It shows that the newspaper evinced a keen interest in scientific experiments and discoveries being made in the West.

Abdus Salam Khurshid asserts that *Aubdatul Akhbar* was held in such high esteem that its excerpts appeared even in the English newspapers including *Bengal Harkaru*. This was the unmatched distinction and no other Persian newspaper of that time had such a reputation.

The official report prepared by the Government of North Western Provinces informs that editor of *Zubdatul Akhbar*, Munshi Wajid Ali Khan was a well-known Persian scholar. He wrote impeccable and euphonious prose and people subscribed to it for reading the mellifluous Persian prose of Munshi Wajid Ali Khan.

Munshi Wajid Ali Khan was a profound scholar of both Urdu and Persian and he wrote a book on Urdu grammar, *Guldasta-e-Anjuman*.

Imdad Sabri provides some important details about *Zubdatul Akhbar* and its famous editor Munshi Wajid Ali Khan though he hardly touches upon the content and display pattern of the newspaper. According to him, Munshi Wajid Ali Khan, was the resident of Hoogli, Bengal and since his childhood, he had a flair for writing. At the age of 12, he left his house and led a carefree life before settling down in Agra. He spent considerable time in literary pursuits before launching the first Persian newspaper of North Western Province, *Zubdatul Akhbar*. In 1833, he launched the newspaper and edited it for almost two decades. He wrote poetry in both Urdu and Persian.[12]

Zubdatul Akhbar was very popular in 1838 when Sir Syed reached Agra. He had a flair for writing and his articles were published in Agra. Sir Syed used to read *Zubdatul Akhbar* with great interest and he visited the newspaper office quite often to assist Munshi Wajid Ali Khan in the production of the newspaper.

Had the files of the *Aligarh Institute Gazette* (1866 to 1898) not been consulted, Sir Syed's association with *Zubdatul Akhbar* would not have come to the fore. Sir Syed talks about his connection with *Zubdatul Akhbar* in the introductory remarks by the editor that appears before an article or a report. In 1878, Munshi Wajid Ali Khan, editor *Zubdatul Akhbar*, wrote a strongly worded editorial against the *Aligarh Institute Gazette*. Sir Syed showing remarkable poise, reproduced it in his newspaper with the following introduction:

Our Old Friend Munshi Wajid Ali Khan and We

We travelled outside Delhi and reached Akbarabad (Agra) probably in 1838. On reaching here, I started admiring Munshi Wajid Ali Khan. At that time *Zubdatul Akhbar* was being published from Agra and he was its editor. I frequently visited the newspaper office and learnt a lot there. We could not see him for long and believed that he might have forgotten me. But I am delighted to learn that he has not failed to think of me and expressed his views on our newspaper. I got an opportunity to assist him when I was at Agra, it proved to be a highly rewarding experience.[13]

It is an explicit acknowledgement of his association with *Zubdatul Akhbar*, hence no one could doubt it. Sir Sayed was very good at Persian and had already got hands-on training at *Sayyidul Akhbar*, Delhi, hence he might have been found quite appropriate to lend a helping hand to Munshi Wajid Ali Khan. The issues of *Zubdatul Akhbar* are not available, therefore it is impossible to specify or spell out the role of Sir Syed in shaping and producing *Zubdatul Akhbar*.

Early Persian newspapers hardly made use of news items but *Zubdatul Akhbar* published news stories on its front page, which were reproduced by another newspaper, *Asadul Akhbar*, Agra. It seems that the newspaper got a cue from *Sayyidul Akhbar*, which published news stories, and other material borrowed from reputed English newspapers. Sir Syed was responsible for picking up news stories from English newspapers, which he also did for the *Aligarh Institute Gazette*. Further, *Zubdatul Akhbar's* deep interest in publishing reports on scientific discoveries and experiments indicates Sir Syed's involvement. Since the files of *Zubdatul Akhbar* are no longer available, nothing can be said authentically about the nature of Sir Syed's stint with the newspaper. Nevertheless, Sir Syed's disclosure makes it clear that he did work for *Zubdatul Akhbar* but his role cannot be spelt out.

THE LOYAL MAHOMEDANS OF INDIA

Sir Syed worked with two newspapers *Sayyidul Akhbar* and *Zubdatul Akhbar* before starting his bilingual periodical, *The Loyal Mahomedans of India* which is erroneously described either as a pamphlet or as a book. Three issues of *The Loyal Mahomedans* appeared in a span of two years at an interval of little over six months. A close look at all three issues of *The Loyal Mahomedans of India* makes it clear that it was a bilingual journal as all the three issues carried an assortment of themes. The description of Muslims who fought for the British, Islamic concept of *jihad* and the treaty signed during the time of the Holy Prophet carried the same title—*The Loyal Mahomedans of India*. Had it been a pamphlet or book, it would have carried different titles for different topics. Further, pamphlets and books are usually not published without the name of the author. The first issue of *The Loyal Mahomedans of India* did not carry the name of the author. Here, Graham and Hali seem to be mistaken; it was essentially a biannual journal.

Explaining the purpose of *The Loyal Mahomedans of India*, Graham says it was started to remind the British of invaluable services rendered by the Muslims during the cataclysmic events of 1857. Graham says:

> During and for long after the mutiny, the Mohamedans were under a cloud. To them, were attributed all horrors and calamities of that time and this prejudice was to a very great extent unjust and was regretted and resented by the Mahomedans at large. No one being apparently willing to take up cudgels in their defence, Sayed Ahmed threw himself into the breach and did all in his powers to rehabilitate their reputation.[14]

Graham (1885) certainly has a point as Muslims were subjected to unprecedented atrocities; their deplorable plight prompted Sir Syed to take up cudgels against the terrible onslaught. He took up the pen for the daunting task of salvaging his co-religionists who were suffering under a reign of repression unleashed by the conquering British. He wrote in order to remove the widely held view of the rulers that the Muslims played a pivotal role in the rebellion as they considered it their religious duty to a wage war against the British. Having written the book *The Causes of the Indian Revolt* in 1859, Sir Syed realized that the misconception about Muslims still persisted, hence he decided to publish a bilingual journal—*The Loyal Mahomedans of India* from Moradabad, where he wanted acquaint the government with the fact that Muslims in several cities whole-heartedly supported the British in their hour of crisis. They even jeopardized their lives trying to save the British from the rebels.

According to Hali, Sir Syed wanted to write a lengthy book on the subject in Urdu and English to be published in parts in India and Britain but it did not happen. As a result, *The Loyal Mahomedans of India* was launched. It was a biannual journal aimed at portraying Muslim loyalty to the British. It also carried the certificates, recommendations and other letters issued by the officials of the government to Muslims for their unflinching loyalty. The description was also appended by the full description of the remuneration or award.

Sir Syed wanted to get it published in Urdu and English simultaneously but many difficulties came in his way which are enumerated by Hali:

> At that time translation from Urdu into English was an expensive business and the cost of printing by type rather than the traditional lithographic process was much higher. Therefore, Sir Syed proposed that each man whose name was to be included should bear the cost of printing the section concerning himself. It is pity that very few people showed any enthusiasm for the project and the result was that only three installments (273 pages in all) were finally issued. These appeared from 1860 to 1861.[15]

The first issue *The Loyal Mahomedans of India* appeared in 1860 from Moradabad. Its size was demy 8vo and each page was divided into two equal columns. Each column 2 inches wide and 6 inches long. Sir Syed chose movable type instead of popular calligraphy. Urdu text and its English translation appeared on the same page; the front page carried the name of the journal both in Urdu and English. The English title—*The Loyal Mohomedans of India* was printed in bold type and occupied 75 per cent space of the front page. Its Urdu title, *Risala Khair Kjuwahan-e-Musalmanan* was displayed in smaller type. The first issue (part I) was composed in gothic type. The name of the editor or the author is conspicuous by its absence. The print line was printed in English and read: Printed by J.A. Gibbson at the Mofussilite Press, Meerut 1860.[16]

The first issue began with the narration of the services rendered by Sir Syed himself during the turbulent and unsettling period of 1857. In order to lend credence to the description of the unprecedented and unflinching loyalty shown by the Muslims, Sir Syed referred to his own example. The narration began with a truism:

It is an controvertible truth that in the revolutions of time a general calamity arises some times of a nature so mightily overwhelming that man is completely prostrated and unhinged there by and rendered utterly helpless in his extremity. There is then as it were a powerful weight upon his soul tearing it down into the gulf of despair for at that season of crushing trial neither virtue nor learning, nor skill not talent is of any avail. His nature is thoroughly changed in the estimation of his fellowmen, none has a good opinion of his, and nothing that he does claim from others any respect. Assuredly when a man is guilty of a really culpable act, there can be no extenuation for that, but when he is enveloped by the somber mantle of misfortune even his good deeds are obnoxious to suspicion and misconstruction are either condemned *in toto*, or said to be found in every class and creed.[17]

The maxim was extended too far, and the introduction in Urdu and its English rendering seem to be tedious and sluggish. The opening sentence ran into more than 40 words both in Urdu and English. It highlighted the deplorable plight of socially and economically ruined Muslims. Here Sir Syed was at his best penmanship:

The advise of this axiom is equally true so far as much as those men who are not under the influence of the blighting shadow of misfortune succeeded in maintaining a fair reputation; and notwithstanding that their hands may be sullied by crime yet they escape reprobation. Now the reason of dire extremity to which I allude is that which befell the Mahomedans in 1857–8. There was not an atrocity committed then of which the blame was not imputed to Mahomedans although the parties really guilty may been Ramadeen or Matadeen.[18]

Then Sir Syed ponders upon the reasons that contributed to the crisis. Turning the table on those who propagated the rumour that the Muslims wanted to overthrow the British rule, Sir Syed asserted:

Some of the acts of horrible drama have already been exposed, but as day by day all the particulars are gradually brought to light when the naked truth stands revealed—then will this glorious fact stand out in prominent relief and become patent to the universe that if in Hindustan there is a class of people above another, who from the principles of their religion, from habits and associations, and from kindred disposition, were fast bound with the Christians in their dead hour of trial and danger in the bonds of amity and friendship, those people were the Mahomedans and they alone—This will actually silence the tongue of slander so loud in their condemnation.[19]

Sir Syed's assertion despite its polemical rhetorical mein was unerring in nature as he cited various instances which were supplemented with the letters of British officials. He rightly pointed out that the rebellion was not a predominantly Muslim uprising.

In line with Sir Syed, the Judicial Commissioner of Oudh, Sir George Campbell (1824–92) termed the rebellion truly Indian in nature as both Muslims and Hindus joined it with equal vehemence. It was not the Muslim alone who waged a war against the British as Campbell refers to Mopala Muslims of south India and Farizi Muslims of Bengal who did not join the rebellion.[20]

Campbell's views are also endorsed by S.N. Sen, who produces a long list of loyal Muslim rulers. He mentions the name of the Nizam of Hyderabad, Muslim rulers of Rampur, Karnal, Moradabad, and Dhaka. They stood by the British in their hour of crisis. Many prominent Muslims such as Qazi Ramzan Ali, Syed Ahmad Khan, Maulana Baksh and Shah Kabeeruddin were close associates of the British.[21]

The history of the rebellion makes it clear that the Muslims did take part in it but they did not spearhead it in Oudh, Bihar, and the Central Provinces. Those who revolted against the British were mostly Hindus. The Muslims did join them as they had lost their empire to the British. A number of prominent rebels who led a fierce battle against the British—Jhansi ki Rani, Tantya Tope, and Nana Saheb—were all non-Muslims. This aside, a number of historical evidences unfailingly endorse Sir Syed's views.

This is not to deny fact that the Muslims in some areas especially in Rohilkhand and the western part of the north India led the rebellion and Sir Syed holds no brief for them. He hardly makes an effort to get them absolved of the charge of rebellion. Sir Syed wrote:

> I am no advocate of those Mahomedans who behaved and joined the rebellion, on the contrary I hold their conduct in utter abhorrence as being in the highest degree criminal and wholly inexcusable. Such unworthy Mahomedans have well deserved the righteous indignation of all right thinking people; but at the same time I must deprecate that wholesome denudation against the entire class of Mahomedans.[22]

Sir Syed was appalled at the frequency of newspaper reports that unabashedly represented the Muslim as being everything that is vile, treacherous and contemptible. In order to thwart such attempts, Sir Syed highlighted the cases of extreme loyalty shown by some Muslims, more especially by those in the service of the government. He began with the specific example of himself though he believed in self-effacement. Sir Syed found it pertinent to refer to his own example to stem the rot. The beginning of narration revealed a measure of modesty:

> It was not originally my intention to say concerning myself, since it did not seem to me that my humble services had been of sufficient importance to merit the gracious notice of the Government, who have done many great things for me as to surpass immeasurably my expectations. Indeed, I blush to compare my sense of unworthiness with the magnitude of the favours and considerations with which I have been honoured. Upon more mature reflection it has however seemed desirable that the author of his work should certainly make mention of certain particulars affecting himself personally, to enable the public to judge from his antecedents, his position, his character and his conduct during the rebellion, what amount of credit should be conceded to his representation and to what extent he proved himself, in the hour of peril, to be faithful and zealous adherent of the Government, he serve.[23]

Having jotted down such introductory lines, Sir Syed went on to narrate his family background and his employment with the government. He briefly mentioned the books he had written and then gave a graphic and a matter of the fact account of the dreadful events of 1857. At that point of time, Sir Syed held the office of Sudder Ameen at Bijnore. During the violent uprising, he decided to stand by the government, no matter what may come in his way.

Sensing the imminent threat, Sir Syed decided to remain with A. Shakespeare, Magistrate, all through and for that he forsook his residence. He did not forsake from his person the weapons which he carried with himself.

The above-mentioned description does not amount to self-exaltation as whatever Sir Syed had said about himself, is authenticated by the letters and certificates issued by the British officials. Alexander Shakespeare's lengthy letter appends the narration:

> All the three officials on whom I am reporting have shown conspicuous loyalty but I were required to draw a distinction, I should do so a favour of Syed Ahmed Khan whose clear sound judgment and rare uprightness and zeal could scarcely be surpassed. I feel assured his official character is so well established the independent of his official services during this crisis, his promotion to a Principal Sudder Ameen might be looked upon as certain and I trust he may soon obtain his promotion but in addition to this I recommend that in appreciation of his peculiar claims to reward, as having been mainly instrumental in securing the escape of the whole of the Bijnore

party of Europeans and of his subsequent services when the district was made over to him.[24]

The letter of Shakespeare also makes mention of Sir Syed's losses in Delhi where his property was ransacked as the rebels came to know that he was a loyal subject of the British. His loss at Delhi and Bijnore was estimated at Rs. 30,000.

Sir Syed's exemplary courage and devotion to his official duties was acknowledged by the Government and subsequently he was raised to the rank of Principal Sudder Ameen. He was also provided with a pension of Rs. 200 per month for as long as he lived but also transferred to his eldest son. Further, a robe of honour (*khilat*), three gems and a donation of Rs. 1,000 was also awarded to him.

The first issue of *The Loyal Mohamedans of India* carried the official correspondence verbatim which makes the text quite tardy. The whole episode concerning Sir Syed was spread over thirty-five pages.

Sir Syed went onto narrate the unprecedented courage of an officer—Zuqeera Khan—posted at Jehanabad, Pilibhit district, who laid down his life in defending the British officials. Zuqeera Khan, a native of Rampur, held the office of Peshkar at the time of the outbreak of violence. Sir Syed wrote about him:

> He displayed zealous loyalty, and performed many good services attaching himself to the Magistrate's person, and was present at his house at all hours. When the revolt gained strength and the continued residence of the Magistrate's wife and children at that station was held to be fraught with peril he escorted them in safely to Nayneetal having been joined by several other Mahomedans who were his friends. At Nayneetal, Zuqueera Khan made himself very useful and was present at the engagement of Churpoora and Sooltangunge on 1 February 1858, conducting himself with indomitable gallantry. On the reoccupation of Pilibhit he was promoted to the Tehsildar, but it was alas! Only a short lived dignity for he was soon slain by a rebel and thus perished for his loyalty.[25]

Later on, the Government gave lands to him and a robe of honour (*khilat*) was also awarded to him. This description is also supplemented with a detailed report of C.P. Carmichel, Magistrate, Pilibhit. Zuqueera Khan's tale was spread over five pages in the first volume of *The Loyal Mahomedans of India*.

The subsequent pages of the first volume narrate the tales of gallantry of Abdul Khan, Kotwal, Pilibhit, Alee Mohamed Khan, soldier,

Safooullah Khan, soldier, Ullay Yara Khan, soldier, Mohammad Khan, soldier and also an extract from the list of persons well known for their loyalty in Pilibhit is also published.

The first issue also carried a fairly detailed account of Moonshi Mohammed Hussain, *Serishtdar*, Dewany Court, Moradabad, when the prisoners broke open the jail. The certificates of J. Wilson, Commander on special duty Moradabad, and John Wilson, Judge, are testament to his unmatched courage.

The pages of *The Loyal Mahomedans of India* were not exclusively meant for highlighting gallantry and exemplary courage of the Muslims serving the Government but were also elaborated on the valuable services rendered by the Muslim elite—the landlords and nawabs. The last ten pages were devoted to highlighting the bravery of Sheikh Shurfooddin, a resident of Shekhpoora, Badaun district. His description was wrapped in rhetorical language; it began with: 'It would be a hopeless task to attempt a delineation of his mental sufferings to portray his load of anxiety for the safety of his precious charge amidst the surroundings or to exhibit with adequate force, ingenuity and courageous firmness with which he baffled the design of the enemy and finally triumphed over the difficulties. These things surpass the power of description.'[26]

The troop revolted on 31 May 1857 at Barielly, and the next day the troops stationed at Badaun mutinied and the soldiers abandoned their allegiance. Soon the district administration caved in. Edward, Magistrate and Collector of the district, was left with no choice but to seek the help of Sheikh Shurfooddin. *The Loyal Mahomedans of India* explained:

> Amidst this state of things, Mr Edwards, Magistrate and Collector of Budaon dispatched a Mahomedan Sawar to Sheikhpoora to summon Sheikh Shurfoodeen to his assistance. This worthy man at once responded to the call and hastily arming his relatives, friends and retainers, some 200 men in all, he proceeded to Budaon. There, meanwhile anarchy had made fearful strides, for the prisoners had been set free, the mutineers were in possession of the Government treasure, and plunder and license prevailed as every side, while the air was rent with the firing of musketry. Through scenes of fire and outrage the Shaikh made his way to the Magistrate's house and taking him under his protection together with three other European gentlemen, viz., Mr Donald, indigo planter, his son and his friend at his own house in Sheikhpoora, and kept them there. Thence, he afterwards conducted them all in safety to another village of the name Kurkora.

Soon the rebel troops carrying guns, 500 cavalry and an entire regiment of infantry reached Budaon then the European wished to go Puttealee, a nearby town, where the English force was posted. The Sheikh escorted them across the Ganges.[27]

Here the letters and certificates appreciating Shurfooddin's gallantry issued by A.M. Phillips, Joint Magistrate Etah; W. Edwards, Judge; C.P. Carmiechal, Officiating Magistrate; W.J. Bramly, Magistrate and Collector of Aligarh; Elliot Colvin and R. Alexandar, Commissioner Rohilkhand Division lent credence to the description.

The first volume ran into eighty-two pages in which a number of specific instances were quoted where the Muslims alone protected the British. The detailed description called attention to the invaluable services rendered by the Muslims during this period of unprecedented peril. The gallantry shown by the Muslim justified the claim of Sir Syed that he made at the beginning of the first volume:

> It is the Mahomedans alone the credit belongs of having stood the staunch and unshaken friends of the Government amidst that fearful tornado that divested the country, and shook the empire to its centre and whoever ready heart and hand to render their aid to the utmost extremity or cheerfully to perish in the attempt, regardless of home and kindred of life and its enjoyment.[28]

Sir Syed alluded to a plethora of specific instances to refute the view held by the British that the Muslims were convinced that Christian rule in India was about to be over as the prophecy of Shah Naimatullah clearly suggested. Sir Syed quoted religious decrees to explain why the Muslims were enjoined by the precepts of Islam to live together with the Christians peacefully as they also believed in the prophets and respected the word of God.

The second issue of *The Loyal Mahomedans of India* carried a slight but significant change. Now the name of Sir Syed, Sudder Ameen of Moradabad appeared on the title page but there was no change in the print line. As discussed earlier, the first issue of *The Loyal Mahomedans of India* chronicled the services of the Mahomedans who stood by the British, but the second issue proffered a perceptive and analytical discussion on the Islamic concept of *jihad* (Holy War). It started with a customary prayer that every devout Muslim said when he began something. The opening lines appear quite appropriate in that the whole issue was devoted to a religious debate.

At the outset, Sir Syed made it clear that after having published a detailed account of several Mahomedans who by their good conduct and devotion had obtained approbation and reward, that he intended to chronicle the eminent services of another loyal Mahomedan. Further, he wanted to explain the real Islamic concept of *jihad* that gained currency and the many Muslims who were swayed by it. Refuting the allegation that the Muslims enjoined by the tenets of their religion to oppose the Christians, he pointed out: 'Where as indeed the very reverse of this is the fact, for Mahomedans admit, that there is no secret upon earth but the Christians with whom its people may maintain amity and friendship.'

He then proceeded to quote the Koranic injunctions liberally to prove that the Christians were the most amenable to forging friendship with the true believers. Further, they were not elated with pride. He also referred to Islamic history and reminded the Muslims of an incident pertaining to the time of the Prophet when the idolatrous people of Mecca began to harass the faithful. Then the Prophet ordered his followers to migrate to Abyssinia. Quoting the Koran and alluding to several incidents, Sir Syed tried to drive home the point that amity and goodwill always existed between Muslims and Christians.[29]

During the time of rebellion, a rumour gained currency that Shah Naimatullah's prophecy is said to have foretold the dissolution of the Christian empire. Sir Syed described it as completely absurd as Islam abominated prophecies. For Islam, no man had the divine attribute to foretell the future; hence no importance was to be attached to any prediction. Sir Syed gave a point by point rebuttal in his terse prose:

> Now God forbids that the Mahomedans should attach an iota of faith to the prophecies of any but the inspired writers! On the contrary, it is held by us to be a grievous sin to ascribe to any mortal man, the divine attribute of knowledge of future—or to place the slightest confidence in the predictions of astrologers or indulge in the superstitions, observances of auspicious times and seasons. This being the case, how could any sensible man give evidence to the fantasies of some unknown individuals who may have chosen to amuse the credulous of a past age by playing the Prophet.[30]

Sir Syed urged the Muslims to make a difference between *jihad* and rebellion as the two concepts are poles apart. He had a dig at so called *Maulavis* who misled the people as Islam did not give license to practice treachery, cruelty and violence. According to Islam, *jihad* could not be waged against the present rule as there were certain pre-requisities. First there must not be any protection of life and property. Second, there should not be a treaty and engagement between the parties. These two indispensable conditions were not fulfilled in the rebellion, Sir Syed pointed out. He set a lengthy and perceptive debate in motion to illustrate the relations of the protected and the protectors. Explaining the religious point of view, Sir Syed borrowed liberally from a plethora of well-known texts of theology and religious history that included *Alamgeeri* and *Hadaya*. At the end of a fairly-long essay on *jihad* that was replete with quotations from the Koran and other sacred religious texts, Sir Syed defined *jihad* in the Islamic perspective: 'It is needless to expatiate upon its praises, but be it observed that the modus operandi and the rules and regulations connected with it have been carefully and exactly laid down by the unerring hand of Divine wisdom and it is not therefore to be supposed for a moment that fraud, deceit or revolt, enter into the elements that constitute a holy war.'[31]

Sir Syed seemed to be quite emphatic in asserting that the rebellion did not have the remotest connection with *jihad*. His perceptive article, running into twenty-five pages, highlighted the *jihad* and its theo-retical framework.

His long essay on *jihad* was followed by the description of many Muslims who lent a helping hand to the British in their hour of crisis. The second volume of *The Loyal Mahomedans of India* arrived detailed descriptions of Moonshi Imamuddin, Tehsildar of Moradabad; Nawab Nabee Buksh Khan Bhadoor, Delhi; and Sheikh Khairuddin Ahmad Khan Bhadoor, Deputy Magistrate, Ghazipur. Sheikh Khairuddin's efforts were profusely applauded because he kept a tight vigil on the troops posted at Ghazipur. Through his relentless efforts Ghazipur had not fallen to the rebels. The official reports said that the Sheikh's expostulations and persuasion went a long way in allaying the suspicion of the 65th Regiment and it was kept in check.

Unlike the first issue, the narration here is divided into small paragraphs and sentences (both in Urdu and its rendering into English) are short and crisp. The prose is completely devoid of verbosity; obscure words and obsolete phrases are hardly used.

In this issue too, narration was authenticated by a host of official documents and letters. It ran to eighty-nine pages and also contains an appendix spreading over ten pages. It proffered a thought-provoking discussion on *jihad* for which Sir Syed sought the help of one of his learned friends who suggested that some other equally important texts previously unnoticed by Sir Syed be also be referred to. The second issue also appeared in the same year (1860).

The third volume of *The Loyal Mahomedans of India* was published in 1861 from the Mofussilite Press, Meerut. Instead of J.J. Robinson, J.A. Gibbon, takes over as the publisher.

The third volume too is devoted to a central theme. As we are aware Sir Syed left no stone unturned to fulfil his objective of a warm rapport with the Christians. Friendship between Muslims and Christians was very close to his heart, as it was a must for the speedy upliftment and development of his community which had erroneously inclined to engage in acrimonious confrontations with the British.

Sir Syed was a avid reader of history, metaphysics, theology and Islamic history. The sweep of his reading was amazing and once he mentioned a book authored by a Christian, Lancelot Addision. The author quoted a treaty signed between Muslims and Christians extensively. It was an old text, written in 1697.

Sir Syed reproduced the above-mentioned treaty verbatim in *The Loyal Mahomedans of India*. He wrote the following introduction before quoting the treaty.

> I have lately been perusing an old book by Mr. Lancelot Addison in which I have found the copy of a league and covenant which in a former era, had been concluded between the Mahomedans and the possessor of Christianity. I, here give this curious document and shall be glad if any of my readers will let me know, whether in the course of their own study of Arabic History, they have seen any mention made of this league.[32]

The above-mentioned treaty, signed by the Prophet himself, had hardly come in for a detailed analysis as its text was not readily available. A copy of the treaty was found in the Monastery on Mount Carmel, a day's journey from Mecca and it was sent to the King's Library in France. The treaty provides equal rights to the Christians and the Muslims and one could hardly find an iota of religious discrimination in the ideal Islamic society set-up by the Prophet. It stipulates:

> If any Christian commits a crime or fault, it shall be the part of the Muslimins to assist him, intercede; and give caution for him and compound for his miscarriage: liberty shall also be given him to redeem his life. Nor shall he be forsaken, nor destitute of help, because of Divine Convenant which is with them; that they should enjoy what the Muslimin enjoy, and suffer what they suffer.

According to this covenant which is by the Christian just request, for confirmation of its authority, you are aligned to protect them from all calamities, and perform all offices of goodwill toward them, so that the Muslimins may be sharers with them in prosperity and adversity.

Moreover, all come ought to be made that no violence be offended to them as the matters relating to marriages, viz., that they should not compel the parents to match their daughters with the Muslimins, nor shall they be molested for refusal either to give a bridegroom or a bride for this an act wholly voluntary depending on their free will and pleasure.[33]

The treaty contained many provisions that provide Christians and other religious minorities with equal rights and the Prophet directed the Muslims to follow it otherwise they would be considered as enemies of God. It was clearly formulated for ushering in a new era of goodwill and mutual trust between the Muslims and the Christians.

The treaty, which lay in oblivion for years, speaks volumes about tolerance, generosity and benevolence of the Prophet during the days of the Muslim glory. At the end of the document, Abu Bakr, Omar bin Alcherab, Osman bin Affawan and Ali bin Abu Talib signed as witnesses. It was signed on the first day of the moon of the fourth month, the fourth year of Hegira in Medina.

The publication of the treaty went a long way in convincing the Muslims to shun their pronounced hostility towards the Christians. The excerpts of the treaty were spread over ten pages.

Similar to two previous issues, the third volume of *The Loyal Mahomedans of India* also called attention to the gallantry shown by six loyal Mahomedans—Sheikh Tajordeen, Daroga, Moradabad; Sayyid Turab Ali, Deputy Collector, Bijnore; Sheikh Ameer Ali, Tehsildar, Pilibhit; Sheikh Badruddin, Tehsildar, Auanla, Bareilly, Munshi Abdul Ghani, Supplier Railways; and Mahomed Ibrahim Khan, Tehsildar, Shamlee. Seventy-eight pages were allocated to their description.

If all three volumes are sifted one can easily conclude that Sir Syed was the first Urdu journalist who sowed the seeds of development journalism as he tried to instill a sense of belonging to the Government of the day among his readers. The first prerequisite of development journalism was to create a sense of belonging and Sir Syed quite successfully achieved it. He wanted to extricate the Muslims from their medieval thinking and to develop a warm rapport with the British—and for this, he used journalism as a vehicle. His pen was entirely directed towards ameliorating the condition of Indians, especially the Muslims. At places, his prose seemed to be highly emotive and persuasive. A dispassionate description with a fair amount of objectivity ran through all the pages of *The Loyal Mahomedans of India*.

Hali points out that the three issues of *The Loyal Mahomedans of India* carry a detailed account of some eighteen people, many of whom had been killed by the rebels and also lost a number of their family members.

Hali is wrong about this as twenty-one people—eighteen government officials, two nawabs and one supplier of railways appeared in the issues of *The Loyal Mahomedans of India*. Ten government official, mostly junior ones, two Deputy Collectors Sayyid Turab Ali, Sheikh Khiruddin, four Tehsildars—Munshi Imamuddin, Mahomed Ibrahim Khan, Sheikh Ameer Ali, and Sheikh Badruddin are picked up and their tales of gallantry and exemplary courage were highlighted. One Principal Sudder Ameen, Sir Syed himself and one Shristadara Moonshi Mohamed Hussain were also given space.

Hali again inaccurately mentions that all three issues contained 273 pages but actually total pages are 277.

At that time (in 1860) the cost of printing by type was very high. Sir Syed proposed that the cost of the printing should be borne by the persons who wanted to get their descriptions published in *The Loyal Mahomedans of India*. The proposal did not evoke much response, and *The Loyal Mahomedans of India* did not survive for long.

NOTES

1. Margarita Barns, *Indian Press*, London: Allen and Unwin Press, 1940, p. 182.
2. Nadig Krishnamurthy, *Indian Journalism*, University of Mysore, 1966, p. 254.
3. Mohammed Ateeq Siddiqui, *Sooba Shumali Maghribi ke Akhbarat wa Matbooat*, Aligarh: Anjuman-e-Taraqqi Hind, 1966, p. 103.
4. *Ahsan-ul Akhbar*, Bombay, 2 January 1846.
5. Mohammed Ateeq Siddiqui, *Hindustani Akhbar-naveesi Company ke Ahed Mein*, Aligarh: Anjuman-e-Taraqqi Urdu Hind, 1957, p. 27.
6. Ibid., p. 28.
7. *Hayat-e Javed*, p. 34.

8. Sir Qadir Abdul, famous Urdu writer quoted in *Hindustani Akhbar-naveesi Company ke Ahed Mein*, p. 57.
9. Tahir Masood, *Urdu Sahafat Uneesvi Sadi Mein*, Karachi, 2003, p. 203.
10. Nadig Krishnamurthy, p. 253.
11. J. Natrajan, *History of Indian Journalism*, Delhi: Publication Division, Govt. of India, 1955, p. 26.
12. Imdad Sabri, *Urdu Sahafat ki Tareekh*, vol. I, Delhi, 1955, p. 72.
13. *The Aligarh Institute Gazette*, November 1878.
14. G.F.I. Graham, *Life and Works of Syed Ahmed Khan*, London: William Blackwood & Sons, 1885, p. 52.
15. *Hayat-e Javed*, p. 65.
16. *The Loyal Mahomedans of India*, Meerut: Mofussilite Press, 1860, title page.
17. Ibid., pp. 1, 2.
18. Ibid., p. 3.
19. Ibid.
20. George Campbell, *Memories of My Indian Career*, Appendix to vol. 1, London, 1893, p. 399.
21. Surendra Nath Sen, *Eighteen Fifty Seven*, Delhi: Publications Division, Govt. of India, 1977, p. 245.
22. *The Loyal Mahomedans of India*, vol. I, Meerut, 1860, p. 6.
23. Ibid., p. 10.
24. Ibid., p. 25.
25. Ibid., p. 63.
26. Ibid., p. 4.
27. Ibid., vol. II, p. 85.
28. Ibid., p. 126.
29. Ibid.
30. Ibid., vol. III, Meerut, Mofussilite Press, 1861, p. 178.
31. Ibid.
32. Ibid.
33. Ibid., vol. III, p. 180.

CHAPTER 10

Sir Syed on Development of Agriculture and its Financing

S.M. WASEEM

Sir Syed was a dynamic person with a vision and a dream and moulded the thinking and destinies of his people. He exhorted his people to do hard work and achieve their objectives. He knew that the capabilities of individuals and that of groups, if harnessed objectively and properly could bring rich dividends. Gifted with a rare sense of understanding, he was astute in evaluating the political, economic, social and cultural urges of the times. He is ranked amongst the best leaders of the world. Basically concerned with the socio-economic, cultural and political degeneration of the Muslims of India, after the First War of Independence in 1857, he started his educational movement in 1859 and continued to push it forward until his death in 1898. He succeeded in initiating changes that had far-reaching effects in the intellectual, political and economic life of Indian Muslims through his educational endeavours which formed the main plank of transition from medievalism to modernism.

Sir Syed was a great man, magnanimous and endowed with extraordinary far-sightedness and acumen to locate, analyse and prescribe solutions to problems. He was '. . . magnanimous, lion hearted, with an extraordinary natural dignity. His talents were very great, but his character was still greater. He was incomparably the noblest man, whom it has been . . . (the) fortune to have ever met intimately.'[1]

A dynamic person, a visionary in the realm of possibilities and above all a social reformer, thinking ahead of his times, this is how one can safely describe Sir Syed Ahmad Khan. He foresaw the political, economic, social, educational and cultural landscape of the future Hindustan. Therefore, he emphasized the importance of scientific and technological education, particularly the one being pursued in the West, as to him it was instrumental in the all-round development and transformation of the Western nations. Keeping in view the outcome of modern scientific and technological education, no one can disagree with his viewpoint that it is education that ignites the drowsy and sleeping mind, otherwise endowed with capabilities. He was absolutely right in emphasizing the need to impart higher modern education to his people, to equip them with abilities and arouse them out of stupor. To him, this was the key for solving the problems from which they were suffering. To quote Shaikh Mumtaz Husain Jaunpuri, '. . . Sir Syed knew that the violent flow of thoughts and knowledge, originating from the Ocean of the West, coming torrentially towards India, would sweep away the Muslims.' Hence Sir Syed desired to equip his people with higher modern education. It is needless to emphasize that education and training of the right type surely helps develop able and efficient minds, but devoid of a moral and ethical foundation, any system of education will be bound to ultimately fail to develop and sustain a truly 'humane' civilization. Therefore Sir Syed began his innovative educational movement, popularly known as the 'Aligarh movement'. He drew the sustenance from both the Western style of higher education and the ethical and moral principles from the teachings of Islam.

This great man intensely felt the despair of backwardness of his people. But he was equally concerned with the collective national development as he was with individual development. Keeping this in consideration, he said 'National development is the sum total of individual labour, individual honour, (and) individual sympathy. Likewise, national retardation is the sum total of individual lethargy, individual dishonour, individual dishonesty, individual selfishness and individual shortcomings.'[2] As national development is the sum total of the efforts, prosperity and development of individuals, each individual effort carries its own significance and importance. Individual efforts simultaneously add to both, individual prosperity and national development. As growth and enrichment in all aspects of human life necessarily chases new targets, individual and collective efficiency continually adds to further individual and national prosperity and development.

Sir Syed, rightly held that:

The purpose of education has always been to develop in a human the dexterity and exuberance in his intellect and understanding, so that he may distinguish between the evil and good in matters that may arise, and he may thus gain the ability to contemplate on the mysteries of divine nature. His morals should be strengthened (by education, so that) he may accomplish his economic matters efficiently and can ponder over matters concerning the (ultimate) hereafter.[3]

Therefore, education should not be merely ornamental but must be of service to the nation, society and individuals. To this end, it must serve to develop the economy, polity and, of course, each individual. In a primarily agricultural country, Sir Syed felt that agriculture needed immediate attention to fulfil its role as the leading economic sector. In his paper on '50 Years of Agricultural Development in India', Sir Syed felt that agriculture had a key role to play as industrialization, even on a small scale, was a long way to come in a subjugated Hindustan.

AGRICULTURE AND ITS DEVELOPMENT

Sir Syed was concerned not merely with education but professional education with a purpose. It was this thought that prompted him to write to Mr Princep, Collector, Aligarh, saying that one of the purposes of his 'Scientific Society' was to acquaint people with better ways of practising agriculture that would lead to the improvement of the condition of the people on the one hand, and also add to the collection of higher revenues in favour of the British Exchequer. He got books by Robert S. Burn and C. Towlison translated into Urdu, and then wrote to the Governor of the North West Provinces, requesting him on behalf of the Scientific Society for a suitable grant to help prepare other books on agriculture. He offered to give to the Government the translated books, in return of the grant. (An aid of Rs. 500 was administered in August 1866 but the books could not be completed.) Then, Sir Syed himself wrote and published a pamphlet in Urdu—*Qadeem Nizam-e-Dehi Hindustan*—in 1878 on the rural economy of India and its structure. The document was devoted to the study of land development, condition of the cultivators, financial institutions to administer credit and famines. He also did an analysis of the existing enactments and the need to amend these to help strengthen the cultivators and add to the development of India's rural economy.

He also wrote on issue of land ownership, various classes of people living in rural India, and the collection of revenue. Describing these, Sir Syed said,

> Those who live with unity together in villages, described by me as community of rural folks in this Pamphlet, are divided into two groups: Firstly, that group which considers itself owner of all the land within the confines of the village, and (therefore) superior to all other village community and 'its right is supreme in comparison to all others.' This group comprises the offspring or successors of all those who initially usurped/controlled the land lying within the confines of the village, and are known as zamindars (land owners) or by any other title given to them as per the custom of the country.

Secondly, that group which is known as 'Ryot', and this (*Ryot*) stands divided into four sub-groups: Firstly, the cultivators, secondly, the artisans, thirdly, the labourers, and fourthly, the *Khush Ba'sh* (the affluent ones).

Sir Syed's thoughts on agriculture and its development are so coherent, so practical and meaningful that one is tempted to say that there lived a well trained agricultural economist in him. He studied the pitiable condition of the farmers, reeling under the heavy burden of debt, their exploitation by landlords and moneylenders, and the deteriorating condition of their land, all adding to their deprivation and ruination. Agriculture to him was the backbone of the economy. Its development should have occupied an important place in any scheme of national economic development and it was imperative to strengthen and develop the cultivators as well.

Sir Syed found that the cultivators were subjected to cruelties by landlords and their functionaries. They were often deprived of their produce, and in some cases from the right to the land they were ploughing. It all happened in violation of the rights of the tillers.[4] It was due to these reasons that the condition of the cultivators had become pitiable. The high rate of interest added fuel to the fire and led to the further deterioration of the financial condition of cultivators. Sir Syed pinpointing the causes of the poverty of cultivators, their deprivation and sufferings, said 'Due to indebtedness and high rate of interest, the condition of the cultivator has become pitiable (indicating his ruination). . . . Whatever is produced due to his sweat and toil, is taken away by the moneylenders without any check; yet, he (the cultivator) is not able to absolve himself of his indebtedness.'[5]

Thus, while the cultivators worked, the benefit of their labour went to the landlords and the moneylenders, who functioned in connivance with each other. Sir Syed divided the rural population into two classes, saying that

> The first one is that class which considers itself owner of the entire chunk of land which falls within the confines of a village, and also superior to the entire village population, nurturing the thought that their rights are supreme. . . .
>
> The second one is that class which is known as *'ryot'*, and this class is divided into four sections, firstly, the cultivators, secondly, the artisans, thirdly, the wage earners, (and) fourthly, the rich and the prosperous ones.[6]

In his Memorandum on Land Development and Help to the Cultivators, and Establishment of Agriculture Banks,[7] Sir Syed wrote 'Land development can be materialized in three ways:

Firstly, by instituting means of irrigation.
Secondly, by making available the facilities for irrigation.
Thirdly, by prescribing or improving the standard of fertility of land.'

He then outlined his scheme of agro-rural development, saying: 'In my opinion the chunks of land which are irrigated with the water, drawn from well, should not be made to invoke levying of Irrigation Cess, which (therefore) should not be realized from (such) cultivators.'

Sir Syed stressed on the development of both, the cultivators and the land alike. He argued that

> The need to develop land and harness resources for helping the cultivators in each district, is so evident that I am afraid that the Government cannot ordinarily meet these requirements out of its own (State) revenues: To achieve this goal, the Government should either raise loans or should give consideration to the method which is generally acceptable and can help achieve the goal—(and) the method is to float limited (joint stock) companies (to help) raise funds for agricultural development. (But), then the Government should also participate as a (contributing) partner.[8]

Then, giving his views on the desired form that financial institutions should take to help rescue and then develop Indian agriculture, and the cultivators too.

1. Banks to Help of Cultivators[9] should be established as separate entities in each District: (Thus, Sir Syed is found dwelling upon the modern district level (Rural Development Banks) which as per his suggestions were required to offer credit, as follows:

   Extending credit facilities to the cultivators for buying seeds and animals, as well as plough and (other) agricultural implements for cultivating their land; for sustaining the cultivators, their children and those who took part in cultivating the land.

   They were also to extend credit (to those who wish) to buy grain (seed), and animals, and plough and other agricultural implements, meant for sale to the cultivators for those purposes which have been mentioned under sub-clause A of this item.[10]

2. Banks for Land Development.[11] These can be well nigh compared with the modern Land Mortgage Banks in India which were later replaced by the Land Development Banks. Sir Syed wanted that these banks when formed, should come forward to provide finance for

   (a) (digging) wells, making tanks and for constructing buildings for cultivators to make available or being helpful in distributing water for purposes of cultivation,
   (b) leveling the land for irrigational purpose,
   (c) constructing buildings (to be used as facility) to
      (i) drain out ground water,
      (ii) drain in water from rivers and other sources to help improve (the condition of) the land,
      (iii) protect land from water coming from rivers or other sources (causing water logging),
      (iv) protect (agricultural) land from losses due to floods and (excessive) water.
      (v) level the land or combing it or to raise enclosure around the (agricultural) land for purposes of irrigation,
   (d) for reconstruction of relevantly mentioned buildings, or doing alteration in these, or taking to their extension.
   (e) for construction of those buildings which are required for the purposes, and are mentioned in this clause.[12]

Sir Syed also suggested floating of (Joint) Stock Companies to undertake the following functions:

To dig wells and construct tanks for purposes of agriculture.

1. To lay a canal or construct a reservoir and to connect it with any river, spring or canal or tank for irrigating the farms.
2. To construct a building for storing water at an appropriate place for irrigating a farm or farms, by linking it with a canal or reservoir.
3. To install mechanical devices on the bank of a river, a spring, a canal or a tank for lift irrigation of those chunks (of land) which are situated at a height.[13]

Sir Syed pinning his hopes on the utility of financial companies, further said '. . . A company can easily experiment with this, provided it foresees a situation yielding profit'. Sir Syed's saying that in the event of these companies offering their shares for sale in the market, it will be obligatory for the Government to buy some of these, is indicative of his idea that Private Sector may also draw resources from the State for sharing its responsibility in the task of national economic development and prosperity of individuals.

If one scans through the present arrangement of agricultural credit, rural development and the financial institutions existing today more than 100 years after the death of Sir Syed Ahmad Khan, who believed in '. . . in the welfare of all, irrespective of their caste or religion . . . ', he would surely perceive that Sir Syed was concerned with the development of the entire economy with particular emphasis on the development of rural sector.

The Aligarh Muslim University which was the epitome of Sir Syed's dream first had established the Institute of Agriculture. Later it was enlarged to include the Departments of Dairy and Horticulture as well.[14] Further, the Faculties of Science and Life Science, Zakir Husain College of Engineering, Ajmal Khan Tibbiya College and also the Jawaharlal Nehru Medical College, should join hands to examine and conduct researches on the efficacy and use of the indigenously available raw materials and medicinal plants, etc., in their quest to find out their commercial uses. Thence after, the researchers, financial institutions, Departments of Commerce and Management Studies and Research as also the Dawakhana Tibbiya College, can all join hands to develop enterprises in their bid to help open avenues of self-employment,[15] as it was assigned an important role by Sir Syed Ahmad Khan in view of the job requirements with the growing 'numbers of the graduates', and the inability of the State to create jobs in required numbers.[16] It will be a great service if an Industrial Estate meant for the budding entrepreneurs from amongst the educated ones from our University, is established at a suitable place, say near Jawan (Aligarh), to help commercialize the researches/inventions by the researchers coming from different departments.

NOTES

1. *The M.A.O. College Magazine,* vol. 6, Aligarh, April 1898, p. 123.
2. *Tahzib-ul Akhlaq,* vol. 6, 1st Ramadan, AH 1292.
3. *Hayat-i Javed,* vol. 2, p. 85.
4. See *Qadeem Nizam-e-Dehi Hindustan, Nayab Rasayel wa Mazameen,* part 15, compiled by Maulana Mohammad Ismail Panipati, Lahore: Majlis Taraqqi Adab, 1963. It was found preserved in the Asafiya Library, Hyderabad.
5. *Ya'd-da'sht Nisbat Taraqqi Haysiyat A'razi wa Imdad Ka'shtkara'n wa Taqarrur Bankhaiy Zara'ti, Maqala't Sir Syed,* part 16, compiled by Maulana Mohammad Ismail Panipati, Lahore: Majlis Taraqqi Adab, 1965, p. 600.
6. *Qadeem Nizam-e-Dehi Hindustan,* p. 519.
7. It was later published in the *Aligarh Institute Gazette*, dated 2 June 1883.
8. *Ya'd-da'sht Nisbat Taraqqi Haysiyat,* pp. 610–11.
9. Earlier in 1876 Sir John Strachey, Lt.-Governor, Northern and Western Districts, had expressed in favour of the establishment of such a bank.
10. *Ya'd-da'sht Nisbat Taraqqi*, pp. 611–12.
11. It will be interesting to make reference to the Central Land Development Bank, organized in Madras (Chennai) in 1929.
12. *Ya'd-das'sht Nisbat Tarraqi*, p. 612.
13. Ibid., p. 613.
14. The author as far back as 1971 in a meeting presided over by the then Pro-Vice Chancellor, Mr Fazlur Rahman, had opined in favour of acquiring the then vacant area of Jamalpur with the help of the Government. When asked by him: 'What for? Young man!', I said: 'Sir, for the establishment of a College of Agriculture and Dairy,' adding that 'it will not only help train our youth but would also be a source of supplying cheaper food items for our Halls, thus rendering the food for Hall inmates cheaper as compared to other Universities. Further, it could be utilized for establishing Industrial Estate.'

15. See author's paper 'Self Employment, Entrepreneurship, and International Trade', Annual Issue, Federation of the Alumni Associations, California, 2005.
16. Also see author's paper, *Jadeed A'la Talim Aur Ma'shi Taraqqi: Sir Syed ki Nazar Mein, Sir Syed Ba'z Ya'ft* (ed. A.A. Siddiqui), Aligarh: Sir Syed Academy, AMU, 1990, pp. 282–94.

CHAPTER 11

Sir Syed and Muslim Identity

TABIR KALAM

The post-Mutiny (1857) period—after the British government had brutally crushed the revolt, the Indian Muslims were regarded as culprits of the entire phenomenon—was one of introspection and reflection for the Indian masses, for which the British blamed the Muslims more than the Hindus. The Muslim intellectuals bloomed during the last four decades of nineteenth century. The central figure in this movement was Sir Syed Ahmad Khan, who being conscious and aware of the fragile condition of the Muslims argued, that the Muslims would do better to understand the objective reality and strive to create space for themselves inside the power structure of the time. The Aligarh movement was, therefore, premised on educational, cultural and political empowerment of the Muslims with Anglo–Muslim rapprochement, and keeping Muslim masses de-politicized.

In this paper an attempt has been made to present Sir Syed's concept of *qaum* and his attitude towards Indian National Congress; and his attempt towards giving the Muslims an identity.

He founded the Mohammedan Anglo-Oriental College at Aligarh, precursor of the University, in 1875, to educate Muslim youths in Western sciences through the medium of English, but in an Islamic environment. This endeavour culminated in the dissemination of modern Western culture and science along with Islamic religion. His vision of the future of Muslims, to be produced by the new institution, was that of a man who would have: 'The Koran in one hand, modern science in the other and on his head the crown of *La Ilah a Illallah*.'

Sir Syed prepared for the confluence of religion and education and his own programme of public action. His *Essays on the Life of Muhammad* were completed in late March of 1870.[1] And a month after that he was making plans for a journal *Tahzib-ul Akhlaq* or the *Muhammadan Social Reformer* to be a vehicle of the new movement.[2] Reformist articles in this journal, as well as extensive religious writings, went hand in hand with his efforts to start a Muslim college. The preface to *Essay on the Life of Muhammad* stated that 'the work was specially intended for the use of those Muhammadan youths who are pursuing their English studies'.[3]

Referring to his book *Asar-us-Sanadid,* Sir Syed lamented that it contained descriptions of Muslim monuments which reflected the grandeur of our ancestors; today they deserved to be viewed only with anguish. We are the decadent descendants who failed to preserve them. The capital city Delhi, where our forefathers ruled for centuries, today the Muslim could fix his eyes on it with shattered hopes and sorrow.[4] There is one point we may note, and that is that Sir Syed Ahmad's heart embraces Delhi and does not travel to the Persian and Arab territories his ancestors left behind. Compiling a chronology of the Delhi kings, he begins with the ancient Hindu ones. Looking for a figure to study and admire, he selected Akbar rather than Aurangzeb.[5]

He says 'no worship, no charity, no good deed is better than the love of your *qaum* (nationality)'.[6] Sir Syed used *qaum* as nation for both Hindus and Muslims, which, in the terminology also connoted a nationality. He argues that

> [T]he word *qaum* is used for the citizens of a country. Various peoples of Afghanistan are considered a *qaum,* and different peoples of Iran are known as Iranis. Europeans profess different religions and believe in different ideas, yet they are all members of a single nation. In a nutshell, since olden times the word *qaum* is used for the inhabitants of a country, even though they have characteristics of their own.[7]

Sir Syed expressed the same view at the welcome address presented at the Indian Association of Lahore:

> [B]y the word *qaum*, I mean both Hindus and Muslims. That is the way in which I define the word nation (*qaum*). In my opinion, it matters not whatever be their religious belief, because we cannot see anything of it; but what we see is that all of us, whether Hindus or Muslims, live on one soil, are governed by one and the same ruler, have the same sources of our benefits, and equally share the hardships of a famine. These are various reasons why I designate both the nationalities (*qaumun*) that inhabit India by the term (*ayk lafz*) Hindu that is nation (*qaum*), which lives in India.[8]

The best example of Sir Syed Ahmad Khan's efforts at creating a rapprochement between the British government and his *qaum* was in the form of *Asbab-i Baghawat-i Hind* (The Causes for India's Revolt), which was frank enough to point our the lacunas and misgovernance perpetrated by the government. He even cited an example of ruler-subject cordiality of Akbar's Era, comparing with the tyranny done to the Indian subjects and their alienation during Aurangzeb's time and further added 'the English government has existed for more than a century and to the present hour has not secured the people's affection'.[9] He also wrote, 'the manner of punishment given to the Indian soldiers who had won medals for loyalty to the East India Company but who out of religious scruple had refused to bite cartridges was most wrong, these soldiers saw their hands and feet manacled, looked at their medals and wept'.[10]

Keeping in mind that the British will live in India and there was no way out to dismantle the government, Sir Syed started extending his loyalty toward the government for the betterment of Indian Muslims. In 1866 inspired by the British Indian Association started in 1851 in Calcutta, he launched a British India Association in Aligarh. He says at the inauguration. 'The association's petitions were educational, economic and non-communal. It seeks a vernacular non-Muslim university in the North West Provinces (UP) where, the arts, sciences and other European literature may be taught in Urdu.'[11]

He believed that contemporary Muslim society was oriented towards the past, while the Indian environment had been completely changed by British rule. In the middle ages Muslims came from far away places and settled in India. They contributed to the advancement of science, that many of them had learned from the Greeks. Today our men, instead of endeavouring to make their own contributions, take pride in the achievements of their ancestors.[12] Sir Syed was opposed to pan-Islamism, isolating Indian Muslims from the rest of Dar-ul-Islam, especially from the Turks, and also hostile to the concept of a universal Muslim *Khilafat.*[13]

The illustration of *qaum* in a broader sense does not mean that Syed Ahmad Khan was not aware of Hindu nationalism, specially in the form of Arya Samaj, Bharatwarsha National Association, Shivaji festival by Tilak and the formation of various cow protection societies.[14] At the same time India witnessed another movement by the Hindus—demanding the use of Hindi in place of Urdu in the courts. Hindu *sabhas* (associations) sprang up in Benaras and with a central office in Allahabad to promote the adoption of Hindi as an official language of India.

Sir Syed argued that Urdu, although developed during the period of Muslim rule, was a product of Hindu–Muslim interaction and was widely spoken in India by Hindus and Muslims. In his letter to Mehdi Ali he wrote,

> I understand, Hindus are roused to destroy the Muslims' [cultural] symbol (*Musalmanun key nishani*) embodied in the Urdu language and the Persian script. I have heard that they have made representation through the Hindu members of the scientific society that the society's *Akhbar* should be published in Devanagari rather than in the Persian script, and that all translations of foreign language books should likewise be in Hindi. This proposal would never accept Hindi and if Hindus persistently demanded the adoption of Hindi in preference to Urdu it would result in the total separation of the Muslims from the Hindus.[15]

When the Indian National Congress was founded (1885) Sir Syed remained conspicuously aloof. Surendra Nath Banerjee had written him that 'no assembly of national delegates would be complete without your presence.'[16] However, when Badruddin Tayyabji was named the Congress President, Sir Syed came out publicly against the Congress. Once again, in December 1887, the two organizations, Indian National Congress in Madras and the Mohammedan Educational Congress (started in 1886 by Sir Syed Ahmad Khan) in Lucknow, met simultaneously. To maintain the non-political character of his own organization, he chose to make his speech at a separate public meeting. In it he bluntly denounced the Congress.[17]

His opposition to the Congress was against their demand for election, because population of Hindus was four times as numerous. How would the Mohammedan guard his interests?[18] He was also afraid of the open exams and said it would be unfair because Bengalis were far ahead of the others in Western education and it would be very difficult for the Muslims to compete with them in higher education.[19] Badruddin Tayyabji pleading the case of the National Congress in his letter wrote, 'if any proposal is made which would subject the Mussalmans to the Hindus or would vest the exclusive power in Hindus to the detriment of the Mussalmans, I would oppose it with all my strength, but the Congress proposed to do no such thing. Its aims are and must be for the benefit of all communities equally'. He also, mentioned that it is not composed of Bengali Babus alone, however, 'not only the Hindus but Muslims of Bombay and Madras Presidency were taking an active part in it'.[20] This argument was countered by Sir Syed: 'I do not understand what the word "National Congress" means. . . . You regard the doings of the misnamed National Congress as beneficial to India, but I am sorry to say that I regard them as injurious not only to my community but also to India at large.'[21]

Jawaharlal Nehru was of the opinion that Syed Ahmad 'was not opposed to the Indian Congress because he considered it predominantly a Hindu organization; he opposed it because he thought it was politically too aggressive'.[22] W.C. Smith says 'Syed Ahmad's opposition to the National Congress and advice to Muslims to stay out of it because it was too disrespectful, not because it was too Hindu'.[23] On the other hand Hafeez Malik is of the view that it was because 'the Hindu middle class which was the main prop of the Indian National Congress'.[24] However, there is no reference in Sir Syed's numerous criticism of the Congress to its supposed Hinduness. He was against the Congress because he did not want to disrupt the Raj-*qaum* equilibrium for which he had carefully and successfully laboured.[25]

The truth of Jawaharlal Nehru's view is substantiated by the fact that Sir Syed sought and obtained Hindu backing for his opposition to the Congress. Many a Hindu raja and talukdar of north India expressed himself against the Congress's 'disloyal demonstrations'.[26] Like Sir Syed, the Maharaja of Banaras argued that the 'representative institutions was an occidental idea.'[27] Rajmohan Gandhi criticizing Malik mentions that 'Malik is wrong. Sir Syed Ahmad had mounted a Hindustani, not a Muslim, campaign against Congress.'[28] Mushirul Hasan clearly mentions that, the stereotypical figure of Syed Ahmad Khan as the architect of Muslim separatism, mesmerized by the British, remains unaffected by the knowledge of his role in introducing rationalist ideas and English education in the last quarter of the nineteenth century. As a result, his reformist endeavours, which were of far-reaching significance, are obscure and neglected.[29]

Sir Syed Ahmad Khan's first concern was his *qaum* and for the betterment of his *qaum* he articulated his policy of aloofness from the Congress. In the wake of turmoil his main concern was consolidation and reformation of the Muslim community. At this political juncture he was very much convinced that the British government was not going to leave India and he was also witness to the Revolt of 1857 with its dire consequences. The total blame was put on the Muslims and the great Mughal rule was put to an end. He wanted to awaken Muslim society and the best means was education and for that purpose he established *Tahzib-ul Akhlaq* and Mohammedan Anglo-Oriental College, at Aligarh.

His attempt at aloofness from the Congress and later from the development of the Indian National Movement and its culmination in the partition of India made Syed Ahmad a pioneer of separatism in India. After the 1947, with the efforts of some Pakistani historians, it has been argued that the genesis of Pakistan was traced to Sir Syed and from this arrangement he was considered the pioneer of separatism in India. The Muslim *qaum* in India was no doubt his first concern but Jinnah's biographer Bolitho surely went too far when he called Sir Syed Ahmad Khan 'the first Muslim in India who dared to speak of "partition"'.[30] Neither the idea nor the word had suggested itself to Sir Syed. Some have held that the concept of Pakistan, even if never mentioned by him, was implicit in his attitude.[31] However, 'it is very difficult to discern even a "hidden" or latent Pakistan in the following statements, all made in the last twenty years of his life, when he was objecting to "election, pure and simple" campaigning against Congress'.[32]

The image of Sir Syed that emerges from the discussion above, is that he was a Muslim social reformer who was primarily a man who was aware of the failings and strength of both the traditional and the modern he was not opposed to modernity, as is evident by the initiative he took in providing Muslim youth with the facility of achieving the knowledge of Western science coupled with the learning of their own Islamic beliefs under one roof. What he was looking for was a way and method to establish a concept of nationality (*qaum*): both Muslims and Hindus. He was rational enough, at that point of time, to realize the fact that only by remaining loyal to the ruling British power could he achieve the much-needed facilities like education and employment for the Muslims. As a visionary he could foresee that the time was not ripe for India to go against the British, especially for the Muslims who were still grappling with the problem of education and employment.

Unfortunately, historians reinterpreting the reasons behind Sir Syed's pronounced loyalty toward the British and his open denouncement of the Indian National Congress, read in this gesture the birth of the idea of creating a separate nation for Muslims. They failed to see that Sir Syed's objective was the formation of an educated, cultured, self-respecting and modern minded Muslim youth and to give shape to this vision he founded the Mohammedan Anglo-Oriental College at Aligarh and started *Tahzib-ul Akhlaq*. If we go through the history of the nineteenth century there is host of religio-revival movements in Bengal, Maharashtra and Punjab, and their deepening anxieties over the future of, or the evangelical threat to their Hindu identity. Going further, history is witness to various religious associations like the Hindu Mahasabha, RSS and numerous Hindu caste associations.[33]

It becomes imperative in the present time to re-examine the interpreted ideas and actions of Sir Syed Ahmad Khan in order to judge him in the right perspective when various marginalized groups are involved in asserting their identities on the basis of caste, creed and region. It would be unjust to put Sir Syed in the category of 'separatist', for what the different groups are struggling to achieve for themselves today is what he tried to achieve for the Muslims in the late-nineteenth century. It is ironical that in India one can be regarded as nationalist/patriot even if he is a Hindu fundamentalist, but if one champions the cause of marginal sections (Muslims), he is only regarded as a separatist/unpatriotic. At this political and social juncture when we are talking about the minority rights and accepting the caste-based political parties it would be unjust to doubt Sir Syed's identity formation and reformist policies. Mushirul Hasan is right to say: 'how an inappropriate expression—"nationalist Muslim"—is widely used to describe the activities of those Muslims who were wedded to a broadly secular polity and to the idea of composite nationality. Its inappropriateness lies in the majoritarian view of nationalism, a view which assumes that partriotism/nationalism comes "naturally" to the majority of non-Muslims and not to others.'[34]

NOTES

1. Syed Ahmad to Mehdi Ali, London, 22 April 1870, *Maktubat-i-Sir Syed*, ed. Shaikh Muhammad Ismail Panipati, Lahore: Majlis-i-Taraqqi-i-Adab, 1959, p. 99.
2. Ibid., April 1870, p. 106.

3. Syed Ahmad, *Essays on the Life of Muhammad*, rpt., Lahore: Premier Book House, 1968, p. xii.
4. Ibid., p. 51.
5. Rajmohan Gandhi, *Eight Lives: A Study of the Hindu-Muslim Encounter*, New Delhi: Roli Book, 1986, p. 22.
6. Ibid., pp. 176–7.
7. Sir Syed Ahmad Khan, 'Ta'lim Awr Atfiq', *Maqalat-i-Sir Syed: Taqrir-i Maqalat,* Lahore: Majlis-i-Traqqi-i-Adab, 1963, p. 160, Quoted in Hafeez Malik, 'Sir Sayyid Ahmad Khan's Contribution to the Development of Muslim Nationalism in India', *Modern Asian Studies,* 4, 2 (1970), pp. 137–8.
8. Syed Iqbal Ali, *Syed Ahmad Khan ka Safar-i-Punjab,* Aligarh, n.d., pp. 140, 167. Quoted in Hafeez Malik, 'Sir Syed Ahmad Khan's Contribution', p. 138.
9. Ibid., p. 121.
10. Shaikh Muhammad Ikram, *Modern Muslim India and the British Pakistan,* Lahore: Institute of Islamic Culture, 1965, p. 25.
11. Hafeez Malik, *Sir Syyid Ahmad Khan and Muslim Modernization,* New York: Columbia, 1980, p. 93.
12. *Syed Ahmad Khan ka Safar-i-Punjab,* p. 88.
13. Quoted in Aziz Ahmad, *Studies in Islamic Culture in the Indian Environment,* New Delhi: Oxford Univesity Press, 1964, p. 56.
14. Hafeez Malik, 'Sir Sayyid Ahmad Khan's Contribution', p. 139.
15. Syed Ahmad Khan to Mahdi Ali Khan Muhsin-ul-Mulk, 29 April 1870 in *Maktubat-i-Sir Syed,* p. 103, quoted in Hafeez Malik, 'Sir Sayyid Ahmad Khan's Contribution', p. 139.
16. Aligarh Archives, 5 December 1885, quoted in Devid Lelyveld, *Aligarh's First Generation Muslim Solidarity in British India,* New Delhi: Oxford Univesity Press, 1996, p. 305.
17. Ibid., p. 307.
18. S.M. Ikram, *Modern Muslim India,* p. 45.
19. Shan Muhammad, *Sir Syed Ahmad Khan,* Meerut: Meenakshi Prakashan, 1969, pp. 145–6.
20. Ibid., pp. 147–8.
21. Ibid., pp. 148–9.
22. Jawaharlal Nehru, *Discovery of India,* Calcutta, 1946, pp. 410–11.
23. Wilfred Cantwell Smith, *Modern Islam in India,* London: Victor Gollancz, 1946, p. 25.
24. Zaheer Malik, *Muslim Nationalism in India and Pakistan,* Washington, D.C.: Public Affairs Press, 1963, p. 211.
25. Rajmohan Gandhi, p. 38.
26. J.N. Das, quoted in Shan Muhammad, *Sir Syed Ahmad Khan,* p. 145.
27. Ibid., p. 150.

28. Rajmohan Gandhi, p. 38.
29. Mushirul Hasan, 'Introduction', in David Lelyveld, *Aligarh's First Generation*, p. xxxi.
30. Hector Bolitho, *Jinnah*, Westport, Connecticut: Greenwood Press, p. 38.
31. S.M. Ikram, p. xiii.
32. Rajmohan Gandhi, p. 44.
33. Mushirul Hasan, 'Introduction', p. xxxiii.
34. Ibid., p. xxxii.

CHAPTER 12

Sir Syed on the Future of India

SHAN MOHAMMAD

The post-Revolt period found Sir Syed occupied with many issues of which the recovery of India's greatness was foremost. This was possible only when his countrymen acquired Western education, avoided social evils and moved continuously in politics. After the Revolt of 1857, Sir Syed wrote *The Causes of the Indian Revolt* and while describing the many causes, held the British responsible for the revolt and suggested the inclusion of Indians in the Viceroy's Council to find out what India was thinking. He pointed out, 'It is from the voice of the people only that the government can learn whether its projects are likely to be well received. The voice of the people can alone check errors in the bid and warn us of dangers before they burst upon and destroy us. All causes of rebellion, however, various can be traced to this one.'[1] Thus he staunchly pleaded for the admission of Indians in the Viceroy's Council.

Though Sir Syed made the suggestion for the inclusion of Indians in the Council, he was afraid lest they prove unworthy of the post in view of the educational backwardness of the people. But Sir Syed's fears were unfounded as the Indian members of the Council performed their duties well.[2]

Sir Syed always felt that Indians should take modern education to be a part of the administration. After the revolt, his sole effort was to introduce Western education and sciences and he told the people that 'No religious prejudices interfere with our learning any language spoken by any of the many Indians of the world. From remote antiquity, have we studied Persian and no prejudice has ever interfered with the study of that language. How then, can any religious objection be raised against our learning and perfecting ourselves in England . . . ?'

Sir Syed firmly believed that the English had come to stay in India and no power could oust them from here. Cooperation and conciliation was the only way through which Indians could get a place in British administration and hate and hostility was not going to gain them anything.[3]

As stated earlier, from the outset of British rule, the thing that was foremost in Syed's mind was how India could emerge from the curse of medievalism. He believed that India was not a backward country but needed reforms in all walks of life. Apart from education which was his chief concern, natural philosophy, political economy, agriculture, commerce, representation of the views of Indians were some of the issues on which Sir Syed devoted his entire energy. In 1864 he founded the Scientific Society and got the best English works on agriculture, political economy, history and natural philosophy translated into the vernacular. Through the lectures in the Scientific Society, he apprised the people of India of the new techniques of agriculture that were very essential to meet the shortage of food and check famines. He was in charge of the Relief Camp at Moradabad and was deeply touched by the starving poor people. He arranged exhibitions of agriculture instruments to provide more knowledge to the farmers. He wrote treatises on agriculture and submitted memorandum regarding the progress of agriculture, provision of facilities and the establishment of agricultural banks for the farmers.[4] Sir Syed had received much knowledge in this from his maternal grandfather, Khwaja Fareeduddin Ahmad, who had been the Chief of Revenue during the later Mughal kings.

He thought and wrote on the trade and commerce in the development of Indian economy that had received a setback under the British. He was shocked to learn that the British had taken over commerce and industries in India and exhorted Indians to take commerce back into their hands and open agencies in European markets. A country cannot progress by hoarding money but investing it in business, and by exporting Indian commodities to European markets would bring good returns. 'We must snatch business from the English hands. Tell them not to take the hides of our country to England to sell it there'.[5]

On the social plane he wanted Indians to do away with social evils like *sati*, polygamy, infanticide, child marriage, *jhaggi*, etc., that obstructed their progress. He favoured widow remarriage and discouraged polygamy and child marriage and in his journal *Tahzeeb-ul Akhlaq* wrote much to enlighten Indians of these evils. He wanted Indians to move with the times and learn good social practices.

Sir Syed raised the slogan of modern education and opened schools wherever he was transferred to impart Western education and sciences.

In 1864 at Ghazipur with the help of Raises Sir Syed founded a school which soon became the Victoria College. At its foundation ceremony, Sir Syed made a remarkable speech and expressed his future expectations for the people of India.

He firmly believed that if Indians had Western education they would have a bright future. 'The day is not far distant, I trust', he said, 'and when it does come, you will remember my words, when that Council will be composed of representatives from every division or district, and that thus the laws which it will pass will be the laws enacted by the feelings of the entire country. You will, of course, see that this cannot come to pass unless we strive to educate ourselves.'[6]

To Sir Syed of all the disciplines, education was the root of progress. He said that those who held that their cause would be promoted by discussing politics were wrong. He considered modern education to be the only means for their progress and told Indians not to strive for anything other than education. Education creates in a nation determination, discipline, struggle and self-help.

Hindus had taken English education much before the Revolt of 1857 but Muslims did not embrace it. They continued with their oriental system of education. He, therefore, appealed to his countrymen in general and Muslims in particular to acquire Western education. In the midst of opposition from his conservative community, he started the Aligarh movement and founded the Mohammedan Anglo-Oriental College at Aligarh in 1877 and busied himself in promoting modern education.

In 1878, he was nominated to the Vice-Regal Council where he sponsored a few Bills for the benefits of the people of India. Meanwhile, the Bills for Local Self Government and representative institutions were introduced in the Council. Sir Syed welcomed the Bill and said,

> To that noble scheme, I am proud to give my hearty though humble support, for I rejoice to feel that I have lived long enough to see the inauguration of the day when India is to learn at the hands of her rulers those principles of self-help and self-government which have given birth to representative institutions in England and have made her great among the nations of the world. My Lord, I sincerely believe that all the intelligent classes throughout India, sympathizes with the feeling which I have expressed, that they feel grateful to the government for the privileges which the scheme of local self government will confer upon them.

While supporting the Bill he had few reservations also and expressed them frankly. He said

> I am convinced that no part of India has yet arrived at the stage when the system of representation can be adopted to in its fullest scope even in regard to local affairs. . . India, a continent in itself, is inhabited by vast population of different races and different creeds, the rigour of religious institutions have kept even neighbours apart, the system of caste is still dominant and powerful . . . whilst one section of the population commands wealth and commerce, the other may possess learning and influence. One section may be numerically larger than the other. . . . One community may be fully alive to the importance of securing representation on the local boards and District Council, while the other may be wholly indifferent to such matters. Under these circumstances it is hardly possible to deny that the introduction of representative institutions in India will be attended with considerable difficulty and socio-political risks.[7]

Two years after the introduction of the Bill, the Indian National Congress was formed. Sir Syed opposed it for he felt it was politically much too advanced for its time.

As we know, Sir Syed from the beginning of his movement did not touch politics. To him any political movement would lead Indians to revolution that would bring the country on the brink of a confrontation with the government. Events like that of 1857 would be revived and Indians would suffer from the political upheaval. What Sir Syed felt was that unless all the communities were educationally at par, political agitation would take India back by a century. He wanted British supremacy in India as long as it took Indians to become fully conscious of their responsibilities.[8]

Scholars have misrepresented Sir Syed's opposition to the Representative Institution and the Indian National Congress. They have not seen his speeches in the spirit in which they were delivered. Sir Syed held that unless all the communities were educationally advanced, political agitation would bring no good results. Political enlightenment would be achieved not in a day or two, it would take many years and till then, Indians would have to wait. Educational accomplishment and political maturity were to take place simultaneously for the realization of India's independence.

Sir Syed was very objective in his approach. Secularism was as fresh air to him and he rejoiced when he found both Hindus and Muslims working together. There is no dearth of passages in the speeches and writings of Sir Syed which go to prove his non-communal approach to Indian problems. Sir Syed lived at a time when any political movement could be suicidal to Indians. Educational disparity and political maturity in different communities could unbalance India. Sir Syed was a loyalist but his loyalty was that of a unique type. His loyalty to the British demanded allegiance to the government but his patriotism forced him to think of ways and means for his country's progress so that in future when they are educationally and economically at par with the advanced nations, so that they may fight for the independence of their country. Sir Syed was a dreamer of democracy in India which could not be gained unless India became independent. He did not like India to be a slave country forever. But he wanted British presence so long as Indians did not get educational accomplishment and political maturity. He also wanted British presence because if the British withdrew, some other European power like Germany, Portugual, and France would conquer India.

Sir Syed appreciated the people of Ireland who were struggling for their independence from the British but lamented, 'The people of Ireland are carrying on their struggle for independence, where are the men who can launch such a struggle in India'. Thus, his goal was India's independence.

Sir Syed's was a dynamic personality. His association with the British administration had enlightened him on many counts but his first devotion was to make and see India great, and he directed all his energies to achieve this. The work done by Sir Syed and the suggestions rendered by him have great relevance today. What Sir Syed had visualized for his country in the nineteenth century was achieved in the twentieth. Because of his indefatigable efforts to make India great that he is called one of the builders of modern India.

NOTES

1. See Sir Syed Ahmad Khan, *Asbab-e Baghawat-e Hind,* with an Introduction by Fauq Karimi, Aligarh: Aligarh Muslim University, pp. 13–14.
2. *Majmoa*, 'Lectures Vs Speeches', Lahore, 1900, p. 19.
3. Colonel G.F.I. Graham, *The Life and Work of Syed Ahmad Khan,* pp. 36, 39, 74.
4. See 'Memorandum Regarding the Agriculture Land and the Establishment of Banks', in *Aligarh Institute Gazette*, 1883.

5. *Aligarh Institute Gazette*, 20 October 1876. See also Shah Mohammad Waseem, *Sir Syed: Maashi Ifkar aur Tarraqiyati Mansubey*, Aligarh, 2001.
6. Graham, p. 86. See also *Majmoa*, 'Lectures', p. 20.
7. See Shan Mohammad, *Writings and Speeches of Sir Syed Ahmad Khan*, pp. 153–8.
8. See *Majmoa*, 'Lectures', pp. 297–311.

CHAPTER 13

Sir Syed's Social Reforms: A Defence

PARWEZ NAZIR

Sir Syed's social reforms should be understood within their proper socio-historical context. The Revolt of 1857 had led to large scale persecution of Muslims by the British government.[1] Under the discriminatory policies of the British government the Muslims lagged behind their non-Muslim brethrens in education and employment.[2] The Bengal Renaissance, under Raja Rammohun Roy and his successors, had led to the expansion of modern education among the Hindus,[3] while the Muslims were still reluctant to replace traditional learning with modern education.

In the nineteenth century, Raja Rammohun Roy laid emphasis on the needs for modern education. To initiate the process he took a bold step through the medium of the press, persuaded and convinced his countrymen to pursue modern Western education.[4] To him, future progress of the country would be possible only through modern education. His sincere efforts succeeded in fostering a cultural regeneration, often termed the 'Bengal Renaissance', and the development of modern education in India.

The educational and cultural regeneration created by the endeavours of Raja Rammohun Roy inspired Sir Syed Ahmad Khan. Lord Mayo's policy of 'distributive justice' might have also worked as an inspirational force.[5] Addison and Steele, the editors of the *Tattler* and *Spectator* also influenced his ideas on education and social reform. The socio-political and economic condition of the Indians in the early nineteenth century, that of Muslims in particular, was deplorable,[6] and this forced Sir Syed to think about ways to improve the condition of his fellow countrymen, in particular, the Muslims. He was also quite perturbed by the British policies towards Muslims, and the way it excluded them from education and employment opportunities, after the Revolt of 1857. Altaf Husain Hali put it wryly:[7]

Yahi hal duniya mein is qaum ka hai
Bhanwar mein jahaz aa ke jis ka ghira hai
Kinara hai dur aur tufan bapa hai
Guma hai par har dam keab dubta hai
Naheen lete karwat magar ahle kashti
Pare sote hain bekhabar ahle kashti

The same is the condition of this *qaum*;
Whose ship is caught in a whirlpool.
The coast is away and everywhere there is tempest;
It seems that the ship is about to sink.
Yet, the people in the ship are not awake;
They are fast asleep uncaring of their ship.

The question that concerned him was how to liberate the minds and consciousness of Muslims from the suicidal syndrome of *Pidram Sultan bud* (our forefathers were rulers) as they were not ready to accept any change, bound as they were by the fetters of tradition. The Muslims in the late-eighteenth and nineteenth centuries were far behind in every walk of life when compared to the other communities. Hali described the condition in the following verses:[8]

Tanazzul ne ki hai buri gat hamari
Bahut dur pahunchi hai nakbat hamari
Gayee guzri duniya se izzat hamari
Naheen kuch ubharne ki surat hamari

Decadence has led us to so miserable condition;
That our ignominy has reached to great extent.
We have greatly lost our honour in the world;
There is no hope of our re-emergence.

The Muslims were backward and conservative in their outlook and traditional in their approach, unaware of the ongoing changes and developments brought about by Industrial Revolution in Europe and elsewhere in the world. They were not at all ready to change themselves according to the needs of modern contemporary society. Toynbee has rightly argued that in Europe the advent of science marked the development of a rational outlook and secularization of thought that paved the way for the rise of Protestantism, and reforms in Christianity.[9] In Indian Muslim society such a development begins with Sir Syed. In this regard Sir Syed accepted the framework of Muslim social reform that was set by Shah Waliullah, Shah Abdul Aziz and Syed Ahmad Shahid.[10] These religious thinkers paved the way for Sir Syed's Aligarh movement.

In the nineteenth century, Sir Syed Ahmad Khan was after Raja Rammohun Roy the first to take up the challenge of modernization, and considered education indispensable for a respectable position in the modern and competitive industrialized world. No doubt, the process of modernism in Indian Islam can be traced back to the activities of Karamat Ali, a student of Shah Abdul Aziz. However Sir Syed discarded orthodoxy and attempted to synthesize modern rationality with Islam.[11]

The print media, especially the Urdu press, was for the first time extensively used by Sir Syed to persuade the Muslims to change their attitudes and social behaviour. Ayesha Jalal stresses that, 'while the domain of education concentrated most of his energies, he did not fail to manipulate the print media to articulate a conception of Muslimness consistent with the colonial state's epistemology of communatarianism in South Asian Islam'.[12] To arouse the sentiments of the Muslims, Sir Syed asked his friend Altaf Husain Hali to write his magnum opus *Musaddas-e-Hali/Maddo-Jazar Islam,* which constitutes one of the instruments of his persuasive agenda. One cannot deny the impact that Hali's work had on the Muslim mind. Iqtidar Husain Siddiqui rightly argued that 'this well known poem served its purpose of awakening the social consciousness of the readers and this led to enlightment of the community'.[13] Ayesha Jalal regards it 'as a crowning achievement of Syed Ahmad Khan's school in deploying the poetic medium to proclaim a distinctive Muslim cultural identity. A rousing message to his co-religionists to shake off the slumber into which they had fallen, the poem was a stinging critique of the Indian Muslim community that had lost its moorings because of its educational backwardness, internal jealousies, religious bigotry, aristocratic avarice and cultural decadence. Having lost sovereignty, wealth, intellect and self respect, Indian Muslims existed by virtue of their religion alone'.[14] He struggled throughout his life for Muslims to gain a dignified existence. Sir Syed believed that the benefits from progress and advancement brought by the Industrial Revolution was not possible without acquiring modern scientific education.

The quality which distinguished Sir Syed from contemporary reformers was his practical approach to every problem. In the first phase of his reform he started the *Aligarh Institute Gazette* or *Akhbar Scientific Society* which was published by the Scientific Society at Ghazipur.[15] With the help of the Urdu press he launched a campaign first to make Muslims think and then to reorient them. The Scientific Society catered to the immediate need of those who showed their interest in acquiring modern scientific knowledge. Sir Syed did a pioneering work for the Muslim elite by getting English works translated into Urdu that opened an window for the Muslim mind to broaden its horizon and its outlook. Now they had an access to Western culture and their ideologies through translations. The Society laid emphasis on introducing improvement in agricultural sector with an objective to improve the economic condition of the people.[16] Sir Syed practically demonstrated the mechanical appliances to improve the agricultural output.[17] Critics of Sir Syed Ahmad Khan deliberately try to denigrate his contributions by contrasting them with the achievements of Delhi College, Delhi College Vernacular Translations Society, Ramchandra, Munshi Zakaullah and the newspaper *Fawaid-un Nazerin.*[18] But what they ignore is the impact of Sir Syed, Scientific Society, *Aligarh Institute Gazette* and *Tahzib-ul Akhlaq* that covered a much larger area.

During his stay in England, he came across two newspapers, namely, *Tattler*[19] and *Spectator*.[20] These papers worked as a catalyst and an effective instrument to revolutionize eighteenth century English society by creating socio-political awareness. These papers exhorted the masses to accept rational ideas of modern thought. Sir Syed Ahmad was impressed by the efforts made by the editors of these papers and fully convinced that nineteenth century India needed this sort of initiative to reform its society. Sir Syed decided to reach his countrymen through the medium of the press and convince them that the liberation from social degeneration and deplorable economic condition was possible with modern Western education. He used the Urdu press as an instrument to realize his goal of reforming and modernizing Indian Muslim society. On 7 May 1870, Sir Syed Ahmad Khan wrote a letter to his friend Nawab Mohsin-ul-Mulk from England in which he expressed his desire to publish a newspaper on lines similar to the *Tattler* and the *Spectator* with the objective of making the Muslims realize the need of change in thinking and develop a positive attitude towards modern Western education.

On his return to India in October 1870, he started a paper *Tahzib-ul Akhlaq*.[21] His objective, as he made clear in the very first issue.

The aim of publishing this magazine is to persuade the Muslim of India to adopt the values of a perfect civilization, to remove all those vagaries for which they are looked down upon by the civilized nations, so that they also may be regarded as one of the respected and civilized people of the world. It is true that sometime a religion makes a nation civilized. There are certain religions which are hindrance to civilization. We have to analyse whether the religion of Islam is one of them? Those custom and habits which are unfortunately adopted and assimilated as a part of religion and become hindrance in the process of progress should be given up. All this should be compared with the original teachings of the religion and checked whether omission or reform is in conformity with the injunction of the *Sharia*. In this way we and our religion may escape the contempt of other religions.[22]

The *Tattler* and *Spectator* too were not spared from criticism by the conservative section of English society for their reformist endeavours. A similar hostile response welcomed Raja Rammohun Roy when he criticized *sati* and other evil practices. Sir Syed was not spared either. To question the authenticity of certain customs and traditions practiced by Muslims for centuries was equal to throwing a stone in troubled waters. He was criticized by the orthodox section of the Muslims who exhorted the people not to read Sir Syed's papers for they were misleading and corrupting.

The fundamental difference between *Tahzib-ul Akhlaq*, and the *Tattler* and *Spectator* was over religion. The *Tattler* and *Spectator* avoided religious issues whereas in *Tahzib-ul Akhlaq*, Sir Syed Ahmad Khan deliberately discussed issues of religious reform. Through his writings he asked the Muslims to discard fanaticism, conservatism, traditionalism and all other religious and social practices that were not permitted by Islam.[23]

Sir Syed started his career as journalist by writing articles on various issues in *Syed-ul Akhbar*.[24] In 1864 he started a paper himself, which was published by the Scientific Society at Ghazipur named *Akhbar Scientific Society*.[25] Later, it came to be known as the *Aligarh Institute Gazette*. The 1857 revolt had a deep impact on Sir Syed's mind. This incident changed Sir Syed Ahmad Khan and forced him to take up the issue of Muslim upliftment in particular and Indians in general. He went to England from where he got the inspiration to reform the society through the mass media. With the help of the Scientific Society and the publication of *Tahzib-ul Akhlaq,* Sir Syed launched his agenda of social reform and intellectual resurgence.

Sir Syed's educational agenda was always surrounded in controversies. He was criticized by his own community for being heretical and by others as 'parochial', some even arguing his venture was for Muslims alone, and led to communal solidarities. Later on, his critics called him the first Muslim to advocate the partition of the country. Jawaharlal Nehru justified his approach of giving preference to Muslims in the post-1857 era.[26] In 1857, the revolt took place for which Muslims were held responsible. The British vindictiveness resulted in terrible suppression of the revolt and the Muslim community. This made the Muslim population withdraw into a cultural isolation.[27] Sir Syed tried to revitalize the Muslim elite and make a quest for improving the means of existence through education. Farhat Hassan rightly remarks that, 'the early reform movements were actually seeking to create conscious Muslim identity'.[28] He worked tirelessly for the educational advancement of the Muslim though his policy was of course integrationist and not isolationist as it is perceived.

The publication of *Tahzib-ul Akhlaq* was not continuous because of the preoccupation and engagement in other ventures which required more attention from Sir Syed. But within a short span of time, it created social and political awareness among the Muslims to the extent that Nazir Ahmad requested Sir Syed to restart its publication. Because of forceful writings, its impact was so deep that people no longer regarded the learning of English as heresy as it was previously presumed. To Sir Syed the English language was essential in getting a job, participation in national and international trading activities, knowing the political development in and around the world. If Indians were to be given a share in the governance they could not enjoy it effectively without knowing English.[29] Articles published in *Tahzib-ul Akhlaq* dealt with multifarious issues, but religious reform received particular attention. Though the *Aligarh Institute Gazette* became very popular among the masses, Sir Syed Ahmad expressed his desire to bring out yet another journal which could bring awareness among Muslims towards modern life that would enable them to shed the conservative and negative attitude which they had developed with the passage of time. Sir Syed Ahmad was the first among Indians to make print media a constructive instrument for the reform of society. The publication of these two journals proved to be a turning point in Muslim journalism. Through *Tahzib-ul Akhlaq* he fostered among Muslims who had now become an idle lot, the spirit of self-respect, self-help. The *Khawab-e-Ghaflat* (dream causing negligence) of Muslims is described in these words by *Hali*:[30]

par us qaum e ghafil ki ghaflat wahi hai
Tanazzul pe apne qanaat wahi hai
Mile khak mein par rawoonat wahi hai
Hui subh aur khawbe rahat wahi hai
Na afsos unhen apni zillat pe hai kuch
Na rashak aur qaumon ki izzat pe hai kuch

The careless community remains asleep as usual,
They have resigned to their plight.
Though they have been so much deteriorated,
Yet their laxity is the same
Though the morning has arrived, they are still in deep sleep
They have been rended to dust, yet have not shed their vanity.
They are not ashamed on their disrespect and insult;
Nor they are proud of other quam's respect and dignity.

Sir Syed told them to learn how to live in adverse situations. He always tried to convince the Muslims not to waste time and money, but utilize them properly to build a healthy environment for the developments of society. His commitment to social reform found an expression in *Tahzib-ul Akhlaq* through which he launched a sustained campaign against illiteracy, superstition, conservatism and dogmatic approach. His concept of social reform was all round development of personality which included moral values, manner, truthfulness, honesty, modesty, humility, punctuality, devotion and commitment for the good of society.

Sir Syed's social reform programme encompassed every aspect of life—polygamy, extravagance on the occasion of marriage and birth ceremony, Hindu customs and practices which had taken deep root in Muslim society, emancipation and equal opportunity in education for women.[31] Sir Syed accepted the truth that Islam has given more rights, honour and dignity to women as compared to other religions. He spoke about gender equality more emphatically.[32] This was not even imagined by the nineteenth-century women in the West. Simultaneously Sir Syed admitted the truth that Muslim women are an oppressed lot in India. Sir Syed tried to bring them out of their degraded condition and provide them a respectable position in society. On property related issues he supported the Family Endowment Bill to prevent the fragmentation of landed property. The move was opposed by others, who were not in association with Sir Syed Ahmad Khan. They called it, 'un-Islamic',[33] 'demand by a microscopic minority',[34] and an 'obstacle in improving material condition', a 'threat to culture' from Anglicized Muslims led by Sir Syed Ahmad,[35] calculated to arouse 'intra-familial feud'.[36] In the educational sphere he laid emphasis on combining religious and secular education by adopting Western science and technology and home science. Sir Syed's curriculum of modern education was designed to be liberal and scientific.

In the religious arena he emphasized purification of religious beliefs and rituals, discarding irrational dogmas and discouraging all those practices not permitted by Islam. He always thought that without sound economic condition social life will not change much and therefore, he advocated modern techniques in agriculture. To supplement income he suggested the promotion of trade and commerce. He was of the opinion that without the application of technology, all-round development was not possible.

Sir Syed's entire emphasis was to discard those superstitions, rituals and heresy which had no religious sanction and stood as a great obstacle in the progress of the Muslim community. He often cited from the Holy Koran that its teachings are in no way against learning science and technology. He clarified the prevalent misunderstanding among non-Muslims that Islam is against all scientific learning. He wanted Muslims to live a dignified as well as civilized life and adopt whatever is beneficial from others.

Tahzib-ul Akhlaq, really succeeded in shaping the overall outlook of the Muslims on modern education. Muslims came out from the century-old stagnation and decadence to action and mustered the courage to embrace Western education and modern thought. Like Raja Rammohun Roy, he faced stiff opposition from his co-religionists, but *Tahzib-ul Akhlaq* remained very popular among people because of the constructive and beneficial role it played, and by the virtue of its simple and lucid style. What the *Tattler* and *Spectator* did in England, *Tahzib-ul Akhlaq* did in India. To make Muslims self-reliant in every walk of life, he tried to attract them towards scientific learning. To Sir Syed, science and scientific knowledge was helpful for all the round development and progress of society.[37]

The impact of *Tahzib-ul Akhlaq* on the minds of Muslims was lasting, it revolutionized their socio-politico and religious life.[38] Many Muslims readily accepted English and modern scientific education, that in turn broadend the horizon of their outlook. His move was opposed by the tradionalist Muslims on the ground that modern and Western education deviated from the true path of Islam. Sir Syed argued that education, and only education, was the remedy to their socio-political and economic backwardness. He popularized his ideas through the print media, the only instrument to reach the people. This worked, and in spite of the opposition his voice was heard and got wider acceptability. Unlike the contemporary *ulama* and intelligentsia, Sir Syed preferred to write in simple Urdu, which was easily understood by the common people. In this way his contribution towards the development of Urdu literature, and in particular Urdu journalism, is noteworthy, Shafey Kidwai emphasizes that 'Sir Syed displayed his consciousness by liberating journalism from the emotional stresses and enabled it to grasp modern sensibilities.'[39]

He was a man with a mission, worked tirelessly for the development of education among Muslims so that they could play a greater role in the socio-political life of the country. His dream was translated into reality with the establishment of Mohammedan Anglo-Oriental College. Education was to be main instrument to fulfil the agenda of social reform and the only effective medium to convince Muslims to opt for modern education and Sir Syed succeeded in this.

One remarkable aspect of Sir Syed's personality was the practical approaches he took. For instance, when he asked the Muslims to pursue modern and Western education, he sacrificed his comfortable life, went to England, to study the English system of education. He returned to India with a clear-headed single objective to open an institution on the model of Oxford and Cambridge. He travelled far and wide to collect funds for the college[40] and finally in 1877, at the hands of Lord Lytton, the then Governor-General of India, the foundation stone of the college was laid which served the future need of Muslims of India.

Once Sir Syed's endeavour to provide Muslims a dignified existence got the momentum, his opponents lost no time to target his concepts of progress. His every effort to modernize the community, whether it was clothes or his rejection of customs and tradition, or his belief in maintaining cordial relation with others including the Christians was criticized. The orthodox Muslims branded him *Kafir* and had a *fatwa* of *Kufr* issued against him.[41]

The greatness of Sir Syed Ahmad Khan lies in the fact that without caring for what the opposition said, he continued his mission through the *Tahzib-ul Akhlaq, Aligarh Institute Gazette* and the Muslim Educational Conference.

Sir Syed was the first to persuade the Muslims through the Urdu press. Then through the Scientific Society at Ghazipur he provided them with modern Western knowledge translated into Urdu. At last his mission of establishing Mohammedan Anglo-Oriental College was achieved through the Aligarh movement. Today in north India, AMU, Aligarh caters to the educational needs of the Muslims. One vital legacy of Sir Syed was the creation of an infrastructure for excellence in modern education which has become a source of self-confidence for Muslims today.

The most crucial agenda of his reform was in the religious sphere. He, according to Percival Spear, 'launched a Muslim modernism which sought to reconcile traditional Islam with modern needs'.[42] To him the Koran and *Hadith* were the real sources of Islam. Things should be interpreted rationally according to these scriptures. Regarding *Hadith* he was of the view that its authenticity should first be verified and then followed. He argued that traditions contrary to Islamic principles, which Muslims in India had adopted under the influence of Hinduism were impious innovation and should be rejected; any tradition contrary to Koran must be rejected.[43]

To Sir Syed, the only sources of Islamic teachings are the Koran and the *Hadith*. These should be interpreted in the light of modern needs and in conformity.

With the rational standpoint of the scientific age, Sir Syed described that man is not a machine to perform certain specific functions. But he is like a tree which develops on all sides because of inherent power that Allah has bestowed upon him. Man is guided by reason which enables him to distinguish between evil and good. A man is said to be rational when he uses his reason and performs his duty in that light.[44] The *ulama* on account of his approach towards religion criticized Sir Syed; they held the opinion that application of reason to understand religion is not correct, particularly those aspects which are part of the *iman* or *aqeeda*. To them reason was not perfect, so that what Allah and *Rasul* has revealed is beyond the purview of the common man. Sir Syed, under Western influence did not agree with this opinion. He expected that educated Muslims should believe only what satisfied their reason. He argued that the rationalistic explanation of the teachings of Islam could be helpful in emerging from the existing problems of the nineteenth century India. It is true, that reason and rationalism save mankind from being superstitious and develop the spirit of enquiry which is helpful for progress.

Sir Syed believed that true religion did not hamper the progress of mankind because Allah never desired that his creature should stagnate. If Allah had thought of degrading man then there was no need of creating him.[45] Muslims came to India, introduced a new dynamic culture totally different from the previous, which survived for centuries, then came a phase of decadence. Islam, in no way was not responsible for it, but the law of nature, i.e. *Har urooj-e-ra zawal ast.*

Indian Muslims were religious-minded and traced everything to religion and got their inspiration from the teachings of Islam. Vambery criticized the Muslim on the ground that for them religion was the basis of every action, and for every thing they turned towards it and this the reason for their decadence.[46] Strachey was also critical of the common Muslim for the same reason.[47] Sir Syed was critical of the *taqleed* as it put restriction on interpreting religious teachings in a modern perspective. Instead he pleaded for *Ijtehad* which meant developing a new *Ilam-al-Kalam* contested by orthodox Muslims. 'Put him,' Ayesha Jalal said, 'at logger heads with the Ulema. Who considered it as an assault on their self proclaimed right as the religious guardian of the Muslim community.'[48] Institutions like polygamy and slavery had lost its relevance in the West but it was still prevalent among the Muslims. This is partly true because slavery was abolished everywhere in the world but continued in one form or the other in the world. Why was Islam to be blamed? Asked Sir Syed if it was abolished altogether[49] Muslims were being criticized for their firm belief in traditionalism and they were not ready to accept science because of their conservatism. It is true but there was hardly any attempt before Sir Syed to persuade the Muslims and convince them that Islam is not opposed to science and scientific knowledge.

The Holy Koran exhorts to understand the creation of Allah with an open mind. Sir Syed did what others failed by persuading as well practically establishing a centre of learning to pursue education in every branch of knowledge. To come cut from the shadow of backwardness, it was Sir Syed who provided them a base.

To remove religious conservatism, traditionalism, narrow mindedness, etc., education was the only way to liberate the Muslim mind. The Muslims in the nineteenth century developed hatred for Western culture, their etiquette and manners; they did not even approve of shaking hands or dining with Christians. To Sir Syed this attitude of the Muslims was not acceptable as Islam regarded the Christians as *Ahl-e-Kitab*. He wrote a lengthy essay *Resala-Ahkam-e Towam Ahl-e-Kitab* on this theme. He tried to reconcile Muslims with the Christians and Christianity.[50] His commentary on the Bible was strategically designed to bridge the gulf between the two communities, and to develop a better understanding and rapprochement.

Allama Iqbal appreciated Sir Syed as first among the Muslims to feel the need of reconstruction in religious thinking. Sir Syed's efforts at constructive reform and betterment necessitated the acceptance of Western education in accordance to the reformed religious principles of Islam.

Sir Syed's approach to persuade the Muslims to discard the prevalent evils that brought degeneration in the society was unique. He first listed them, then analysed their injurious effects on society, then suggested the remedies to save society from their evil effects. Sir Syed accepted the truth that Islam has given women more respectable position and rights than Christianity, but their existing condition was really deplorable at present in India, for which Islam was in no way responsible but the ignorance of the Muslims and the media. Sir Syed advocated women's education. His advocacy finally culminated in the establishment of the Women's College was founded by Shaikh Abdullah under the aegis of the AMU.[51]

The activities of Christian missionaries created an atmosphere of antagonism between Muslims and Christians. The missionaries were given a free hand to propagate their religion and condemn the religious beliefs of Hindus and Muslims and this created mutual distrust and intolerance in society. William Muir in his book attacked the life of Muhammad (PBUH), and he declared that the moral principles of Islam were not compatible with modern ideals. He attributed political and social decadence among Muslims to Islam. There is hardly anything to be called civilization and cultured in Muirs' description about Islam and the Prophet. Muir's work was a fanatical approach to arouse the sentiments of Muslims and to make them reactionary and intolerant. Sir Syed wrote *Khutbat-e-Ahmadiya* to refute Muir's charges labelled against Islam and the Prophet. He wrote a commentary on the Bible, *Tabaa-in-ul-Klam*. He accepted the Bible as a revealed book but believed that over centuries it had suffered from continued interpolations.

He was the first Muslim in modern India to realize in true sense the necessity for a reinterpretation of Islam to make it more accommodating to ideas like liberalism, modernity and progress. He was opposed in his attempt to reinterpret those Islamic beliefs by the orthodox and conservatries *ulama*. Sir Syed and Mohsin-ul Mulk wrote articles refuting the allegations of opponents and explained their position regarding religious beliefs.

The task of restructuring the social and religious life of the Muslims is described by Hafeez Malik as 'Muslim renaissance for a competitive existence in future'. He further says that 'as a consequence of his intellectual exposure to Western sciences, Sir Syed developed an entirely new set of religious orientation. To the orthodox this was not only an affront to Islam but also a challenge to the socio-political position of the *ulama*.'[52] Gradually, however, modern Muslim youth internalized these new religious values and orientations and discarded the old one, which Hafeez Malik regards as Sir Syed's greatest achievement.[53] For instance, the traditional orientation is 'scientific knowledge suppresses religion'. The modern orientation is that 'scientific knowledge reveals the truthfulness of a true religion'. Similarly the traditional notion that 'man should search God with the eyes completely closed' was replaced by a modern one 'with eyes wide open man should investigate the phenomena of nature in order to comprehend God'.[54] Sir Syed continued his mission, vigorously and enthusiastically and succeeded against all odds. As Hali said, *Hum bat karte hain Syed kam karte hain*. I conclude this essay with the following verses of Hali:[55]

Bas ai na ummeedi nay un dil bujha tu
Jhalak ai ummeed apni aakhir dikha tu
Bahut tunne paston ko bala kiya hai
Andhere mein aksar ujala kiya hai
Nawaza bahut be nawaon ko tune
Tawangar banaya gadaon ko tu ne

Oh! Disappointment, do not discourage us;
Oh! hopefullness, show your face to us
[Oh! hopefulness] you have risen many depressed to high position;
You have often lightened the dark.
[Oh hopefulness!], you have blessed many destitutes;
Beggers have been made rich by you.

NOTES

1. William Dalrymple, *The Last Mughal*, Delhi: Viking, 2006, p. 69.
2. Mushirul Hassan, *Nationalism and Communal Politics in India 1885–1930*, p. 5; Paul R. Brass, *Language, Religion and Politics in North India*, 1974, p. 178; Francis Robinson, *Separatism Among Indian Muslim: The Politics of the United Province Muslims, 1880–1923*, p. 59; W.W. Hunter, *Indian Musalmans*, p. 164. He argued that the number of Muslims declined drastically in the services between 1851 and 1969.
3. Saumyendranath Tagore, *Rammohun Roy: His Role in Indian Renaissance*, Calcutta, 1975, p. 25. See also Bruce Carlisle Robertson, *Raja Rammohun Roy: The Father of Modern India*, p. 43; R. Tagore, *Inaugurator of the Modern Age in India,* p. 4; D. Koft, *The Brahmo Samaj Intelligentsia and Bengal Renaissance: A Study of Revitalization and Modernization in the Nineteenth Century Bengal; Transition in South Asia: Problems of Modernization*, ed. R.I. Crane, Durham, 1970.
4. Rammohun Roy, the pioneer of modern Indian journalism, started publishing and editing two newspapers: *Sambad Kaumudi* and *Mirat-ul Akhbar*. These two papers were the main instruments of his social reforms. *Sambad Kaumudi* first published in 1821 was a Bengali weekly newspaper. *Miraat-ul Akhbar*, first published in 1822, was a Persian weekly newspaper. See *The Essential Writings of Raja Rammohan Roy*, ed. Bruce C. Robertson.
5. Hafeez Malik, *Sir Syed Ahmad Khan and Muslim Modernization in India and Pakistan*, Karachi, 1980, p. 125.
6. Syed Tufail Ahmad Manglori, *Musalmano ka Roshan Mustaqbil*, pp. 216–17, Shah Waliullah, *Shah Waliullah key Siyasi Maktubat*, ed. and tr. Khalique Ahmad Nizami, Delhi, 1969. *Tarikh-e Ahmad Shahi* described that every class of society was a victim of penury. See also Percival Spear, *Twilight of the Mughals*.
7. Altaf Hussain Hali, *Maddo Jazzar-e Islam Maktaba Jamia*, 1995, p. 14.
8. Hali, p. 47.
9. Arnold Toynbee, *A Study of History*, abridged by D.C. Somervell, vol. 2, Oxford Univesity Press, 1957, p. 148. See also C.E. Black, *The Dynamics of Modernization: A Study in Comparative History*, 1967, p. 6. David Apter, *The Politics of Modernization*, 1966 emphasized the process of commercialization and industrialization as the evidence of modernity in the West, p. 43. W. Wilson Hunter to Miss Murray 17 December 1862, in Francis Henry Skrine, *Life of William Wilson Hunter*, 1901. Lucian W. Pye, *Aspects of Political Development*, 1965. To Pye modernization is based on advanced technology and a spirit of science, on a rational view of life, a secular approach to the social relations and feeling for justice in public affairs. For Syed Ahmad Khan,

Britain's political domination in India was not ensured merely by brute force, rather it reflected the triumph of modernity over tradition. In India modernity came very late. The Muslims were exposed to modernity only after 1857, when they accepted a change from traditional to modern ways of life.

10. Hafeez Malik, p. 261.
11. Ali Yusuf, A. Karamat Ali, *The Encyclopedia of Islam*, Lieden, 1975, vol. 4, p. 265.
12. Ayesha Jalal, *Self and Sovereignty: Individual and Community in South Asian Islam since 1850*, Delhi: Oxford University Press, 2001, p. 61.
13. Iqtidar Husain Siddiqui, 'Sir Syed Ahmad's Approach to History', in *Sir Syed Ahmad Khan: A Centenary Tribute,* ed. Asloob Ahmad Ansari, p. 126.
14. Ayesha Jalal, p. 65.
15 . The Scientific Society was established by Sir Syed Ahmad Khan at Ghazipur in 1864. Later Sir Syed was transferred to Aligarh and the office of the society moved to Aligarh and hence came to be known as the Aligarh Scientific Society. A large number of scientific texts were translated by the Society into Urdu. It was a twin effort to help the Muslims of India to acquaint themselves with Western scientific knowledge and Western classical literature, apart from being a centre for the promotion and dissemination of knowledge. It also served as an effective instrument for Sir Syed Ahmad to realize future schemes of social reforms and intellectual awakening. The Society translated books on diverse subjects agricultural sciences, algebra, geometry, calculus, hydrology, meteorology, geography, history, political economy, polity, mathematics, etc. On science and technology the works of Robert Burn Tomlinson and Harris were translated which proved to be very beneficial. The chief translator was Munshi Zakaullah. See *Aligarh Institute Gazette* for further details. The Society started publishing a newspaper, the *Aligarh Institute Gazette* in 1866. It was bilingual and published twice a week.
16. *Aligarh Institute Gazette*, 20 April 1866.
17. Ibid., 25 May 1966.
18. S. Irfan Habib, 'Syed Ahmad and Scientific Society', in *Sir Syed Ahmad Khan: A Centenary Tribute*, ed. Asloob Ahmad Ansari, pp. 217–18.
19. *Tattler*, an English newspaper, edited by Sir Richard Steele and Joseph Addison. First published on 12 April 1709. Without assigning any reason Steele stopped the publication. This annoyed Addison and he started another newspaper.
20. Once the publication of *Tattler* stopped abruptly, Joseph Addison, the co-editor of the *Tattler* started the *Spectator*. The first issue appeared on 1 March 1711. These two newspapers changed the face English society. They propagated ideas like liberty and enlightment and

developed the spirit of scientific temper exhorted people to discard ignorance, immorality and advocated women's education.

21. *Tahzib-ul Akhlaq* or Mohammedan Social Reformer was first published on 24 December 1870. It was published in three phases. 752 articles were published on diverse subjects out of which 363 were written by Sir Syed himself. (Original copies of *Tahzib-ul Akhlaq* are available at Maulana Azad Library, AMU, Aligarh.)
22. *Tahzib-ul Akhlaq*, 1870; *Tamheed,* vol. I, pp. 1–2.
23. Ibid., p. 58.
24. *Sayyidul Akhbar* was a Urdu newspaper edited and published by Sir Syed Ahmad's elder brother, Syed Mohammad. Most scholars mentioned the year of its publication as 1838 . Contesting the opinion, Shafey Kidwai in his article 'Aligarh Institute Gazette: Zu Lesani ya kaseer lesani Akbar', published *Tahzib-ul Akhlaq*, October 2006 stated its year of publication was 1841. Sir Syed started his journalistic journey by writing articles for *Sayyidul Akhbar.* After the sudden demise of his brother he edited it but it closed down soon.
25. *Akhbar Scientific Society* later became the *Aligarh Institute Gazette.* First published on 30 March 1866. It was the main voice for Sir Syed Ahmad and his Society for the dissemination of progressive and modern ideas. It is interesting to note that this weekly was the first to publish editorials, book reviews and advertisements. This shows Sir Syed's entrepreneurship to raise funds in the market in the absence of a sound financial basis.
26. Jawaharlal Nehru, *Discovery of India*, pp. 347–8.
27. Hafeez Malik, p. 125.
28. Farhat Hasan, 'Quest for Identity', in *Zubaia Mustala*, ed., *The South Asian Century, 1900–99*, Oxford University Press, 2000, p. 84.
29. Sir Syed Ahmad Khan, *Maqalat-e-Sir Syed: Madhhabi wa Islami, Madamin,* 16 October 1863, p. 274. See also Sir Syed Ahmad 'Need for Development of Science and Civilization Amongst Indian People', *Selected Lecture of Sir Syed Ahmad* (tr. by M. Abdul Manan, vol. I, pp. 26–7.
30. Hali, p. 14.
31. Contesting the opinion that Syed Ahmad was not in favour of female education, Ayesha Jalal described him as a 'strong proponent of women's education, after his visit to England and France', *Self and Sovereignty*, p. 69. The *Aligarh Institute Gazettee*, 8 July 1870, declared in clear words that we wish our women to be educated but not at the cost of morality, privacy and above all honour. For detail see Ashraf Ali Thanwi, *Perfecting Women: Maulana Ashraf Ali Thanwi's Bahishti Zewar*, tr. and ed. Barbara Metcalf, Berkeley, 1982. Also see Gail Minault, *Secluded Scholars: Women's Education and Muslim Social Reform in Colonial India*, Delhi: Oxford University Press, 1998. Syed Ahmad's

advocacy culminated in Nazir Ahmad's novel *Miratul Urus* wherein Asghari represents the role model of a modern educated women. Further this movement found an appreciation in Hali's *Majalis-un-Nisa*.

32. *Tahzib-ul Akhlaq*, 3 August 1971.
33. *Awadh Akhbar*, 23 February 1880.
34. *Agra Akhbar*, 21 February 1880.
35. Ibid.
36. *Awadh Akhbar*, 23 February 1880.
37. David Lelyveld, *Aligarh's First Generation*, Delhi, 1996, p. 108.
38. Sir Syed, '*Tahzib-ul Akhlaq ka Asar Dilon par*' (Recollection of the Mazaamin), *Tahzib-ul Akhlaq*, pp. 519–20.
39. Shafey Qidwai, 'Sir Syed as a Journalist', in Asloob Ahmad Ansari, ed., *Sir Syed Ahmad Khan: A Centenary Tribute*, 2001, p. 403.
40. See his lecture delivered on 29 December 1873 in Punjab to propagate the idea of the MAO College. He was received with honour and people generously contributed. Sir Syed admired them in *Zindah Dilan-e-Panjab*, Hali, *Hayat-e Javed*, pp. 632–3.
41. Imdadul Afaq, *Imdad Ali*, pp. 78–84.
42. Percival Spear, *India*, *Pakistan and the West*, p. 190.
43. *Tahzib-ul Akhlaq*, 1872, vol. 2, no. 1, p. 10.
44. Ibid., p. 304.
45. Ibid., pp. 147–9.
46. Vambery, *A Western Culture in the Eastern Lands*, London, 1906, p. 236.
47. Sir John Strachey, *India: Its Administration and Progress*, 3rd edn., London, 1903, p. 305.
48. Ayesha Jalal, p. 68.
49. *Sir Syed Ahmad, Ibtal-e Ghulami*, p. 2.
50. *Tahzib-ul Akhlaq*, vol. 1, p. 32.
51. See for details of 'Education Movement and the Foundation of Women's College, A.M.U., Aligarh', S.R. Abdullah's autobiography: *Mushahedat and Tassawarat (1954)* and biography *Sevaneh-e-Umri-e-Abdullah Begum*. Tufail Ahmad Mangalauri, p. 246.
52. Hafeez Malik, p. 279.
53. Ibid., pp. 278–9.
54. Hali, p. 89.
55. Ibid., p. 90.

CHAPTER 14

Sir Syed and Christianity

IQBAL SABIR

Sir Syed Ahmad Khan, who was one of the towering personalities in the galaxy of nineteenth-century reformers, occupies a significant place in the modern history of the Indian subcontinent. He zealously worked to bring about a change in Muslim thought and behaviour. According to my revered teacher (late) Professor K.A. Nizami, 'he ushered in the dawn of an era of intellectual renaissance in India and contributed many essential elements to the development of modern Indian society'.[1] He applied his mind to the task of creating conditions in which his community could come up to par with other communities of India. He paid attention to almost all aspects of contemporary social life and left a deep impact of his thought and personality on everything that he touched. No doubt he found in education the solution to all the ills of Muslim society in those days and made sincere efforts to create an environment conducive to education.[2] But at the same time he also applied himself with great devotion to several other issues and problems prevalent in the then Muslim society. Of these problems, the Christian–Muslim relations also was seriously drawing notice of religious-minded people of both the communities. The British rulers' attitude towards their Indian subjects in general and towards Muslims in particular. The appearance of scholarly works not only criticizing and refuting Islam and Islamic traditions but also hurting the religious sentiments of Muslims,[3] and above all the role of the Christian missionaries in different parts of the country,[4] on one hand, and, on the other, the response of Muslim *ulama* and religious scholars such as issuing religious verdicts (*fatwas*), against Christians and Christianity, holding the polemical debates (*munaziras*),[5] and also the publication of the brochures and the treatises proving Christians and Christianity as great threat to Islam and the Muslims[6] had created an atmosphere of doubt and hatred among the followers of the two religions. Sir Syed Ahmad Khan could not keep himself away from the prevailing situation and, therefore, turned to it with complete determination, devotion and sincerity. His intention was no doubt to provide an entirely appropriate and vastly accepted solution to this socio-religious problem being faced by Christians and Muslims alike. He firmly believed that both the religions and their followers had a lot in common—both in the form of ideas and practices. In this connection he was strongly of the view that both Christian and the Muslims would have to sympathetically, sincerely and warm-heartedly understand each other's religions and their teachings in order to develop an atmosphere of compassion, harmony and brotherhood. Without which it would be very difficult, especially for the Muslims, to lead a trouble free life. Accordingly, he devided to work out in this field mostly through his intellectual approach. This paper is an attempt to bring to light Sir Syed Ahmad Khan's contribution in this regard.

Sir Syed's interest in Christians and Christianity may be traced back to the events during his posting as Sadr Amin at Bijnaur, when he saved and supported the families of the English (Christian), officers of the district throughout the uprisings of 1857. It was undoubtedly on account of his efforts that the British officers and their ladies and children safely reached Rurkee.[7] Alexander Shakespeare, who was the Collector of Bijnaur at that time, admired and expressed his deep indebtedness to Sir Syed for this act of generosity and humanism. According to Altaf Husain Hali whatever was done by Sir Syed was done in accordance with the principles of Islamic morals.[8]

Subsequently, Sir Syed's posting at Moradabad provided him with an opportunity to study the views and behaviour of the Christian missionaries. When there arose a controversy over the issue of Hindu and Muslim orphans children whose parent had lost their lives during the severe famine in Moradabad, and surrounding areas in the pre-Mutiny period, the Christian missionaries wanted these orphans to be handed over to them whereas Sir Syed Ahmad Khan favoured the demand of the local people, that the Hindu children should be given to interested Hindu families and Muslim orphans be given to interested Muslim families. In the beginning Sir Syed succeeded by convincing John Strachy, the then Collector of Moradabad district. But when on the latter's transfer, the new Collector Power assumed the charge, Sir Syed had to ultimately hand over these children to the

Christian missionaries.[9] Although he was very disgusted and felt deeply hurt on surrendering these Indian children to the missionaries, he did not give up his interest and curiosity in the basic tenets of Christianity. As he had visualized the future of Indian subcontinent to be dominated by Western ideas and conventions, he was really desirous of getting the sympathy of Western people—the Christians, in favour of his co-religionists. Accordingly, he took the task of bridging the gulf between Christianity and Islam, and their followers. In this connection he first thought it necessary to remove the doubts and the false impressions prevalent amongst them about each other's religion, culture, social and moral values. His object was that the followers of the two religions should live in harmony. He, therefore, decided to write from different angles on various aspects of socio-religious thought and values of both the communities.

The compilation of the treatise (*Risala*) *Tahqiq-i Lafz-i Nasara*[10] (An Inquiry into the Word Nasara), was the first most effective intellectual step in this direction. This work was in fact a refutation of the writings of some Muslim *ulama* calling British (Christian) people Nasara. Sir Syed, endeavoured through it to clear up the misunderstanding of the Christians about this term—Nasara. In earlier works by Muslims authors, Christians or issues related to them were referred to as Nasara. One must mention here that Muslims since very beginning of Islam addressed Christians as Nasara. Unfortunately the British took it as an insult and a humiliating term. Therefore these works had drawn the serious notice of the British. The government regarded the use of this word as an act of sedition. The writers who employed it were punished.[11]

In the *Risala*, the *Tahqiq-i Lafz-i Nasara*, Sir Syed made it clear that the word Nasara had been derived not from the word Nasera, as the British had misunderstood. Rather, it had been derived from the Arabic verb root Nasara, that means, to help. He argued that the term Nasara has been used in the Koran in the sense of a helper. In this connection he quotes Koranic verse in which it is stated that Hazrat Isa (Jesus Christ), asked his disciples, *Man ansaarii ilallaah*? (Who are my helpers for God?)[12] The disciples (*hawariyin*) replied, *Nahnu ansaarullahi* (We are Allah's helpers).[13] For this reason, those who followed the disciples and those who believed in Jesus were known by the name 'Nasara'. The disciples themselves had accepted this name and were thus called Nasara. He says that in the Koran no mention has been made of the 'Village of Nasera',[14] and similarly,

Hazrat Isa, the Prophet of God, has not ever been referred to in the Holy Koran as the Naseri, the 'person belonging to the village of Nasera'. Arguing further in this context Sir Syed maintains that the Koran makes it very clear that the Christians who lived in *yathrib*, later known as 'Madinat-un Nabi'—the City of the Prophet—also called themselves Nasara. For example, it is stated in the *Surah* Maaa-Idah (The Table Spread), Oh Muhammad, you will find that best friends the Muslims have, are those who say Ana Nasara means 'we are Nasara' (Christians).[15]

لَتَجِدَنَّ اَشَدَّ النَّاسِ عَدَاوَةً لِّلَّذِيْنَ اٰمَنُوا الْيَهُوْدَ وَالَّذِيْنَ
اَشْرَكُوْا وَلَتَجِدَنَّ اَقْرَبَهُمْ مَّوَدَّةً لِّلَّذِيْنَ اٰمَنُوا الَّذِيْنَ قَالُوْٓا اِنَّا
نَصٰرٰى ذٰلِكَ بِاَنَّ مِنْهُمْ قِسِّيْسِيْنَ وَرُهْبَانًا وَّاَنَّهُمْ
لَا يَسْتَكْبِرُوْنَ ○

Thou wilt find the most vehement of mankind in hostility to those who believe (to be) the Jews and the idolaters and thou wilt find the nearest of them an affection to those who believe (to be) those who say: Lo We are Christians. That is because there are among them priests and monks, and because they are not proud.

Altaf Husain Hali writes in his *Hayat-i Javed* that after the publication of the *Risala* no one else was punished for using the word Nasara. He says that an English newspaper once reported that Sir Syed was mistaken and no one had been punished for using the word Nasara. But this statement was contradicted by a fair-minded British officer who wrote that he had seen someone with his own eyes, hanged to death in Kanpur for using the word Nasara.[16]

The next great step Sir Syed Ahmad Khan took was to resolve the religious misunderstandings between the Christians and the Muslims was the compilation of his commentary on the Holy Bible—the *Tabiyin-ul Kalam*.[17] As pointed out earlier, the polemical debates (*munaziras*), between Christian missionaries and Muslim *ulama*, were frequently held during the nineteenth century in which the Christian missionaries, harshly attacked Islam, the Prophet Muhammad and the Koran. The Muslim divines of the time, particularly on account of their ignorance of the teachings of Christianity, unaware of the history of the Christian–Muslim relations especially during the early centuries of Islam, and the lack of knowledge in the rational as well as modern sciences, found themselves unable to intellectually face these Christian preachers. An atmosphere of sorrow and disruption gradually descended and the whole Muslim community of the subcontinent was in a dilemma.[18] It appears Sir Syed felt deeply affected and he took serious notice of these activities of the Christian missionaries. It is to be pointed out here that before the uprising of 1857, he had planned to write in the defense of Islam, and, for this purpose, he had prepared notes on different topics. But unfortunately, these records were destroyed during the disturbances in 1857.[19] When the situations returned to normal, he decided to undertake the task but from different angle. He was of the view that the Muslims, were defeated in these polemical debates because of their lack of knowledge of Christianity. Sir Syed did not agree with the generally prevailing Muslim point of view that the passages in the Bible concerning the miracles of Jesus Christ, etc., had been altered and tampered with. He thought that the disputes between the Christians and the Muslims over the question of abrogation (*naskh*), were nothing more than a war of words. He was also of the opinion that much of the evidence which the Christians derived from the Bible to attack the tenets of Islam was based on their misunderstanding of Islam.[20]

Sir Syed's decision to write a commentary on the Bible required deep study of Islam and Christianity, and also a great deal of time and money. While he was posted at Ghazipur he employed a Jew, Salim, to teach him Hebrew. He also studied for some time under the guidance of Maulana Inayat Rasool Chirraiyakoti who was a renowned scholar of Christian, Islamic and Jewish sciences and also Arabic and Hebrews. It was under the latter's tutelage that Sir Syed became well-versed in above subjects.[21] Finally the *Tabiyin-ul Kalam* was completed, probably the first Muslim commentary, on the Bible.[22] It is divided into three parts. The first part is the Preliminary Discourse on this commentary; the second part is the commentary on the Books of Genesis in Urdu with English translation, the third part is the commentary on the first five chapters of the Bible in Urdu only. The first part of this monumental work, i.e. the 'Preliminary Discourse', consists of ten 'Discourses' and two 'Appendices'. In these discourses Sir Syed discusses the issues like the 'Necessity of the advent of prophets' (*Zururat-i Ambiya*), 'Revelation' (*Wahi*) and 'Word of God' (*Kalamullah*), the 'Muslims' faith about Pentateuch (the Touriet)', 'Psalms' (*Zubur*), the 'Books of prophets' (*Suhuf-i Ambiya*) and *Injil* (the Gospel), the number of books included in the Bible, the Islamic principles to enquire into and confirm the authenticity of a religious book, the Muslims' opinion regarding the corruption of the sacred scriptures, the authenticity of the books included in the Bible, the 'Muslims' belief about these scripture, and the 'Naskh' and the 'Mansukh', i.e. one commandment of God cancelling another.[23]

Through these discourses Sir Syed made an attempt to dispel the 'hostile feelings' which were steadily growing more acute on the both sides and which came about largely as a result of mutual intolerance and the ignorance of both Christians and the Muslims regarding the each other's religion. In these discourses, which form the basis for a commentary on the Bible, Sir Syed pointed out that it was as essential for Jews and Christians as it was for Muslims to believe that all the prophets had been sent by Almighty God, and that the Scriptures brought by these prophets are accorded the same importance by Islam as they are accorded by the other two religions.[24] To him, the standard of judging the authenticity of these writings is the same for the Muslims and the Christians. In this connection he quotes the eminent Muslim scholars like Imam Mohammad Ismail al-Bukhari, Fakhruddin Razi and Shah Waliullah of Delhi to prove that the only kind of textual falsification to be found in the Bible is that which Christian commentators have already admitted and it is only in those places where the sacred Books of the Christians differ from the Koran and the *Hadith*.[25] Here he quotes the famous exegesis—the *tafsir*, the commentaries of the Koran, the *Durar-i Mansur,* in which Ibn Munzar and Ibn Abi Hatim have been mentioned as saying that the *Toureit* and the *Injil* are in the same state of purity in which they were set down from Heaven.[26] Sir Syed refers to the passages from the *tafasir* by the above mentioned and other Muslim divines.[27] Afterwards, he gives an account of the efforts made by the Jewish and Christian *ulama* to preserve and authenticate the text of the Old and the New Testaments.[28] In the next discourse he adds a short history of the scholarship that proved the purity of these Revealed Books.[29] As far as the two 'Appendices' (*tatammas*), are concerned, Sir Syed provides a comprehensive list of the principal historical events recorded in the Bible in chronological order and the correspondence (*mutabiqat*), between the Hijri and the Christian eras.[30]

The second part of the *Tabiyin-ul Kalam*, as mentioned above, is the 'Commentary of the Books of Genesis'. This part comprises two Introductions and eleven chapters. Firstly there is an introduction, that is the introduction to the Old Testament[31] in which Sir Syed discusses the 'classification of the books of the Testament',[32] as to who wrote the Pentateuch (Touriet),[33] refutation of the objections raised against the genuineness of the Pentateuch[34] and the origin of the divisions of the Pentateuch into chapter and verses.[35] During the discussion he also makes comparison between the verses of the Touriet and the Koran.[36] Then there is another Introduction to the Book of

Genesis.[37] In this Introduction Sir Syed discusses in the light of the views of eminent Christian and Jewish clerics, the authenticity of the Books of Genesis by shedding light on the significance of the 'Divine Revelations', sent down to Prophet Moses (Hazrat Musa, PBUH). In this connection also he refers to the Koranic verses and other Islamic ideas regarding the Books of Genesis. At this point Syed Ahmad also supports the views of Horne as, according to him (Sir Syed), his ideas are very close to the Islamic conception in this context.[38] As for the eleven chapters of the second part of the *Tabiyin-ul Kalam*, Sir Syed has thoroughly discussed therein the significant events mentioned in the Books of Genesis, by comparing them with the events and the views described in the Koran and the Prophetic Traditions—*Ahadith*. These chapters cover the significant topics like the Creation of 'Earth', 'Light', 'Man', 'Heaven', etc., Trinity, the Sabbath,[39] the knowledge of 'God' and 'Evil',[40] 'Satan' or Devil,[41] whether the whole mankind is from one race,[42] 'the discrepancies in certain points in the Hebrew, Greek and Samaritan texts of the Books of Genesis,[43] the Deluge of Noah, etc.[44]

The third, the *Tabiyin-ul Kalam*, is the most significant part of this monumental work—the commentary on the first five chapters of the Bible. This part is totally in Urdu. Before commencing the *tafsir*, Sir Syed, gives in nutshell the history of Christianity from its origin to the rise of Islam. Describing the birth of Hazrat Masih, in order to show the Muslim point of view on the subject or in other words the respect and regard as well as prophetic greatness of Hazrat Isa, Alaissalam, in the eyes of the Muslims. He quotes the famous Sufi thinker Shaikh-i Akbar Muhiyuddin ibn al-Arabi,[45] who, through Arabic poetic verses, beautifully describes the holy birth and its merits—the prophetic characteristics of this great prophet of God:

God created from the water of Mary and (inflammatory) breath of Gabriel;	عن ماء مريم او عن نفخ جبرين
Who appeared in the form of earthly existence—human being;	فى صورة البشر الموجود من طين
The spirit that entered into the essence that was sacred;	تكون الروح فى ذات مطهرة
Innocent and pure of worldly affairs, and also known as the prison—means Jesus Christ;	من الطبيعة تدعوها بسجين
It was the spirit of Allah, not of any body else;	روح من اللّٰه لا من غيره فلذا
That is why, he (Jesus Christ) use to revive the dead and create the bird from the clay;	احيى الموات وانشاء الطير من طين
So that his lineage from his God may be corrected;	حتى يصح له من ربه نسب
	به يوثر فى العالى وفى الدون
	الله طهره جسما ونزهه
	روحا وصبره مثلًا بتكوين

It was on account of this (lineage) that he was
equally effective on human being and clay;
Allah made Jesus Christ's body sacred
And clean, and purified;
The spirit of Jesus Christ and made his
Birth an example.[46]

Afterwards Sir Syed states that whosoever met Jesus Christ, found him in accordance with his own thinking. Whenever any one looked at his face and tried to get a glimpse of his (other), external features, recognized him as human being and the son of Mary, and any body thought that he (Jesus Christ) had not been born through any external, reason, he realized him the 'ruh'. Similarly, whenever any one thought over his (Jesus Christ's) miracles (*mujizat*)—particularly his miraculous power to revive the dead, which is the exclusively quality of God, held him either as god or as the Son of God. Concluding the discussion Sir Syed very emphatically says that the person who looked at Hazrat Masih, keeping in view all his prophetic merits and qualities, found (and still finds), him as the Prophet of God (*Nabi Allah*), the Word of God (*Kalamullah*), and the Spirit of God (*Ruhullah*), and the same faith (*iman*) is held by the Muslims.[47] In his support Sir Syed again quotes the Arabic verses of Muhiyuddin ibn al-Arabi.[48]

Sir Syed goes on to say that some of the Muslim divines are of the view that Hazrat Masih, was a human being but at the same time he was not a human being.[49] Similarly, the Christian *ulama* also do not mean the term 'Ibnullah' (the son of God), to be understood in its literal sense, rather they believe that 'God is one' and

He is Father; and there is no God except Him. As God is eternal (*Azali*), His attributes also must be eternal. And Genesis also is one of the attributes of God. Accordingly, on account of this attribute, His Son—Jesus Christ, also came into existence in eternity from his Father. But nothing was divided between the essence of Father and the essence of the Son. Consequently, the essence of the Son is just the essence of Father. However, Father did not obtained His Godly essence from anyone else whereas the son—Jesus Christ—received his godly essence from his Father. That is why Father is called Eternal-Reason (*Illat-i Azali*), and the Son, the Eternal-Effect (*ma'lul-i Azali*).

Therefore, the functions of both Father and the Son are separate and different, and a sort of difference really exists between them. And it is due to this reason that the Son, Jesus Christ, has a lesser status than Father. But despite the fact that there is only one essence of both Father and the Son, the Son is that very God and God is that very son.[50] But disagreeing with this opinion, Sir Syed quotes the Koranic verse

لَقَدْ كَفَرَ الَّذِيْنَ قَالُوْٓا اِنَّ اللّٰهَ هُوَ الْمَسِيْحُ ابْنُ مَرْيَمَ[51]

They surely disbelieve who say: Lo! Allah is the Messiah, Son of Mary.

which, according to him, in the same context rejects and discards these ideas.[52]

At this juncture Sir Syed very briefly discusses the status of Angel Gabriel, who is called Ruh-ul Quds (the Sacred Spirit), the positions of Father and the Son[53] or in other words, the Conception of Trinity (*Tathlith*), and finally comes to the conclusion that there is no difference between the views of the Muslims and the Christians regarding the concept of the *Haqiqat-i Iswi*—the 'Reality of Jesus Christ' whether it is termed as the *Ruhullah*—the Spirit of God or as *Ibnullah*—the 'Son of God'.[54]

Furthermore, Sir Syed sheds light on various sects and religious groups that emerged among the Christians before the rise of Islam. For example, he says there was a sect among the Christians during the first century AD whose followers held Jesus Christ neither as the real God nor as the real human being. They rather believed that he was the *Ruhullah*, the 'Spirit of God' and the prophet of God. Referring to the work of Ismail Abul Fida, Sir Syed maintains this group's name was Aananiya. It is significant that Syed Ahmad further says the followers of this sect did not believe Jesus Christ was the 'Son of God'—*Ibnullah*. They believed that all the teachings of Jesus Christ were in accordance with the tenets of the Torah—the *Touriet*.[55] Mentioning another Christian sect of the same century, the Lipo Claptical Nicoli Tens, based on the information supplied by some Christian historians of the early centuries, Sir Syed states that the followers of this sect did not believe in *Hashr-i Ajsad*—the resurrection of human bodies, and most of them would say that the body of Jesus Christ was not made of matter and, that is why, they said, he was not crucified—the *Salib*.[56] Sir Syed is of the opinion that the Christian historians of the later ages may not have included this sect into Christianity. Referring to Abul Fida once again, Syed Ahmad says that in the first century there was another Christian sect whose followers did not accept Jesus Christ as God's Prophet. They looked upon him as a pious person. They also did not believe that the Bible was revealed to him. Sir Syed refuses to accept them as the Christians.[57]

In a scholarly discussion on the religious differences in the sphere of beliefs and the practices among the Christians sects Sir Syed said that they flourished during the pre-Islamic period.[58] It is significant that Sir Syed advises his co-religionists not to form any unfavourable ideas about Christians of those ages without any authentic historical evidence brought to light by Christian clerics and scholars.[59]

Subsequently we come across learned discussion on the significance of the Bible of Mathew (*Injil-i Mata*).[60] Sir Syed says the word *Injil*, (the Bible), literally means 'good-news'.[61] Disagreeing with the views of the modern Christian *ulama*, particularly Horin, he argues that the original Bible was in Hebrew later translated into Greek. He gives various proofs. For example, he quotes a *Hadith* through which we come to know that Warqa bin Nawfil bin Asad bin Abdul Azd[62] had embraced Christianity before the rise of Islam, and he knew very well to read and write Hebrew.[63] It appears from this *Hadith* that there was another Bible, written in Hebrew. The same *Hadith* also clearly reveals that the Bible of Mathew was in fact in Hebrew.[64]

Sir Syed, as mentioned above, writes the *tafsir*—the 'exegesis' or the 'commentary' on the first five chapters of the Bible of Mathew. During the *tafsir* of the first chapter, mentioning the ancestors of Jesus Christ, Sir Syed, with the intention showing a similarity between the information contained in the Bible of Mathew and in the Holy Koran on this issue, quotes verses 84 and 85 of the *Surah:'AN-'AAM*—(Cattle).

وَتِلْكَ حُجَّتُنَآ ءَاتَيْنَٰهَآ إِبْرَٰهِيمَ عَلَىٰ قَوْمِهِۦ نَرْفَعُ دَرَجَٰتٍ مَّن
نَّشَآءُ إِنَّ رَبَّكَ حَكِيمٌ عَلِيمٌ ۝

That is our argument. We gave it unto Abraham against his folk. We raise unto degrees of wisdom whom. We will. Lo! thy Lord is Wise. Aware.

وَوَهَبْنَا لَهُۥٓ إِسْحَٰقَ وَيَعْقُوبَ كُلًّا هَدَيْنَا وَنُوحًا هَدَيْنَا مِن قَبْلُ
وَمِن ذُرِّيَّتِهِۦ دَاوُۥدَ وَسُلَيْمَٰنَ وَأَيُّوبَ وَيُوسُفَ وَمُوسَىٰ
وَهَٰرُونَ وَكَذَٰلِكَ نَجْزِى ٱلْمُحْسِنِينَ ۝ [65]

And We bestowed upon him Isaac and Jacob; each of them. We guided; and Noah did. We guide aforetime; and of his seed (We guided) David and Solomon and Job and Joseph and Moses and Aaron. Thus do. We reward the good.

Shedding light on the significance of the city of Jerusalem, during the *tafsir* of the second chapter of the Bible of Mathew, Sir Syed refers to a verse of the *Surah* Baniii-'Israaa-'iil (The children of Israel), of the Holy Koran, which reveals the (religious) significance of Jerusalem.

سُبْحٰنَ الَّذِىْ اَسْرٰى بِعَبْدِهٖ لَيْلًا مِّنَ الْمَسْجِدِ الْحَرَامِ اِلَى
الْمَسْجِدِ الْاَقْصَا الَّذِىْ بٰرَكْنَا حَوْلَهٗ لِنُرِيَهٗ مِنْ اٰيٰتِنَا اِنَّهٗ هُوَ
السَّمِيْعُ الْبَصِيْرُ ○[66]

Glorified be He who carried His servant by right from the Inviolable Place of Worship to the Far Distant Place of Worship the neighbourhood whereof. We have blessed, that We might show him of Our tokens! Lo! He, only He, is the Hearer, the Seer.

A *Hadith* of Muhammad (PUBH) is also quoted on this occasion in which the Prophet is reported to have ordained the Muslims to make pilgrimage to the three mosques including the 'Masjid-i Aqsa'—the 'Distant Mosque' in Jerusalem. Therefore, highlighting the point that the Masjid-i Aqsa is the *qibla*, the object of veneration of the *Ahl-i Kitab*, People of the Book, and in the beginning of Islam it was the *qibla* of the Muslims as well. Sir Syed once again tries to show a sort of similarity between the two great religions of the world.[67] Continuing the *tafsir* Sir Syed emphatically describes the greatness of the prophets, in the eyes of the Muslims, who flourished before the rise of Islam. Here he once again refers to the verse no. 13 of the *Sura*: Shuuraa (Council) of the Koran in which Allah says that the religion preached by all those prophets was the same.[68]

شَرَعَ لَكُمْ مِّنَ الدِّيْنِ مَا وَصّٰى بِهٖ نُوْحًا وَّالَّذِىْ اَوْحَيْنَا اِلَيْكَ
وَمَا وَصَّيْنَا بِهٖ اِبْرٰهِيْمَ وَمُوْسٰى وَعِيْسٰى اَنْ اَقِيْمُوا الدِّيْنَ
وَلَا تَتَفَرَّقُوْا فِيْهِ كَبُرَ عَلَى الْمُشْرِكِيْنَ مَا تَدْعُوْهُمْ اِلَيْهِ اَللّٰهُ
يَجْتَبِىْ اِلَيْهِ مَنْ يَّشَاءُ وَيَهْدِىْ اِلَيْهِ مَنْ يُّنِيْبُ ○[69]

He hath ordained for you that religon which He commended unto Noah, and that which We inspire in thee (Muhammad), and that which We commended unto Abraham and Moses and Jesus, saying: Establish the religion, and be not divided therein. Dreadful for the idolaters is that unto which thou callest them. Allah chooseth for Himself whom He will, and guideth unto Himself him who turneth (toward Him).

At the end of the commentary of the second chapter of the Bible of Mathew, Sir Syed Ahmad discusses the meaning of the word *Nasara*.[70]

In short, it may be said that Sir Syed, throughout his *tafsir* of the first five chapters of the Bible of Mathew, has made attempts to prove the sanctity and authenticity of various events mentioned therein by comparing them with the divine commandments and events regarding the life of Hazrat Masih, contained in the Koran and the *Hadith*, and always endeavours to creat harmony between the teachings of the two great religions of the world—Christianity and Islam, particularly by highlighting the reverence and highness of the prophetic personality of Jesus Christ.[71] The whole exegesis reveals its author's deep religious and scholarly insight.

RECEPTION OF THE COMMENTARY

This great work of Sir Syed Ahmad Khan, the *Tabiyin-ul Kalam*, found critics and enemies on all sides. According to Maulana Altaf Husain Hali since Sir Syed had rejected the commonly accepted Muslim view that the text of the Bible had been falsified, the Muslim *ulama* and the religious people discarded this work. Similarly, as its author (Sir Syed), had proved that there was absolute agreement between (pure) Christianity and Islam, and considered that the very fundamentals of (present-day) Christianity—namely the Trinity, the expiation of sins and the rejection of the prophethood, particularly the Christian point of view of the concept of the '*Khatm-i Nabuwwat*'—the completion of the channel of the advent of prophets of God by the advent of Prophet Muhammad, were false, the *Tabiyin-ul Kalam* was not accepted by the Christians as well.[72]

It was only John M. Arnold, the famous Christian scholar, who in his book, *The Koran and Bible* (1866), published a letter of Syed Ahmad Khan regarding the first part of the Commentary. This letter clearly shows the main purpose of writing this work. Sir Syed concludes the letter in these words, 'Of course, I have always desired to see the maintenance of a friendship between Mohammedans and Christians, since, if according to the Holy Koran, there can be any friends to us, they can be the Christians only.'[73]

Commenting on this monumental work of Sir Syed Ahmad Khan, John M. Arnold writes in his same book, 'The commentary, asserting as it does, the authority of the Bible, and providing such from the Koran itself in opposition to the hitherto assumed corruption of the Christian Scriptures, deserves to be translated into every tongue.'[74]

Similarly, the famous French orientalist, Garcien de Tassey,[75] also greatly appreciated Sir Syed's endeavours—the 'compilation and publication of the *Tabiyin-ul Kalam*'. He mentioned and quoted passages from this commentary of the Bible in one of his lectures delivered in 1883 in which he said.

A new book which I commend to your attention is the commentary written by Syed Ahmad Khan, who at this time is one of the most famous Urdu writers. He is the same author, whose work the *Asar-us Sanadid*, I translated for the journal of the Paris Asiatic Society. A short time ago, I informed you that the commentary was being printed, and now I am pleased to announce that the first part has been completed, and a copy has been kindly sent to me by the author. It appears from this work that Syed Ahmad Khan is not only thoroughly conversant with the Holy Quran and our own Sacred Books, but he has also acquainted himself with many oriental and even European works. . . . Indeed, his commentary is the product of his vast learning. . . . This is the first time that a Muslim has written . . . such a complete and comprehensive discussion on this subject.[76]

RISALA AHKAM-I TA'AM-I AHL-I KITAB

The completion and appearance of the *Tabiyin-ul Kalam* was not the final destination for Sir Syed Ahmad Khan, who had embarked on this journey of Christian–Muslim harmony. Khawaja Altaf Husain Hali writes in his *Hayat-i Javed* that in 1866, Sir Syed received a letter through which asked him to give his opinion as to whether Muslims could share meals with the Christians, assuming that the food, the Muslims were offered, contained nothing that was forbidden to them. He answered that according to the Koran and the *Hadith*, it is quite lawful for them to do so. In this connection he pointed out that Muslims in every other part of the world but India shared their meal with Europeans—the Christians. Sir Syed's opinion was published in the *Scientific Society Gazette* on 14 September 1866.[77] Certainly this opinion of Sir Syed Ahmad Khan, as was expected in those days, did not gain much favour from the Muslims of the country. However, he received a letter from a certain Syed Saheb of Lucknow expressing agreement with this opinion. To this letter, Sir Syed replied,[78]

I have never hesitated to eat and drink with English people, so long as wine and pork have not been included in the meal'. He is also reported to have said, 'It was after the capture of Bijnaur, that Mr Palmer, the District Magistrate of Bijnaur, and I were returning from Najibabad. On the way we stopped for a rest in the shade of a tree. Mr Palmer asked me if I would like some tea. When I asked him as to where we could get it, he replied that he had a flask with him. I was delighted and we both had some tea and toast.

After our refreshment, we left and shortly arrived at Nagina. It happened to be the time for the *Asr* (afternoon) prayer and I went over the mosque to join the congregation. After the *namaz* was over, some people made objection as to why, after sharing tea and toast with an Englishman, I should join the prayer. Though I became enraged, I, however, explained them that it was permitted by the Quran. Everyone, in the mosque, was amazed at what I told them.

Likewise, some time later, in Bijnaur I used to visit Mr Palmer during the evening. Once he was just about to have his dinner, he invited me to join him. I, therefore, took my meal there. His servant was astonished to see me having meal with an Englishman.[79]

Maulana Hali goes on to say that although Sir Syed had been eating with English people for some time, yet it had never occurred to him to publicize the idea. But when he realized that one man's example in this direction was not enough, and the Muslims would never lose their fear of the British nor the British their suspicion and hatred of the Muslims until both people came together and established some kind of social basis for learning each other's way of thinking, he compiled and published in 1868 from Banaras, where he was posted at that time, a treatise on the theme entitled: *Risala Ahkam-i Ta'am-i Ahl-i Kitab* (The Treatise on the Ordinances Regarding Eating with the People of the Book).[80]

In the beginning of the *Risala*, the compiler writes that the food of the 'People of the Book' (*Ahl-i Kitab*), provided that it has nothing forbidden, is lawful for the Muslims, they can have it.[81] To provide strong support to his ideas Sir Syed quotes the Koranic verse:

اَلْيَوْمَ اُحِلَّ لَكُمُ الطَّيِّبٰتُ وَطَعَامُ الَّذِيْنَ اُوْتُوا الْكِتٰبَ حِلٌّ لَّكُمْ
وَطَعَامُكُمْ حِلٌّ لَّهُمْ

This day are (all) good things made lawful for you. The food of those who have received the Scripture is lawful for you and your food is lawful for them.[82]

which means: 'Today all clean things and food of those who have the Book (who are Ahl-i Kitab—"People of Book"), have been made lawful for you.'[83]

He also refers to a *Hadith* of the *Tirmize* in which Prophet Muhammad, is reported to have allowed his followers to take food of the *Ahl-i Kitab*.[84] Further, he writes that the prophet of Islam once had a meal prepared by the Jews.[85] Likewise, he mentions a *fatwa* (legal opinion) of Shah Abdul Aziz of Delhi which also proves that it is perfectly in order for Muslims to have meals of and with English people provided that no pork or wine was included in the meal.[86] Subsequently, Sir Syed, in the light of the Koran and the *Hadith*, tries to remove all the doubts which had been raised by the Muslim *ulama* in India about the lawfulness of eating with the 'People of Book'.[87] At last, in the conclusion—the *khatima*, of the *Risala*, Sir Syed advises his co-religionists to realize the need of the time and create an environment of harmony between themselves—the Muslim, and the Englishmen (the Christians).[88]

RECEPTION OF THE *RISALA*

Hali tells us that at first the *Risala* caused a hue and cry. People started to believe that Sir Syed had become a Christian and thought that they should refrain from eating with him.[89] We are also informed that several works were published in refutation of Sir Syed's *Risala Ahkam-i Ta'am-i Ahl-i Kitab*. Some people advised the Muslims not eat with Sir Syed Ahmad Khan. But according to Sir Syed himself, their words were like a whirlwind—a little dust flew but soon settled down again.[90]

Even after this he did not stop or feel tired, but he continued his mission of love and brotherhood, to bring harmony between Christianity and Islam. It was during his stay in England between 1869–70[91] that Sir Syed spent most his time in collecting material for his other monumental work, the *Khutbat-i Ahmadiya,* which was in fact a refutation of Sir William Muir's book; *The Life of Mohammad.*[92] First published in 1870,[93] the *Khutbat-i Ahmadiya* comprises at twelve essays thoroughly discussing different aspects of Islam and the Holy Prophet Muhammad.[94] These essays were also translated and published into English from London during 1869–70 by Trubner & Co.[95] Two of these essays, which form the fourth and the tenth *khutbat* (discourses or chapters),[96] are directly concerned with the theme of the present paper—Christian–Muslim harmony. One of these two essays, published in 1869, is entitled, 'Prophecies Respecting Muhammad as Contained in Both the Old and the New Testament'.[97]

It appears Sir Syed got the idea from the Holy Koran as the essay begins with the words: 'According to the injunctions of the Koran, hereafter to be quoted, we Mohammedans implicitly believe that Advent of our Prophet Muhammad was expressly and indubitably foretold both in the Old and the New Testament.'[98] Then Sir Syed quotes the Quranic verse in which God answers Moses' prayers: 'I will write down good unto those who shall fear me, and give alms, and shall believe our signs, who shall follow the Apostle, the illiterate Prophet, whom they shall find written down with them'.[99]

اَلَّذِيْنَ يَتَّبِعُوْنَ الرَّسُوْلَ النَّبِيَّ الْاُمِّيَّ الَّذِيْ يَجِدُوْنَهٗ مَكْتُوْبًا
عِنْدَهُمْ فِي التَّوْرٰىةِ وَالْاِنْجِيْلِ يَاْمُرُهُمْ بِالْمَعْرُوْفِ وَيَنْهٰىهُمْ عَنِ
الْمُنْكَرِ وَيُحِلُّ لَهُمُ الطَّيِّبٰتِ وَيُحَرِّمُ عَلَيْهِمُ الْخَبٰٓئِثَ وَيَضَعُ
عَنْهُمْ اِصْرَهُمْ وَالْاَغْلٰلَ الَّتِيْ كَانَتْ عَلَيْهِمْ فَالَّذِيْنَ اٰمَنُوْا بِهٖ
وَعَزَّرُوْهُ وَنَصَرُوْهُ وَاتَّبَعُوا النُّوْرَ الَّذِيْ اُنْزِلَ مَعَهٗ اُولٰٓئِكَ هُمُ
الْمُفْلِحُوْنَ ○

Those who follow the messenger, the Prophet who can neither read nor write, whom they will find described in the Torah and the Gospel (which are) with them. He will enjoin on them that which is right and forbid them that which is wrong. He will make lawful for them all good things and prohibit for them only the foul; and he will relieve them of their burden and the fetters that they used to wear. Then those who believe in him, and honour him, and help him, and follow the light which is sent down with him; they are the successful.

Further he quotes another Koranic verse: 'And when Jesus, the son of Mary, said "O children of Israil, verily I am the Apostle of God sent unto you, confirming the Law which was delivered before me, and bringing good tidings of an Apostle who shall come after me, and whose name shall be Ahmad."'[100]

وَاِذْ قَالَ عِيْسَى ابْنُ مَرْيَمَ يٰبَنِيْٓ اِسْرَآءِيْلَ اِنِّيْ رَسُوْلُ اللّٰهِ
اِلَيْكُمْ مُّصَدِّقًا لِّمَا بَيْنَ يَدَيَّ مِنَ التَّوْرٰىةِ وَمُبَشِّرًا بِرَسُوْلٍ يَّاْتِيْ
مِنْۢ بَعْدِي اسْمُهٗٓ اَحْمَدُ فَلَمَّا جَآءَهُمْ بِالْبَيِّنٰتِ قَالُوْا هٰذَا سِحْرٌ
مُّبِيْنٌ ○

And when Jesus son of Mary said: O Children of Israil! Lo! I am the messenger of Allah unto you, confirming that which was (revealed) before me in the Torah, and bringing good tidings of a messenger who cometh after me, whose name is the Praised One. Yet when he hath come unto them with clear proofs, they say: This is mere magic.

Furthermore, going through the sacred Jewish and Christian scriptures, Sir Syed writes that in the Old and the New Testament, there are two kinds of prophecies—one which, if interpreted impartially and without any prejudice, will be found self-evidently to apply to Prophet Muhammed exclusively; while the other, although it refers to some prophet exclusively, cannot be satisfactorily ascertained who that prophet is; so that each nation might justly claim it as referring to a prophet of their own. We shall therefore, pass over those prophecies that are classed under the second head.[101] He quotes verse 20 of chapter XVII, and verses 12 and 13 of chapter XXI of the Book of Genesis, *Kitab-i Paidaish*, in which God promised to bless Ishmael and to multiple his seed. Sir Syed, on this juncture, opines, 'The promise of God to bless Ishmael was fulfilled by appointing Muhammad, a descendant of Ishmael, the Prophet for the entire world.'[102] Later he discusses in greater detail, God's promise to Abraham by exploring verse 18, chapter XV, verses 3 and 4, chapter XXVII; verses 13 and 14, chapter XXVIII; of the Book of Genesis, and the verses of the other Sacred Book, and draws a conclusion in these words:

> In the above-quoted passages our Prophet, Muhammad, is evidently foretold, for God declared to all the Israelites that He would raise up a prophet from amongst their brethren. Now, we hesitate not to affirm that it is impossible that the words—brethren of Israel—could have any other meaning than that of Ishmaelites, and there never had any prophet but Mohammed, Sallallaho Alaihe Wasallum.[103]

Seeking the prophecies regarding Prophet Muhammad, in the Old and the New Testament, Sir Syed concludes the essay with: 'This renowned Prophet (prophesied in the above-quoted holy works), we respect, was Mohammed Sallallaho Alaihe Wasallum, the last, and of all, the greatest.'[104]

No doubt, this essay of Sir Syed Ahmad Khan on the 'Prophecies Respecting Muhammad', was a significant step toward forging harmony between the Christians and the Muslims. He must have written the essay to remove the doubts each had about the other. He was not only successful in educational and political spheres but clearly also on the religious front as well. Another essay entitled, 'Whether Islam has been Beneficial or Injurious to Human Society in General and to the Mosaic and Christian Dispensations' published from London in

1870 by the same Trubner & Co.,[105] consisting of four sections, is a valuable contribution of Syed Ahmad Khan in the field of Christian-Muslim unity. The section I of the essay, 'Advantages derived by human society in general from Islam', contains the passages from the writings of eminent scholars of the modern period, such as Gibbon and Devenport,[106] and in section II, on the 'Refutation of the opinion that Islam has been injurious to human society', Sir Syed Ahmad Khan categorically refutes the ideas, of Sir William Muir, regarding polygamy, divorce, slavery, freedom of judgement, toleration and the reception of Christianity in Islam.[107]

Rejecting Muir's opinion about polygamy, Syed Ahmad says, 'It is a great mistake to suppose that by Islam polygamy is made compulsory upon its followers, on the contrary, the general practice of it, is not even recommended, the privileged use of it being reserved for such as for physical reasons may stand in need of it, but in the absence of such an excuse the indulgence in it is wholly contrary to the virtues and morality taught by Islam.'[108] Quoting the remarks of the famous scholars like Haggins and Devenport, in favour of polygamy, Sir Syed subsequently writes, 'When the subject is considered from the religious point of view, we find that polygamy is nowhere prohibited in Judaism and Christianity, which, at present, are, besides Islam, the only two inspired religions in the world. For the support of our assertion we shall quote the remarks of a few eminent Christian authors in favour of polygamy.'[109] Similarly, for divorce, Sir Syed states,'Our Prophet neither underrated nor over valued divorce. He constantly pointed out to his followers how opposed it was to the best interest of society; he always expatiated upon the evils which flowed form it, and ever exhorted his disciples to treat woman with respect and kindness, and to bear patiently their violence and ill temper.'[110]

Section III of the essay deals with 'Benefits and advantages which Judaism and Christianity derived from Islam'. To begin with, he gives the reasons as to why he includes both Judaism and Christianity in his argument. He writes, 'The reason for mentioning Judaism and Christianity jointly is, because we believe that Jesus Christ did not, for the most part, alter or reject any of the doctrines contained in the Law of Moses; and his own declaration—"Think not that I am come to destroy the Law, or the prophets: I am not come to destroy, but to fulfil"—demonstrates the truth of our assertion.'[111] Then he sheds light on the perfection of the concept of *Tawhid*—'Oneness of God', i.e. the root or the basis of all Islamic teachings, and attempts to show how far Judaism and Christianity have benefited from this concept of Islam —the *Tawhid*.[112]

The topic of the fourth and the last section of the essay is the 'Advantages derived from Islam by Christianity particularly'. This section is in fact the most important part of Sir Syed's essay. In the very beginning of the section he boldly says, 'No religion upon earth is more beneficial to Christianity than Islam and the latter has been to none more beneficial and advantageous than to Christianity.'[113] Afterwards, Syed Ahmad very fearlessly writes, 'The worst of corruptions that crept into Christianity after the Apostles, was the doctrine of the Trinity (the *Tathlith*)—a doctrine which was at once in op-position to eternal truth and contrary to the pure precepts inculcated by Christ.'[114] He further writes, 'It is to the eternal glory of Islam that it re-established the worship of the unity of Godhead, and revived that pure religion inculcated and promulgated by Christ himself; it constantly warned the then-called Christians of their errors, and invited them to accept the true religion—a religion preached by Christ.'[115] He carries on to say, 'Many Christians, whose eyes were opened by the loud watchword of Islam, perceived the degraded state into which they had been plunged, and thenceforward strove to recover their former position in the scale of the religions—in general of the world. This class of men is now distinguished by the proud appellation of Unitarian Christians.'[116] What is most interesting in the whole dis-cussion that Sir Syed is of the view that if for a moment this Unitarian-ism is taken away from the world, the following remarks of Gibbon would be in every respect true: 'If the Christian Apostles, St Peter or St Paul, could return to the Vatican, they might possibly inquire the name of the Deity who is worshipped with such mysterious rites in that magnificent temple.'[117]

Pointing out the beneficence of Islam to Christianity, Sir Syed says:

> The greatest of boons conferred by Islam upon Christianity is the spirit of resistance which it breathed into the Christians against the exorbitant power of the popes, under which they had so long groaned. The Pope was looked upon as the infallible Vicar of Christ. He could open the gates of Hell, Purgatory, and Heaven. He arrogated to himself the power of purging away, by means of Indulgences, the sins of whomsoever he pleased. He was in-

vested with full power to make what was unlawful, lawful. In fact, in the authority he possessed, and the jurisdiction he exercised, he was in no way inferior to Christ himself.[118]

He then quotes a verse of the *Surah*: 'Aali-'Im-Raan—(The family of Imran)', of the Holy Koran and also a *Hadith* of the Prophet of Islam in support of his views.[119] The concerned Koranic verse:

قُلْ يٰاَهْلَ الْكِتٰبِ تَعَالَوْا اِلٰى كَلِمَةٍ سَوَاءٍ بَيْنَنَا وَبَيْنَكُمْ اَلَّا
نَعْبُدَ اِلَّا اللّٰهَ وَلَانُشْرِكَ بِهٖ شَيْئًا وَّلَايَتَّخِذَ بَعْضُنَا بَعْضًا
اَرْبَابًا مِّنْ دُوْنِ اللّٰهِ فَاِنْ تَوَلَّوْا فَقُوْلُوا اشْهَدُوْا بِاَنَّا مُسْلِمُوْنَ[120]

Say: O People of the Scripture. Come to an agreement between us and you: that we shall worship none but Allah, and that we shall ascribe no partner unto Him, and that none of us shall take others for lords beside Allah. And if they turn away, then say: Bear witness that we are they who have surrendered (unto Him).

Sir Syed points out the evils flowing from the worship of the popes, reprimanded the Christians for their slavish servility, and exhorted them to throw off so ignominious a yoke, and to seek out the truth for themselves.[121] Similarly, the *Hadith*, referred to by him, also clearly reveals that the pope was worshipped even before the rise of Islam. In this *Hadith* Prophet Muhammad is reported to have made an inquiry from his companion, Adee Ibn Hatim, who had been a Christian before embrassing Islam, 'Had he (the Pope), not the power to pronounce to be lawful that which was unlawful, according to religion and vice versa?' Ibn Hatim's reply, 'Verily, O Messenger of God, that we used to do', is the perfect evidence to this effect.[122] But what Syed Ahmad concludes at the end of this essay is really of great value and significance. He maintains,

For a time this wholesome truth, inculcated by the Koran, was looked upon by Christians with impatience and hatred; but as truth never fails, at the last, to impress itself upon the minds of men, it gradually engrafted itself upon that of Luther, who, when he came in contact with the above-quoted passage of the Koran, at once comprehended the truth it inculcated, and, clearly perceiving the slavish and degrading position in which his co-religionists were plunged, at once stood up to preach publicly against that servile practice; and although some of his adversaries denounced him as being a Mohammedan at heart, he never desisted from his endeavours, and, at last, succeeded in effecting the grand reform generally known as Protestantism, or the Reformation; and for this emancipation of human mind from the worst of all slavery—a priestly one—Christianity should for ever remain thankful to Islam.[123]

If a sincere analysis is made of the contents of the above, it may rightly be said that Sir Syed was wholeheartedly desirous of bridging the gulf between Christians and Muslims on both ideological and social fronts. He wrote these essays by sitting in the stronghold of the Christian people—England. However, he never hesitated in expressing what he considered true and beneficial to his object—Christian–Muslim harmony. It is significant to note these efforts of Syed Ahmad Khan brought amicable results. It was the same William Muir, in refutation of whose book Sir Syed had written the *Khutbat-i Ahmadiya* and the series of essays in English, who became a great admirer of his socio-educational mission. Muir's address, delivered on the occasion of his visit to the MAO College, Aligarh, on 12 November 1875, clearly reveals his changed intellectual attitude towards Muslims and Sir Syed and his associates.[124] William Muir paid another visit to Aligarh in October 1876. This time a beautifully embossed address (*Sipasnama*), in a sandal-wood box mounted in chased silver was presented to him by the Muslims.[125] His reply to this address[126] is of great value and bears testimony to the fact that Sir Syed's efforts, especially through his valuable writings, brought fruitful results.

Proceeding further in this direction, we come across a lecture delivered by Sir Syed Ahmad Khan on the occasion of the visit of Lady and Mr Blunt, the member of the British Parliament, to the MAO College, Aligarh in 1884. Addressing Mr Blunt, Sir Syed spoke,

> Our desire that there should exist sympathy between the Mohammedans and English nation is by no means an odd one. There never has been a time when there might have happened any occurrence between the Mohammedans and the English nation which could lead to any ground for unpleasant feeling or enmity between ourselves and the English people, or, which could make us feel any way jealous of their increasing prosperity. The English people mostly held aloof even of the Crusades which happened at a time which was productive of all sorts of ill-feeling.[127]

Attracting the sympathy of the English (Christian) people in general and Mr Blunt in particular, Sir Syed, during the address opines, 'In the matter of the establishment of the British sovereignty in India we and the English nation are joined together like the two blades of a pair of scissors; no one could say which of the two blades contributed most towards it.[128]

CONCLUSION

Sir Syed Ahmad Khan, having witnessed the fall of his community—not only the political downfall but the moral and intellectual decay as well—with his own eyes, had reached the point of realization that without maintaining sincere friendly relations with the English people, his co-religionists, the Muslims could not develop themselves either morally or intellectually or in social and political spheres. He thought it necessary to remove misunderstandings from each other's minds about each other's religions, prophets, and customs and practices. He therefore made strenuous efforts in this direction. All his steps and measures, in the way of creating harmony between Christians and Muslims reveal his deep sense of religious sincerity, strong scholarly insight and broad outlook. According to Maulana Altaf Husain Hali, Sir Syed, through his writings and speeches, always desired cordial relations, based on social friendship and brotherhood, between the followers of Christianity and Islam.[129]

No doubt he succeeded to a great extent. His self-determination, broadmindedness, immense patience and tolerance, sincere religious feelings and a high moral character brought him respect and honour in his life. His views and efforts in Christian–Muslim unity and harmony brought a pleasing atmosphere in the country and had far-reaching results and deeply influenced posterity as well. History tells us that his impact on both Muslims and Christians have been equally and deeply felt. The world today is also facing similar crises. The problem may hopefully be solved by bringing to light Sir Syed Ahmad Khan's contribution to Christian–Muslim harmony, and a socio-political environment, based on love, kindness and sincerity may be created in the Christian–Muslim world. The initiative must be taken from the side of the Muslims, particularly those belonging to the Aligarh Muslim University as they have been claiming to be true successors of Sir Syed Ahmad Khan. Setting aside the feelings of sorrow and disappointment, they must come forward on their pioneer's path with the pious intention of reviving his endeavours.

NOTES

1. See, K.A. Nizami's 'Foreword' to English translation of Khawaja Altaf Husain Hali's, *Hayat-i Javed*, by K.H. Qadri and David J. Mathews, Delhi: Idarah-i-Adabyat-i Delhi, 1979, p. vi.
2. A number of works of different scholars, including those of Graham and Hali have appeared in different languages on Sir Syed's life and contributions to the field of Muslim education. Some of them, particularly those in English and Urdu, are really remarkable.
3. For example, William Muir's work, *The Life of Mohammad*.
4. It may be mentioned here that the role of Christian missionaries had been very insensitive. Their way of attracting Indians towards Christianity had deeply hurt Hindus and Muslims. The records of the polemical discussions between the Muslim ulama and the Christian missionaries and also between the latter and the Hindu pandits are available which may prove the best source of our information on this theme.

   We are informed by Altaf Husain Hali, as will be mentioned hereafter in the present paper, that Sir Syed too was deeply disgusted by this attitude of missionaries toward the Indian people. See, *Hayat-i Javed* (Urdu), Lahore: Academy Punjab, 1957, pp. 163–4.
5. As just mentioned above there is lot of material hitherto unexplored in the form of small brochures and treatises, mostly in Urdu, which inform of these polemical debates held from time to time, mostly in north and west India, in between the Christian missionaries and the Muslim *ulama*. These works supply valuable information in this context.
6. See the above-mentioned literature, particularly the works containing the details of polemical debate between the Muslims and the Christians.
7. For details, see *Hayat-i Javed,* pp. 128–37.
8. Ibid., p. 138.
9. For details, see ibid, pp. 163–4, 396.
10. Published from Aligarh in 1899. The original copy of this work was not available to the present author. The information is based on Hali's *Hayat-i Javed*. Moulvi Mohammad Ismail Panipati's information regarding the *Risala Tahqiq-i Lafz-i Nasara* is also based on Maulana Hali's above-mentioned work. See, Ismail Panipati, ed., *Maqalat-i Sir Syed*, part 15, Lahore: Majlis-i Taraqqi-i Adab, 1963, pp. 188–90.
11. *Hayat-i Javed*, pp. 159–60.
12. *Surah* LXI: *Saff* (The Ranks), verse 14; also *Surah*: Aali-Im-Raan (The family of Imran), verse 12.
13. Ibid.
14. It may be mentioned here that Jews have been calling Hazrat Isa, the Naseri, i.e. belonging to the village of Nasera—the Qariya-i-Nasera, to show disrespect to him. That is why Christ's followers took this remark

as their Prophet's humiliation. Accordingly when in India, during the nineteenth century, the Muslim *ulama* and scholars used the word 'Nasara' for the Christians, the British imagined that the Muslims intended to show the same kind of disrespect as the Jews, when they referred to Jesus Christ, as Naseri. In fact, this interpretation of the British was totally based on their misunderstanding and lack of knowledge of Islam.

15. Verse 82 of the *Surah*, Maaa 'Idah (The Table Spread). For details of Sir Syed's arguments, see *Hayat-i Javed*, p. 160.
16. Ibid.
17. The first part of the Commentary was published by Sir Syed himself in AH 1278/AD 1862 from Ghazipur; see Appendix A, enclosed herewith. The second part appeared in AH 1281/AD 1865 from Aligarh (see Appendix B, enclosed herewith). The date of the publication of the third part of the *Tabiyin-ul Kalam* is not known (see Appendix C, enclosed herewith).

    It is necessary to mention here that the Sir Syed Academy of the Aligarh Muslim University has republished the whole Commentary—the *Tabiyin-ul Kalam* in 2004 (see Appendix D, enclosed herewith).
18. *Hayat-i Javed*, p. 165.
19. Ibid.
20. Ibid.
21. Ibid., p. 167.
22. For details, see ibid, pp. 165–9.
23. See the *Tabiyin-ul Kalam*, Aligarh: Sir Syed Academy, 2004, part I.
24. *Hayat-i Javed*, p. 167.
25. See *Tabiyin-ul Kalam*, part I, pp. 64–73.
26. Ibid., p. 73.
27. Ibid., pp. 73–92.
28. Ibid., pp. 92–4.
29. Ibid., pp. 96–155.
30. Ibid. See Tatamma, Appendix 1 of part I of the *Tabiyin-ul Kalam*, pp. 1–72, and Tatamma Appendix 2 of the same, pp. 1–66.
31. Ibid., part II, p. 2.
32. Ibid.
33. Ibid., p. 10.
34. Ibid., p. 16.
35. Ibid., p. 20.
36. Ibid., pp. 8–9, 13–14.
37. Ibid., p. 24.
38. For details, see ibid., pp. 24–36.
39. Ibid., p. 108.
40. Ibid., p. 143.

41. Ibid., p. 145.
42. Ibid., p. 266.
43. Ibid., p. 208.
44. Ibid., p. 281.
45. Born on 17 Ramazan 560/28 July 1165 at Murcia in Spain, Shaikh-i Akbar Muhiyuddin Muhammad bin Ali bin Muhammad al-Arabi, better known as Ibn Arabi (also as Ibn al-Arabi), belonged to the tribe of Bani Tai and was descendant of Hatim Tai. He exerted great influence upon the Sufis of different spiritual orders. His mystic doctrine of 'Wahdat al-Wujud', 'the Unity of Being', or 'the Unity of Existence'; has been considered as the ideological root of Islamic mysticism. His thoughts and terminologies have formed the foundation of subsequent Sufi intellectual discourses. Likewise, his monumental works, the *Fusus al-Hikam* and the *Futuhat-i Makkiya,* have also left deep impact on the followers of Tasawwuf—Sufism, Islamic spirituality through the centuries. For his biographical, ideological and other details see, *Encyclopaedia of Islam*, vol. III, Leiden, 1971, pp. 707–11. Also A.E. Affifi, *The Mystical Philosophy of Muhyid Din-Ibnul 'Arabi*, Cambridge, 1939. Also see William C. Chittick, *The Sufi Path of Knowledge: Ibn al-Arabi's Metaphysics of Imagination*, Albany: State University of New York, 1989; also his article 'Ibn Arabi and his School', in *Islamic Spirituality: Manifestations*, ed. Sayyed Hossam Nasr, New York: SCM Press, 1991, pp. 49–79. Ibn Arabi died in AH 638/AD 1240-1 and lies buried in Damascus.
46. *Tabiyin-ul Kalam,* part III, pp. 2–3.
47. Ibid., p. 4.
48. Ibid., p. 5.
49. Ibid. It may be noted here that there has hardly been any Muslim divine who said that Hazrat Masih, was not a human being. It seems to the present author that Sir Syed might have formed this idea by being impressed by the mystical ideas of Muhiyuddin Ibn Arabi expressed in his above-mentioned Arabic poetic verses.

    But Sir Syed read very widely and deeply. If he has written so, he must have come to know of such Muslim ulama who expressed these views about Jesus Christ that he was a human being but at the same time he was not a human being.

    Anyhow, at this juncture, the present author finds himself unable to make any comment except mentioning this famous poetic verse of Shaikh Sadi Shirazi.
50. *Tabiyin-ul Kalam*, part III, p. 6.
51. *Surah* V: Maaa-'Idah', verse 72.
52. *Tabiyin-ul Kalam*, part III, p.6; what Sir Syed wants to say is that the Koran negates and condemns such ideas and indicates such people who believe in it.

53. Ibid.
54. Ibid., p. 7.
55. Ibid., p. 8.
56. Ibid.
57. Ibid., p. 9.
58. For details, see ibid., pp. 9–15.
59. Ibid., p. 7.
60. For details, see ibid, pp. 16–26.
61. Ibid., p. 16.
62. Warqa bin Nawfil was the cousin of Khadija, the wife of Prophet Muhammad. When the Prophethood was conferred upon the latter through Angel Gebriel, she took him to Warqa bin Nawfil who confirmed that according to the prophecies in the Jewish and Christian sacred scriptures, he (Muhammad, PBUH), was the Prophet of God. For details see Ibn Hasham, *Sirat-un Nabi*, part I (Urdu trans. & ed. Abdul Jalil Siddiqui, Ghulam Rasool Mehr, Delhi: Itiqad Publishing House 1982, p. 264; also William Muir, *The Life of Mohammad* (rpt), New York: A.M.S. Press, 1975, pp. 36, 42, 50, 56; also Shibli Nomani, *Sirat-un Nabi*, part I (4th edn.), Azamgarh: Darul Musannifin, n.d., p. 202; also P.K. Hetti, *History of the Arabs*, New York: St Martin's Press, 2001, pp. 108, 113; also Mohammad Hamidullah, *The Life and Works of the Prophet of Islam*, trans. & ed. Mahmood Ahmad Ghazi, New Delhi: Adam Publishers, 2004, pp. 43, 49, 70, 129, 465.
63. *Tabiyin-ul Kalam*, part III, p. 17.
64. Ibid.
65. Ibid., p. 27.
66. *Surah*: Baniii-Israaa-iil, verse 1.
67. *Tabiyin-ul Kalam*, part III, p. 47.
68. Ibid., p. 53.
69. *Surah*: Shuuraa (Counsel), verse 13.
70. *Tabiyin-ul Kalam*, part III, p. 60. In this connection, Sir Syed's treatise *Risala Tahqiq-i Lafz-i Nasara*, published from Aligarh in 1899 may be seen but it is not available now. Also see, *Hayat-i Javed*, pp. 159–60.
71. *Tabiyin-ul Kalam*, part III, pp. 62–129.
72. *Hayat-i Javed*, p. 168.
73. Ibid., p. 172.
74. Ibid. It may be noted that these remarks of John Arnold are, however, followed by a sentence which is utterly absurd. He writes, 'Let be this done by the Muslims themselves, and it will then demand little ingenuity or zeal on the part of the Christians to prove, that, if the Bible be true, the Koran must be false.' See ibid., p. 173.

    Of course, these remarks hurt Sir Syed Ahmad Khan. But all his distress apart, he did not feel discouraged. He continued his efforts both intellectually and through other means to remove these types of doubts from the minds the Christians and the Muslims.

It is significant to mention here in this connection that rejecting these views of John Arnold, Maulana Altaf Husain Hali states,

> I don't know as to how Mr Arnold came to this conclusion. If he had thought more deeply about the matter, he would have been obliged to admit that if there is agreement between the Bible and the Quran then the Muslims should have no difficulty in showing that since the Bible is true, modern Christianity is completely misleading and goes against the very teachings of the Bible itself. (*Hayat-i Javed*, p. 173)

Mention may be made here of a Christian scholar of Egypt, who was the editor of a Christian newspaper, the *Shahadat-ul Haqq*. It was around 1884 that following the foot-steps of Sir Syed Ahmad Khan, he too, according to Maulana Hali,wrote that the three religions—Judaism, Christianity and Islam, and the three books of these religions had much in common. In another work, on the same theme, entitled *Wahadat-ul Adyan wa Wahdat-ul Islam*, this Christian Egyptian scholar had shown that the differences that are generally acknowledged, have come about through misunderstanding (*Hayat-i Javed*, p. 173).

Similarly, Sir Syed was followed, as is mentioned in the *Hayat-i-Javed*, by another Christian scholar of French origin, Mosio Clafil, who lived in and published a journal, *Ittihad-i Islami* in Arabic and French from Egypt. The purpose of this journal too was to resolve the religious and political misunderstandings that had come up between the Christians and the Muslims, and which had, for many years, embittered the socio-political relation of the people of both the communities. See, ibid., pp. 173–4.

75. Garcien de Tassey was a French orientalist. He had close contact with Sir Syed Ahmad Khan. The latter's famous work on the historical monuments of Delhi the *Asar-us Sanadid,* had been translated into French by Garcien de Tassey. He is said to have mastery over Urdu language and literature, and produced several works including articles in this field.
76. *Hayat-i Javed*, pp. 174–5.
77. Ibid., p. 198; also see the *Scientific Society Gazette*, 14 September 1866.
78. *Hayat-i Javed*, p. 198.
79. Ibid., pp. 198–9.
80. *Hayat-i Javed*, p. 199. Though the brochure *Risala* was first published by Sir Syed himself from Banaras (Varanasi) in 1866, it was republished from Aligarh by Matba-ul Ulum in 1899. That is available to and has been used by the present author in the preparation of this essay (see Appendix E, enclosed herewith).

81. *Risala Ahkam-i Ta'am-i Ahl-i Kitab*, Aligarh: Matba-ul Ulum, 1899, p. 2.
82. *Surah*: V, Maaa-'Idah, verse 5.
83. *Risala Ahkam-i Ta'am-i Ahl-i Kitab*, p. 3.
84. Ibid., p. 3.
85. Ibid.
86. Ibid., p. 5.
87. For details, see, ibid., pp. 6–67.
88. Ibid., pp. 68–71.
89. *Hayat-i Javed*, p. 200.
90. Ibid.
91. Ibid., p. 203; also, G.F.I. Graham, *The Life and Work of Syed Ahmad Khan* (rept.), Delhi: Idarah-i-Adabiyat-i-Delhi, 1974, p. 97.
92. *Hayat-i Javed*, p. 213. Graham, p. 194–204. It may be mentioned here that Sir William Muir's book had deeply hurt the sentiments of Muslims all over the world, particularly Indian Muslims. For details see, *Hayat-i Javed*, pp. 491–546.
93. Ibid., p. 497.
94. Ibid., pp. 213–14, 491–546.
95. Graham, p. 106.
96. *Hayat-i Javed*, pp. 519, 536.
97. See Appendix F (enclosed herewith).
98. See the *Essay*: 'Prophecies Respecting Mohammed as Contained in both the Old and the New Testament', London: Trubner & Co., 1869, p. 1.
99. *Surah* VII: A'Raaf (The Heights), verses 156, 157.
100. *Surah* LXI:, *Saff* (The Rank), verse 6. See the *Essay*, p. 2.
101. See the *Essay*, p. 5.
102 Ibid., p. 9.
103. Ibid., p. 12.
104. Ibid., p. 28.
105. See Appendix G (enclosed herewith).
106. See the concerned *Essay*: 'Whether Islam has been Beneficial or Injurious to Human Society in General and to the Mosaic and Christian Dispensations', London: Trubner & Co., 1870, pp. 1–7.
107. Ibid., p. 7.
108. Ibid., pp. 7–8.
109. Ibid., p. 12.
110. Ibid., p. 14.
111. Ibid., p. 35.
112. Ibid., pp. 36–7.
113. Ibid., p. 37.
114. Ibid., p. 38.

115. Ibid.
116. Ibid.
117. Ibid.
118. Ibid., p. 39.
119. Ibid.
120 *Surah*: Aali-Im-Raan (The family of Imran), verse 64.
121. See the *Essay*, p. 39.
122. Ibid.
123. Ibid., pp. 39–40.
124. Graham, pp. 252–9.
125. Ibid., p. 259.
126. For this reply of William Muir, see ibid., pp. 259–61.
127. See, *Writings and Speeches of Sir Syed Ahmad Khan*, compiled by Shan Mohammad, Bombay: Nachiketa Publication, 1972, p. 177; also *Hayat-i Javed*, p. 403.
128. Shan Mohammad, p. 178.
129. *Hayat-i Javed*, p. 402.

APPENDIX A

امنا بالله وما انزل علينا وما انزل على ابراهيم و اسمعيل و اسحق و يعقوب والاسباط وما اوتي موسى و عيسى
والنبيون من ربهم لانفرق بين احد منهم و نحن له مسلمون .— سورة آل عمران آيت ٨٣

"We believe on God, and that which hath been sent down unto us, and that which was sent down unto Abrahem, and Israel, and Isaac, and Jacob, and the tribes, and that which was delivered to Moses, and Jesus, and the Prophets from their Lord; we make no distinction between any of them, and to Him we are resigned."——HOLY KORAN.

THE

MOHOMEDAN COMMENTARY

ON THE

HOLY BIBLE.

BY

SYUD AHMUD.

PART FIRST.

تبيين الكلام

في

تفسير التوراة والانجيل على ملة الاسلام

الفه

المفتقر الى الله الصمد سيد احمد

حصه اول

GHAZEEPORE,

PRINTED AND PUBLISHED BY THE AUTHOR AT HIS PRIVATE PRESS.

1862 A. D. 1278 H.

APPENDIX B

ونوريحكم بها النبيون الذين اسلموا للذين هادوا
وا من كتاب الله و كانوا عليه شهداء فلا تخشوا الناس
قليلا سورة مايدة آيت ۳۷

We have surely sent down the law, con
tight : thireby did the prophets, who profess
judge those who Judaized ; and the doctors an.
by the book of God, which had been committed to
then were witnesses thereof. Therefore fear not
neither sell my signs for a small price.—HOLY K

THE

MOHOMEDAN COMMENTARY

ON THE

HOLY BIBLE

GENESIS I—XI.

PART II

Syed mad

تبيين الكلام في تفسير التورات والانجيل على ملة الاسلام

[illegible]

[illegible] سورة نوح

[illegible] میں سے پہلی کتاب

[illegible]

[illegible]

[illegible] گیاره

[illegible]

ALLIGURH:

Printed and [illegible] by the Author at his Private Press.

A. D. [illegible] 281 H.

APPENDIX C

تبئین الکلام

في

تفسیر التوراة و انجیل علی ملة الاسلام

حصة سوم

انجیل مقدس متی

از باب اول تا باب پنجم

APPENDIX D

تبیین الکلام
فی
تفسیر التوراة والانجیل علیٰ ملة الاسلام

APPENDIX E

۷۸۶

وطعام الذین اوتوا الکتاب حل لکم

احکام طعام اہل کتاب

مؤلفہ

جناب آنریبل ڈاکٹر سر سید احمد خاں بہادر مرحوم کے سی۔ ایس

ای۔ ایل ایل۔ ڈی

واضح ہو کہ

اس رسالہ میں جہاں کہیں جناب مولوی شاہ عبدالعزیز صاحب کے
فتوے کا ذکر ہے اس فتوے کی نقل جناب مرحوم کو جناب خواجہ
محمد ولی اللہ صاحب غازیپوری سررشتہ دار کلکٹری بنارس سے وصول ہوئی تھی

در مطبع انسٹیٹیوٹ علی گڈھ طبع شد

۱۸ ۶ ۹۹
سنہ

APPENDIX F

ESSAY

ON THE

PROPHECIES RESPECTING MOHAMMED

AS CONTAINED IN BOTH

THE OLD AND THE NEW TESTAMENT.

خطبة

علي بشاراته المذكورات في التوراة والانجيل

الفها

المفتقر الى الله الصمد سيد احمد عفى الله عنه

THE ORIGINAL ENGLISH TEXT OF THIS ESSAY HAS BEEN REVISED AND CORRECTED BY A FRIEND.

يجدونه مكتوبا عندهم في التوراة والانجيل

BY

SYED AHMED KHAN BAHADOR, C.S.I.,

AUTHOR OF THE "MOHAMMEDAN COMMENTARY ON THE HOLY BIBLE," FELLOW OF THE ROYAL SOCIETY, AND LIFE HONORARY SECRETARY TO THE ALLYGURH SCIENTIFIC SOCIETY.

LONDON
TRUBNER & CO., 57 AND 59, PATERNOSTER ROW.
1869

APPENDIX G

ESSAY

ON THE QUESTION

WHETHER ISLAM HAS BEEN BENEFICIAL OR INJURIOUS TO HUMAN SOCIETY IN GENERAL,

AND TO THE

MOSAIC AND CHRISTIAN DISPENSATIONS

خطابة

على ان الاسلام رحمة للانسان وجُنّة لاديان الانبياء باوضح البرهان

الفها

المفتقر الي الله الصمد سيد احمد عفى الله عنه

THE ORIGINAL ENGLISH TEXT OF THIS ESSAY HAS BEEN REVISED AND CORRECTED BY A FRIEND.

اليوم اكملت لكم دينكم و اتممت عليكم نعمتي و رَضِيتُ لكم الاسلام دينا

BY

SYED AHMED KHAN BAHADOR, C.S.I.

AUTHOR OF THE "MOHAMMEDAN COMMENTARY ON THE HOLY BIBLE," HONORARY MEMBER OF THE ROYAL ASIATIC SOCIETY, AND LIFE HONORARY SECRETARY TO THE ALLYGURH SCIENTIFIC SOCIETY.

LONDON:
TRÜBNER & CO., 8 AND 60, PATERNOSTER ROW
1870.

Contributors

MUSHIRUL HASAN: Professor of History, Vice-Chancellor, Jamia Millia Islamia, New Delhi.

S.M. AZIZUDDIN HUSSAIN: Professor of History, Jamia Millia Islamia, New Delhi.

B. SHEIKH ALI: Retd. Professor of History, Former Vice-Chancellor, Goa & Mangalore Universities.

Z.U. MAILK: Retd. Professor of History, CAS, Department of History, AMU, Aligarh.

GULFISHAN KHAN: Reader in History, CAS, Department of History, AMU, Aligarh.

SANAULLAH MIR: Reader in Philosophy, Department of Philosophy, AMU, Aligarh.

ALI AHMAD: Reader in Education, Department of Education, AMU, Aligarh.

HASSAN IMAM: Sr. Lecturer, CAS, Department of History, AMU, Aligarh.

M. SAJJAD: Lecturer, CAS, Department of History, AMU, Aligarh.

SHAFEY KIDWAI: Reader in MJMC, Chairman, Department of Mass Communication & Journalism, AMU, Aligarh.

S.M. WASEEM: Retd. Professor of Commerce, Department of Commerce, AMU, Aligarh.

TABIR KALAM: Lecturer, Department of History, Banaras Hindu University, Varanasi.

SHAN MOHAMMAD: Retd. Professor, Department of Political Science, AMU, Aligarh.

PARVEZ NAZEER: Lecturer, CAS, Department of History, AMU, Aligarh.

IQBAL SABIR: Sr. Lecturer, CAS, Department of History, AMU, Aligarh.